AF292356

TADA's REVOLUTION

MISCHIEF IN MINIATURE

SUSAN CHI

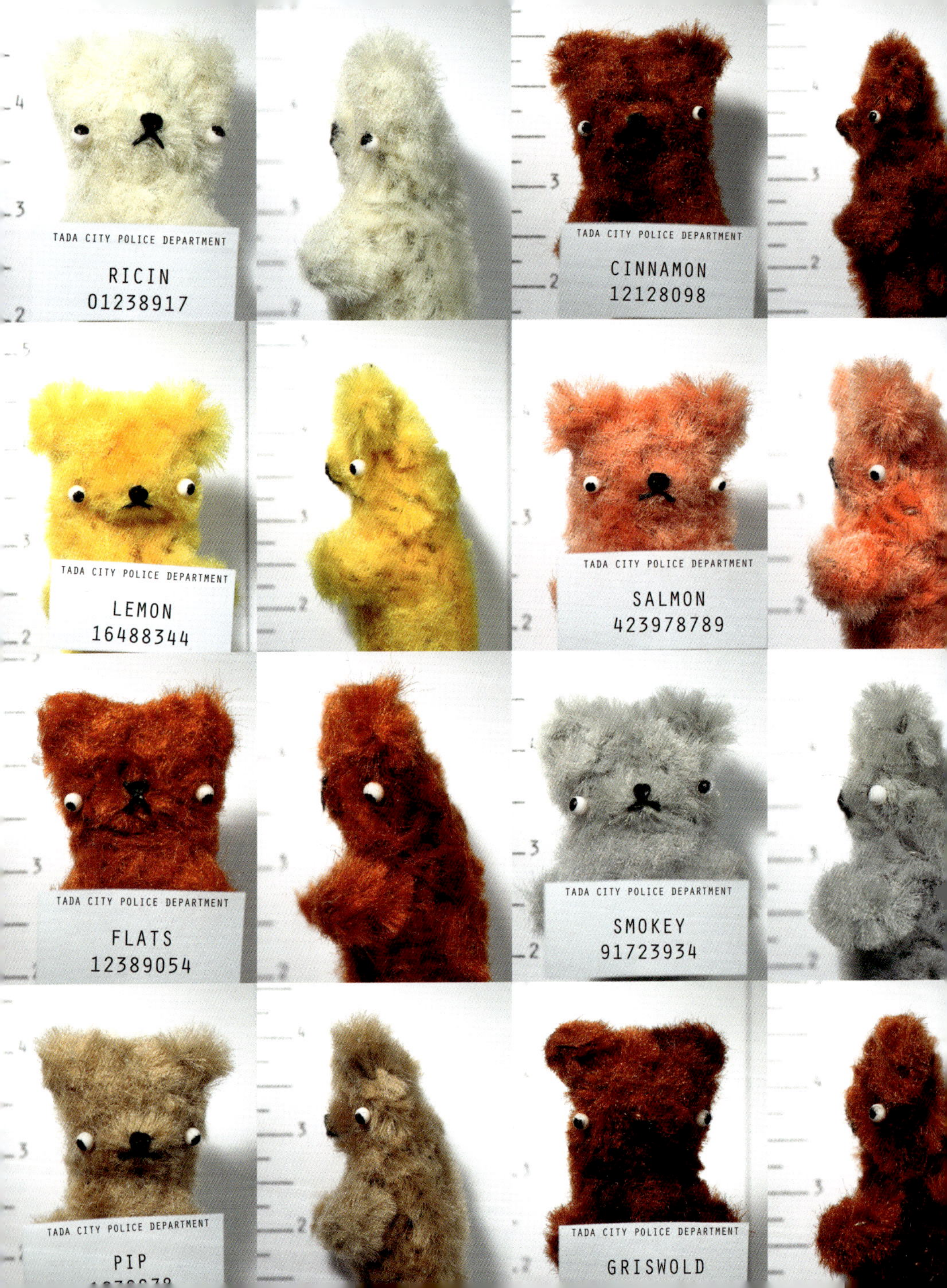

TADA CITY POLICE DEPARTMENT
RICIN
01238917
TADA CITY POLICE DEPARTMENT
CINNAMON
12128098
TADA CITY POLICE DEPARTMENT
LEMON
16488344
TADA CITY POLICE DEPARTMENT
SALMON
423978789
TADA CITY POLICE DEPARTMENT
FLATS
12389054
TADA CITY POLICE DEPARTMENT
SMOKEY
91723934
TADA CITY POLICE DEPARTMENT
PIP
TADA CITY POLICE DEPARTMENT
GRISWOLD

TADA's REVOLUTION

MISCHIEF IN MINIATURE

SUSAN CHI

teNeues

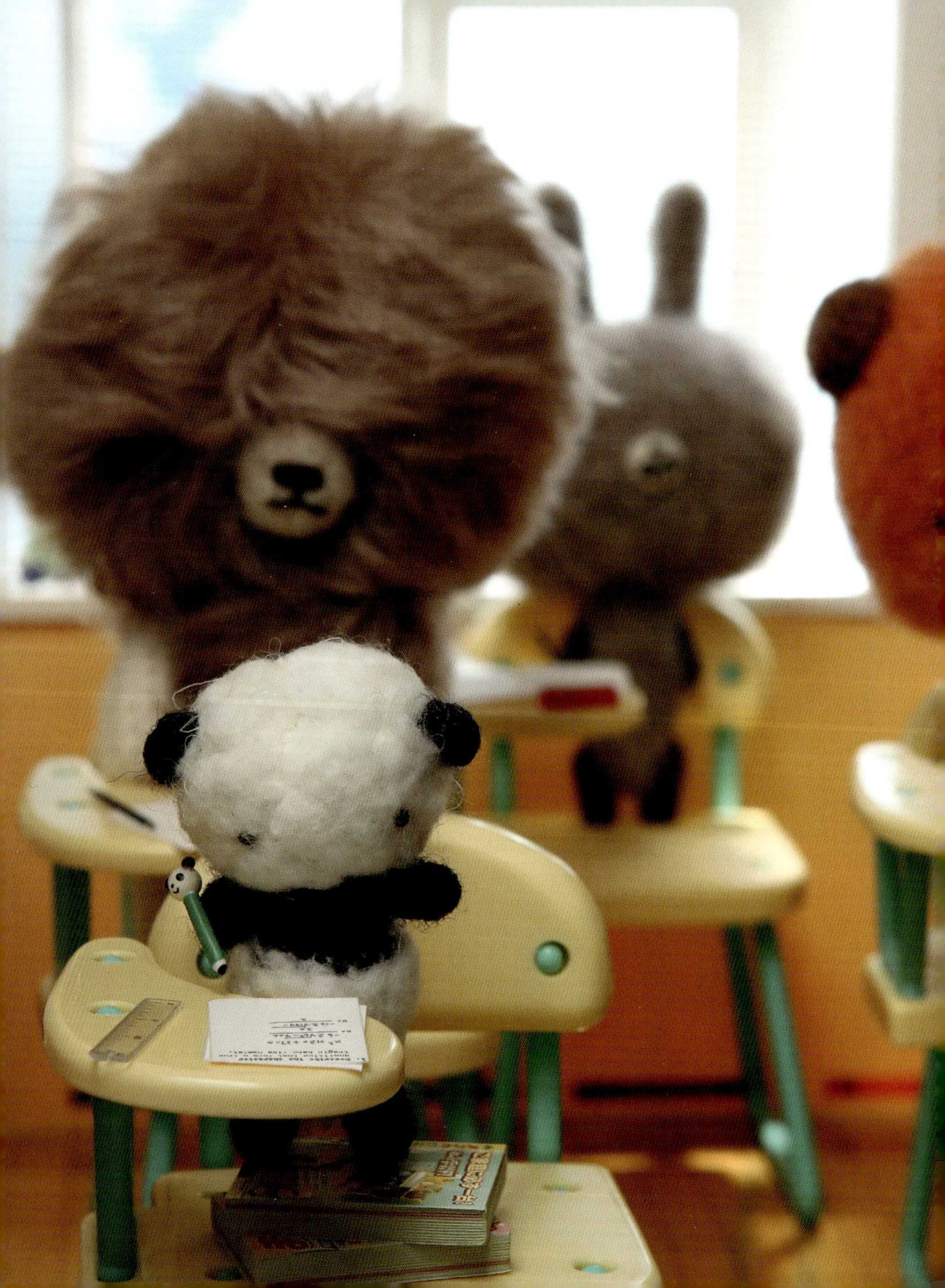

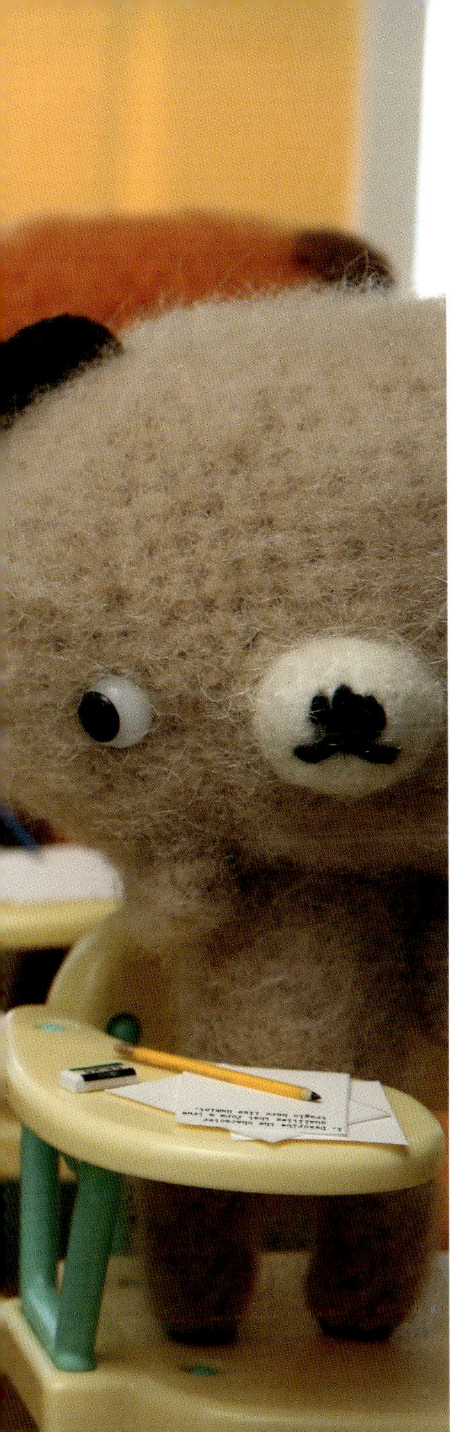

INTRODUCTION

SUSAN CHI

When I began work on TADA's Revolution in 2008, I came from a completely practical, rigid, and structured background of working as a chemical engineer for 12 years. Although I did not have a clear or well-formed vision of what direction my artwork would take, I knew that I wanted to pursue a creative endeavor that was fluid and completely free of constraints.

TADA's Revolution is a continually changing and expanding art project that chronicles the everyday life and adventures of stuffed animals living in a fantastical miniature toy world. Like most children, I grew up playing with stuffed animals. Just like real pets, they each had names and personalities and participated in almost everything I did. I chose stuffed animals to be the main characters in TADA's Revolution because they are childlike and nostalgic and can be as versatile and limitless as our imagination. In my spare time, I taught myself to crochet, sew, and write my own patterns and designs for one-of-a-kind stuffed animals. Each animal is meticulously crocheted, groomed, and outfitted. Their personalities are congruent with their facial expressions, body language, and demeanor.

To create the intricate world they live in, I further expanded my skills in woodworking, polymer clay sculpting, and set building. Along with my already -growing collection of vintage miniatures and toys, I was able to create realistic vignettes resembling places that are familiar to everyone. Soon, TADA's city grew to be like any big city with well-manicured parks, fully stocked grocery stores, high-end movie theaters, and restaurants. And just like any big city, it is a place filled with excitement and wonder, but also mischief and crime. It is the perfect arena for the stuffed animal characters to live, work, and play—just as I had imagined as a child.

In developing the philosophy and approach to TADA's Revolution, a major priority was for the work to be constantly evolving and stylistically dynamic. I wanted to continually advance in my skill and craft, and to develop and integrate new and more complex techniques. It was also important to create pieces that were not predictable or formulaic so each scene could be completely novel and unique. The goal was for the audience to experience something that they had never experienced before. I knew that I did not want to simply emulate the work of other artists or to create a series of derivative works. Simultaneously, I also wanted to create images that told self-contained and universal stories. I did not want to create work that was excessively esoteric, or that would require a complex backstory to fully appreciate a piece. It was important that any individual from any age, background, or culture could look at the images and understand most (if not all) of the story.

Content-wise, we aspire for the work to be playful, funny, and uplifting. Self-honesty and innocence are central and recurrent themes. Many pieces were generated as a reaction to the artificial rules and constraints governed by the economics, society, and politics that bind us all. Ultimately, TADA's Revolution, the art project and the self-titled book, *TADA's Revolution: Mischief in Miniature*, which we are delighted to present here in print form for the first time, is a play on the absurdity of convention, and is a celebration of being honestly and unabashedly who we are.

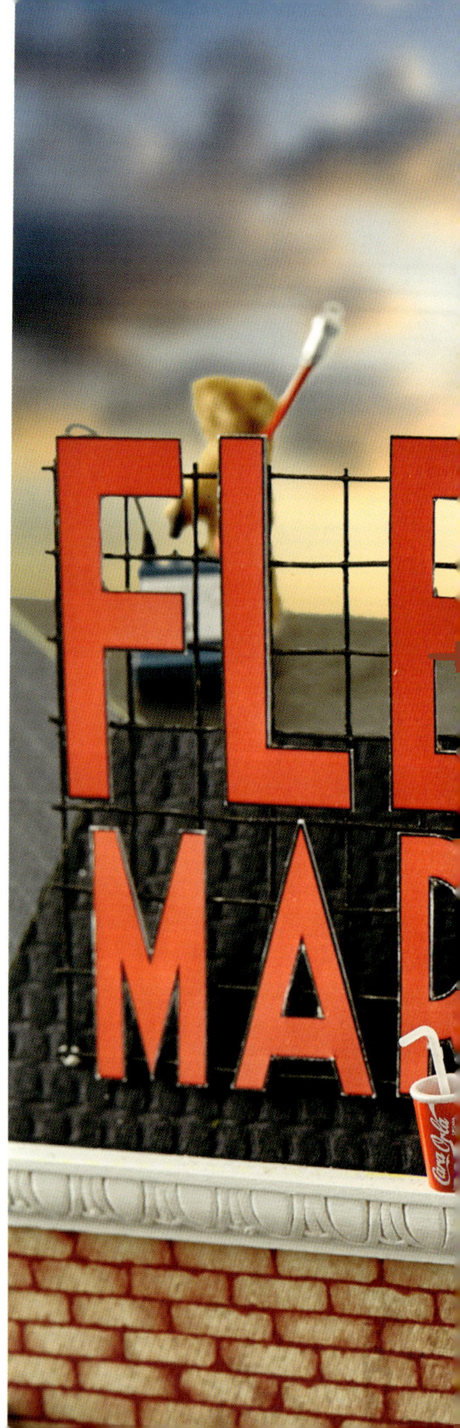

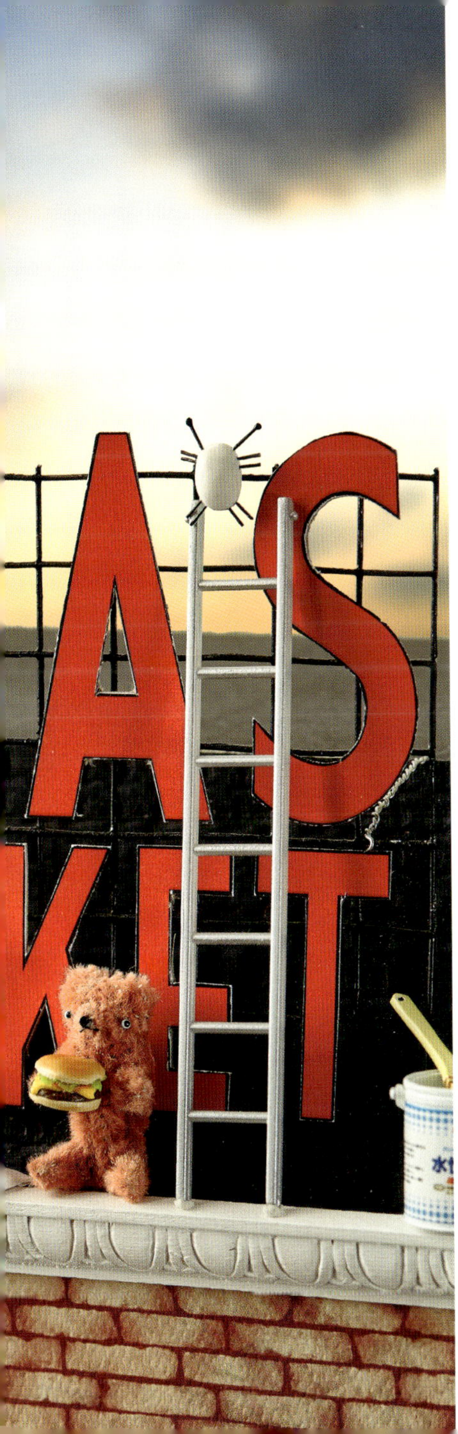

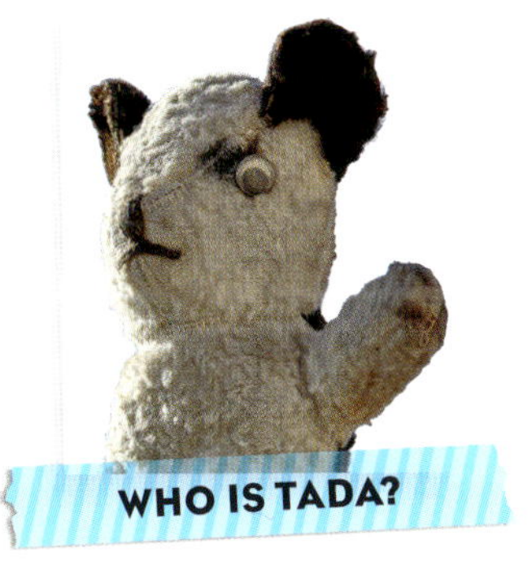

A common question that I get asked is: "Who is TADA?" TADA is a vintage mohair panda bear that I acquired several months prior to the inception of TADA's Revolution. An old, play-scarred veteran of countless adventures, he also began a second career working for TADA's Revolution in 2008. Over the years, he has worked for TADA's Revolution as a lighting assistant, stunt double, and was recently promoted to the Vice President of Operations. He has also served as a consultant on Stuffed Animal Psychology during many executive and planning meetings. TADA has been symbolic of the entire process of rebirth and rediscovery, and has become the figurehead for the Revolution.

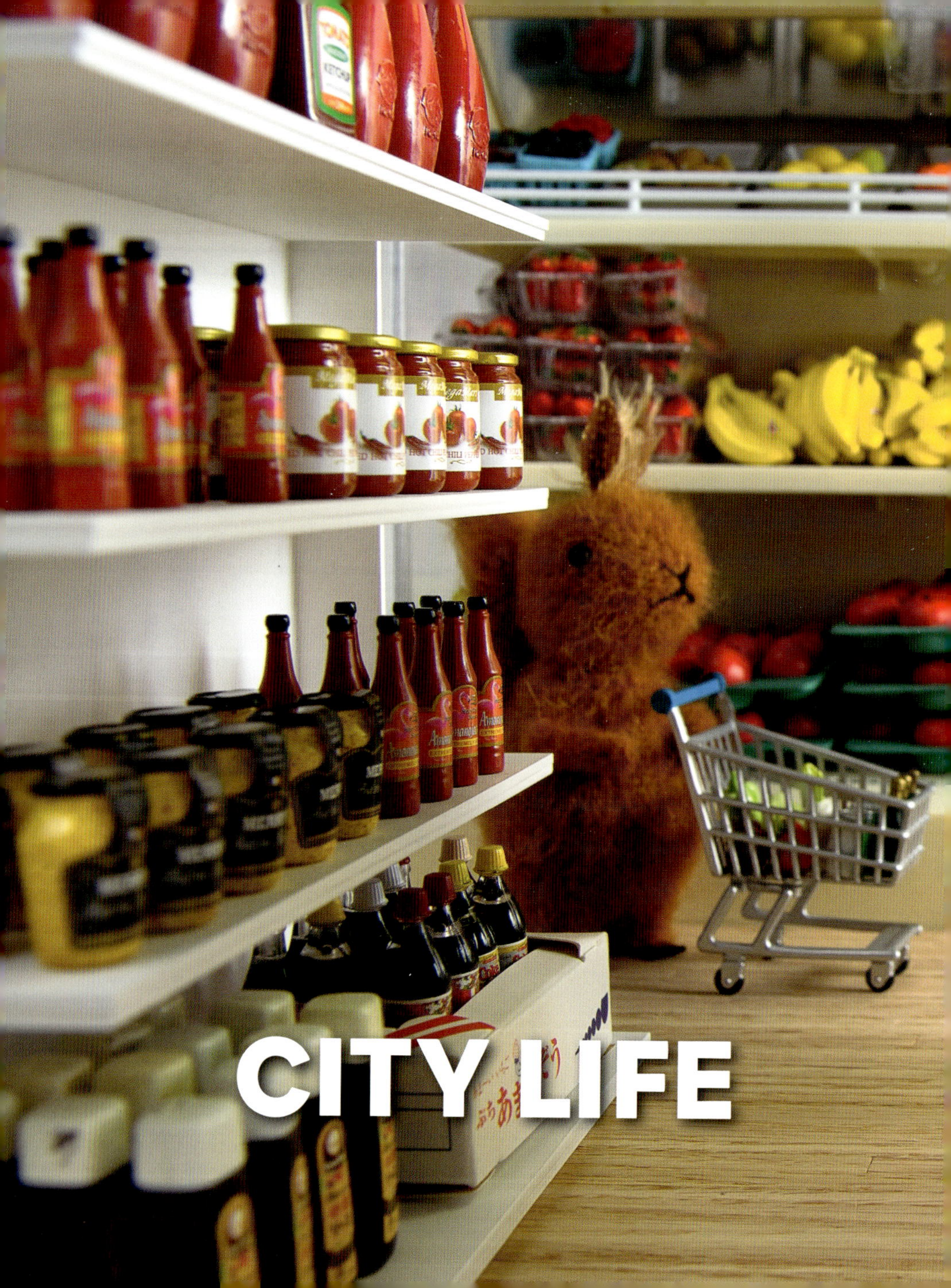
CITY LIFE

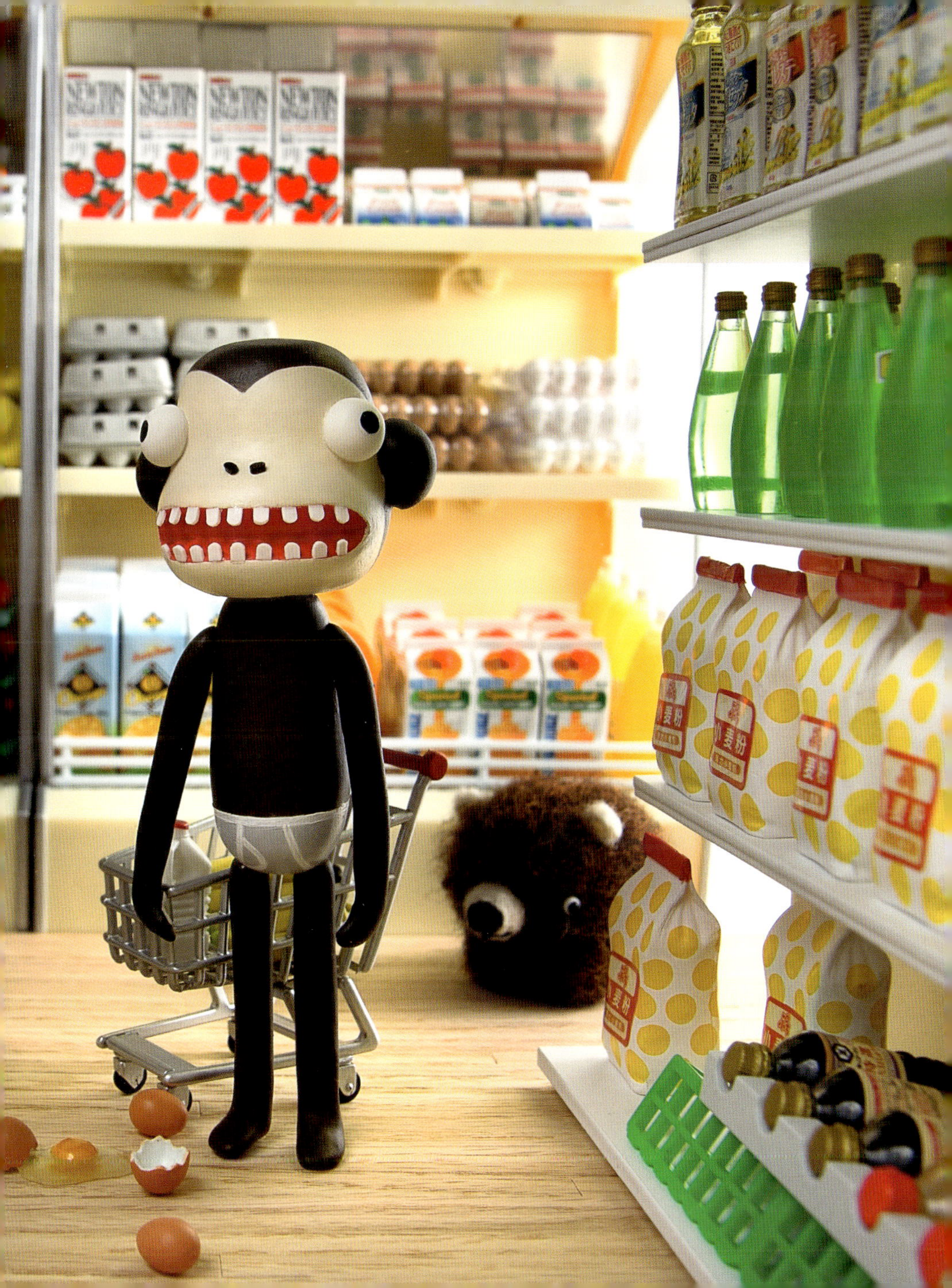

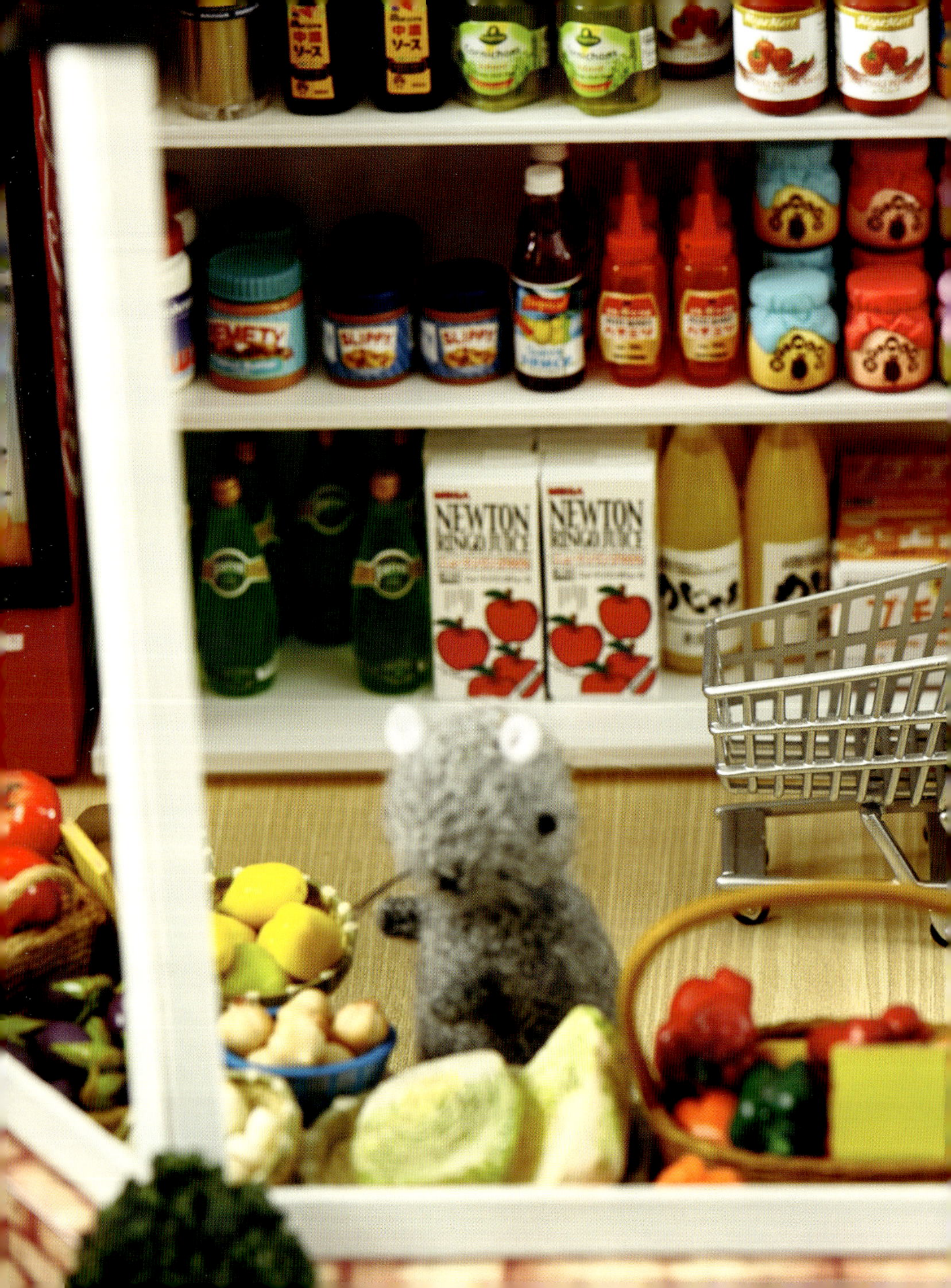
中濃ソース
SKIPPY
NEWTON
RINGO JUICE
リンゴジュース

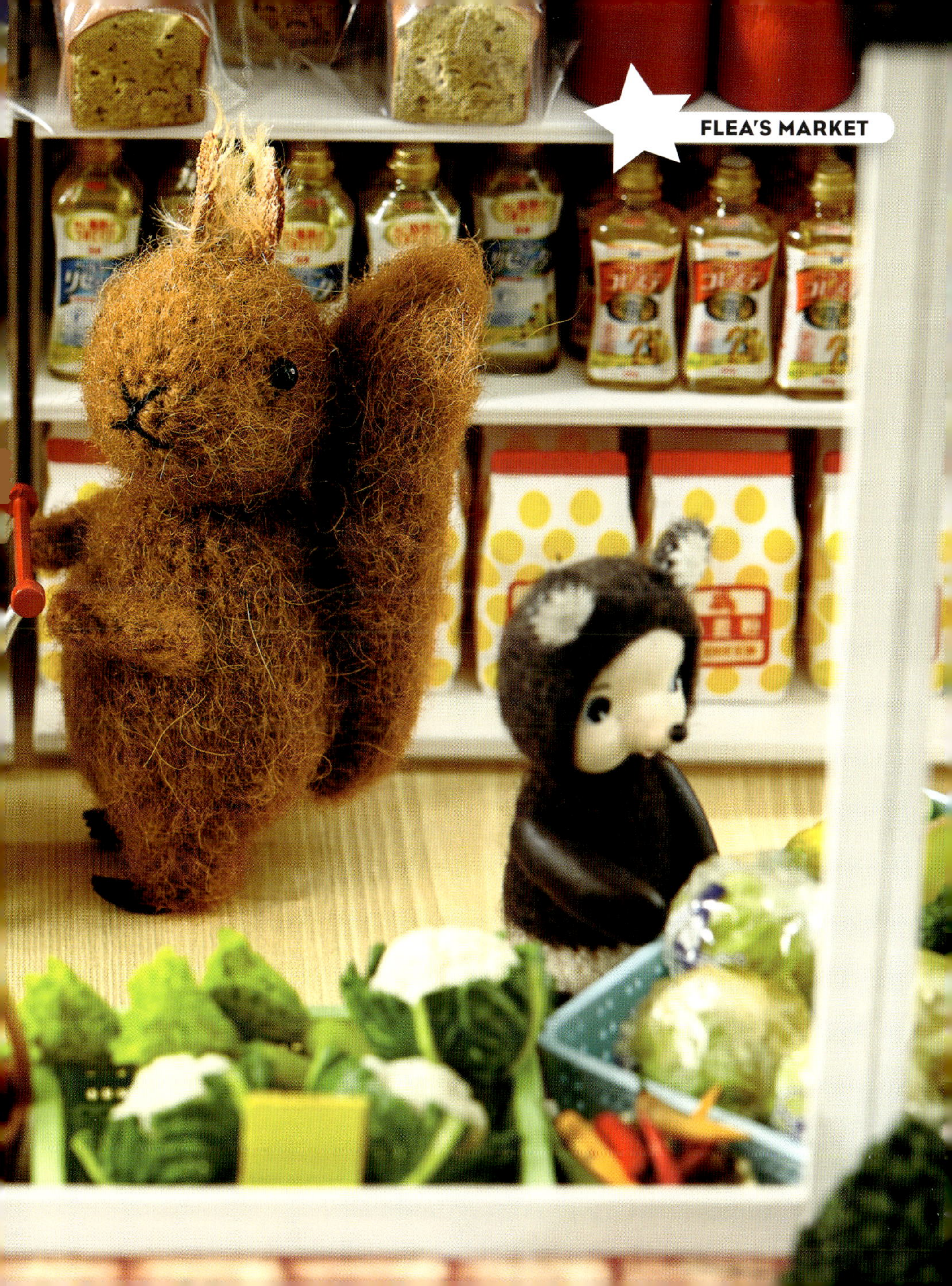

FLEA'S MARKET

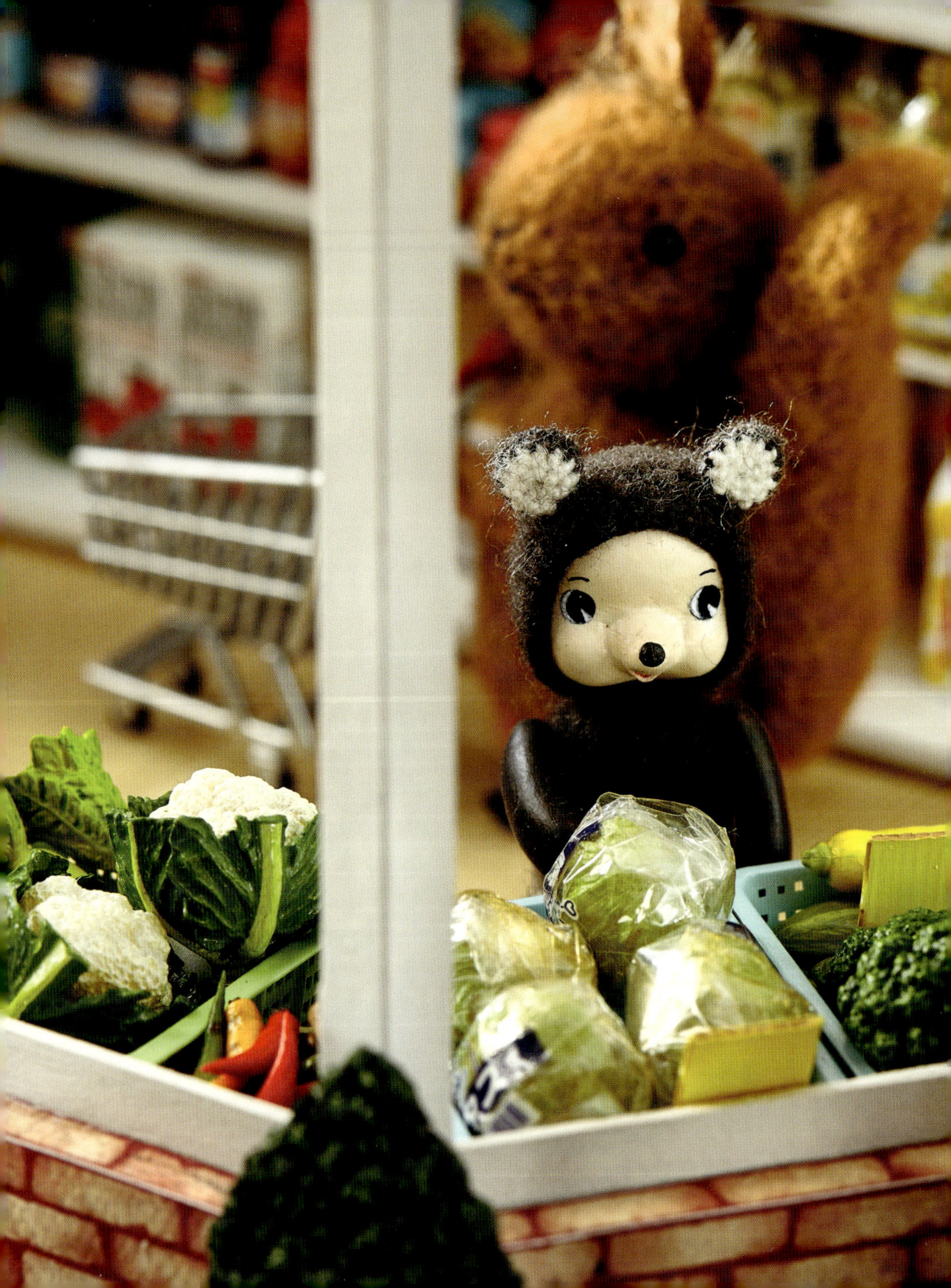

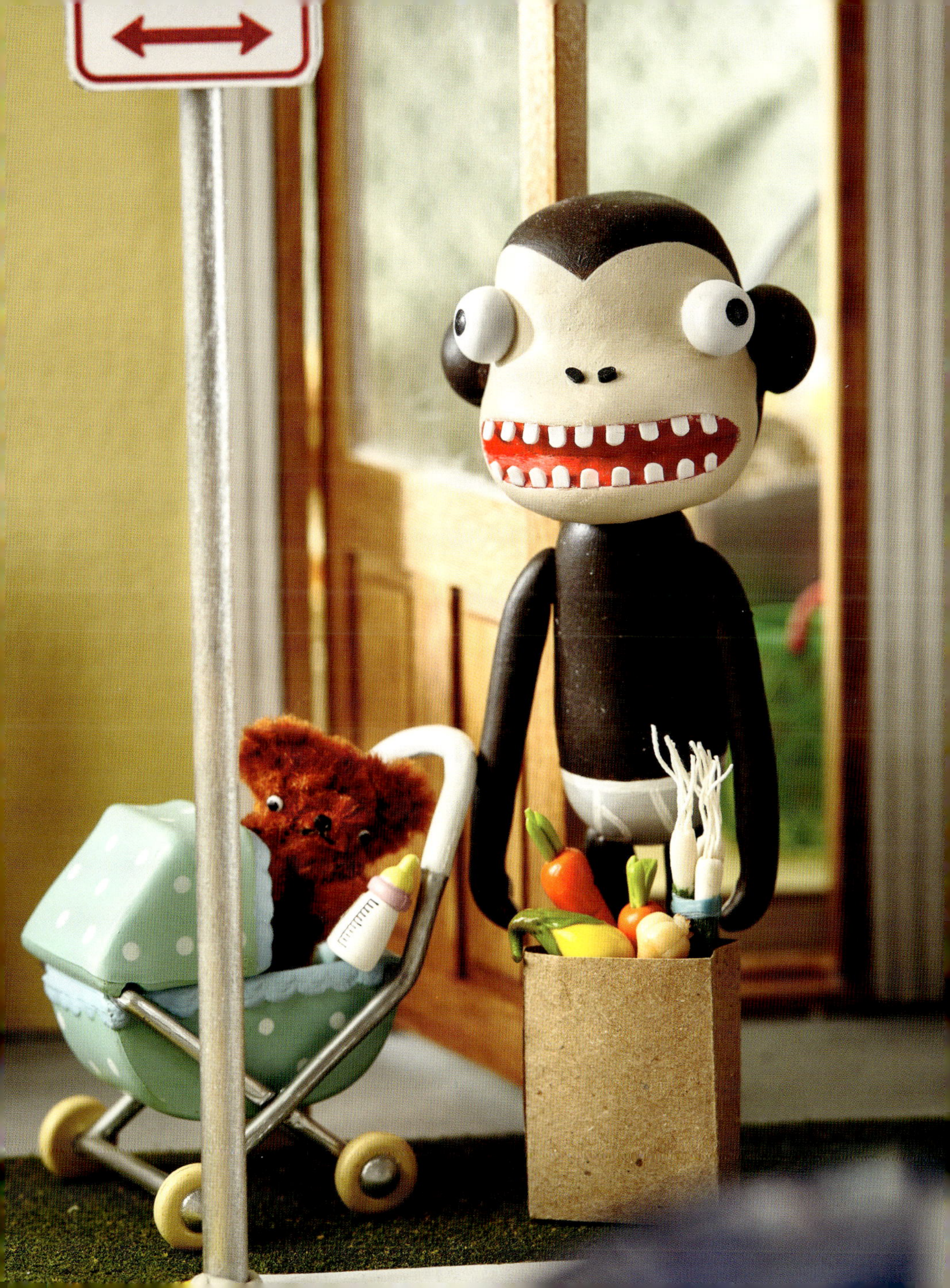

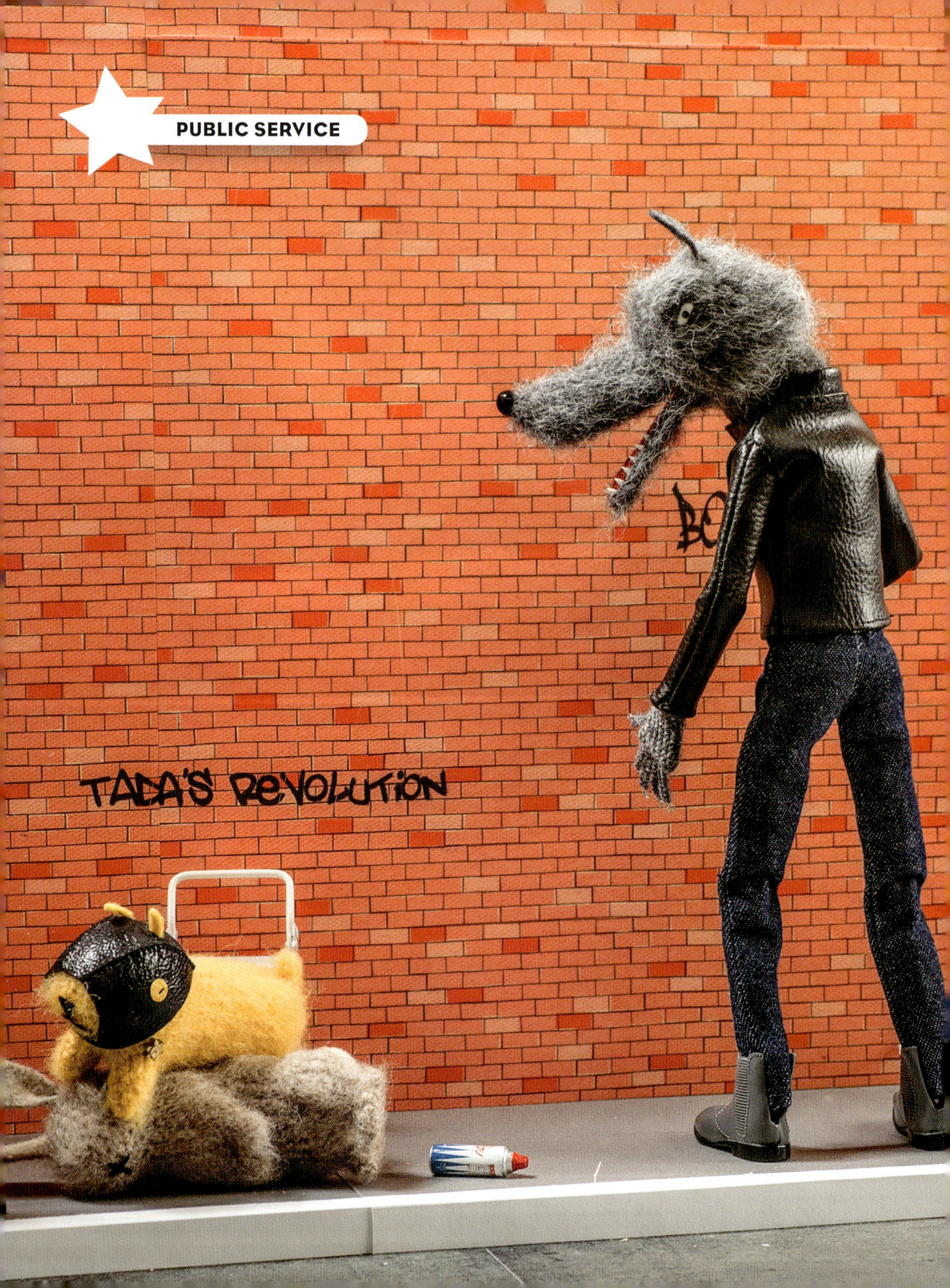
TADA'S REVOLUTION

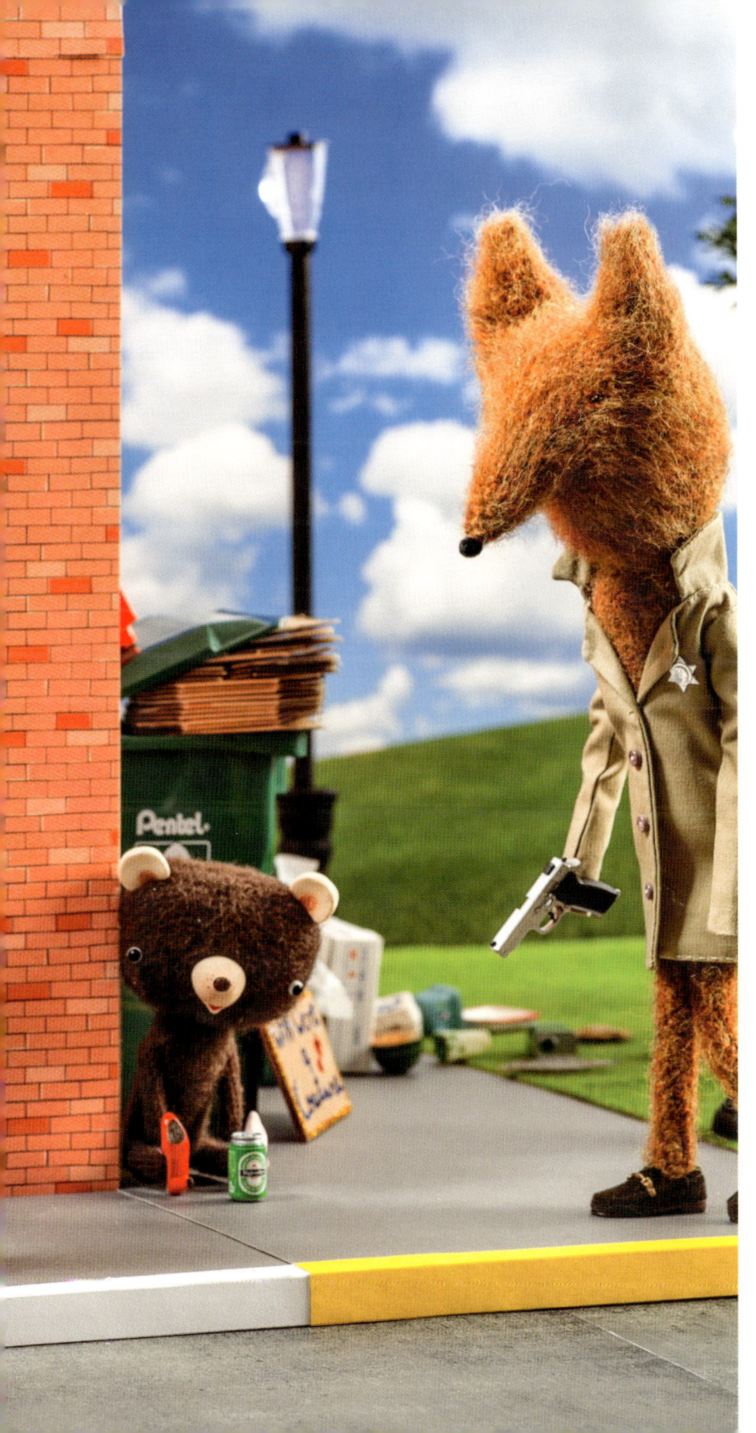

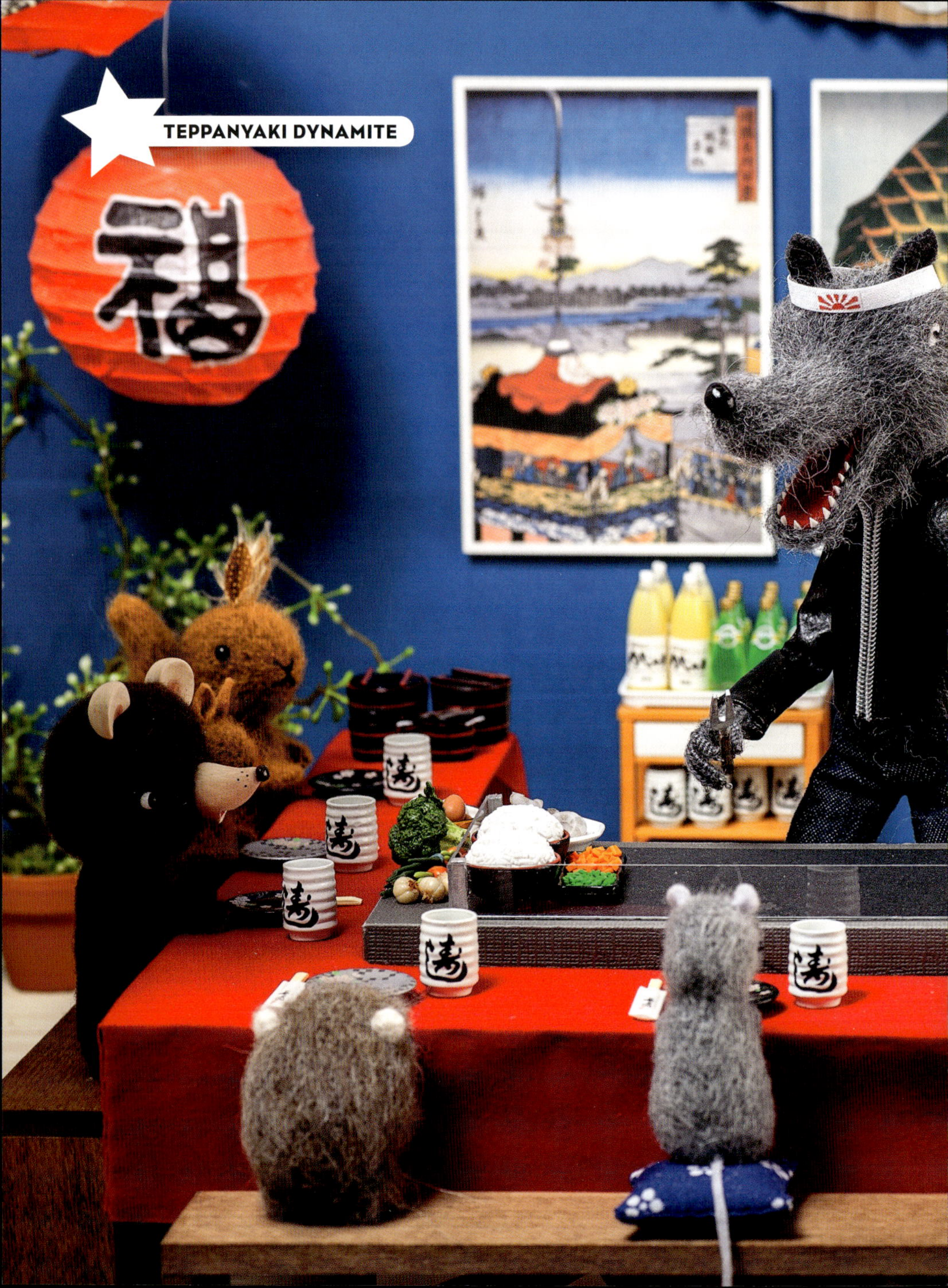
TEPPANYAKI DYNAMITE

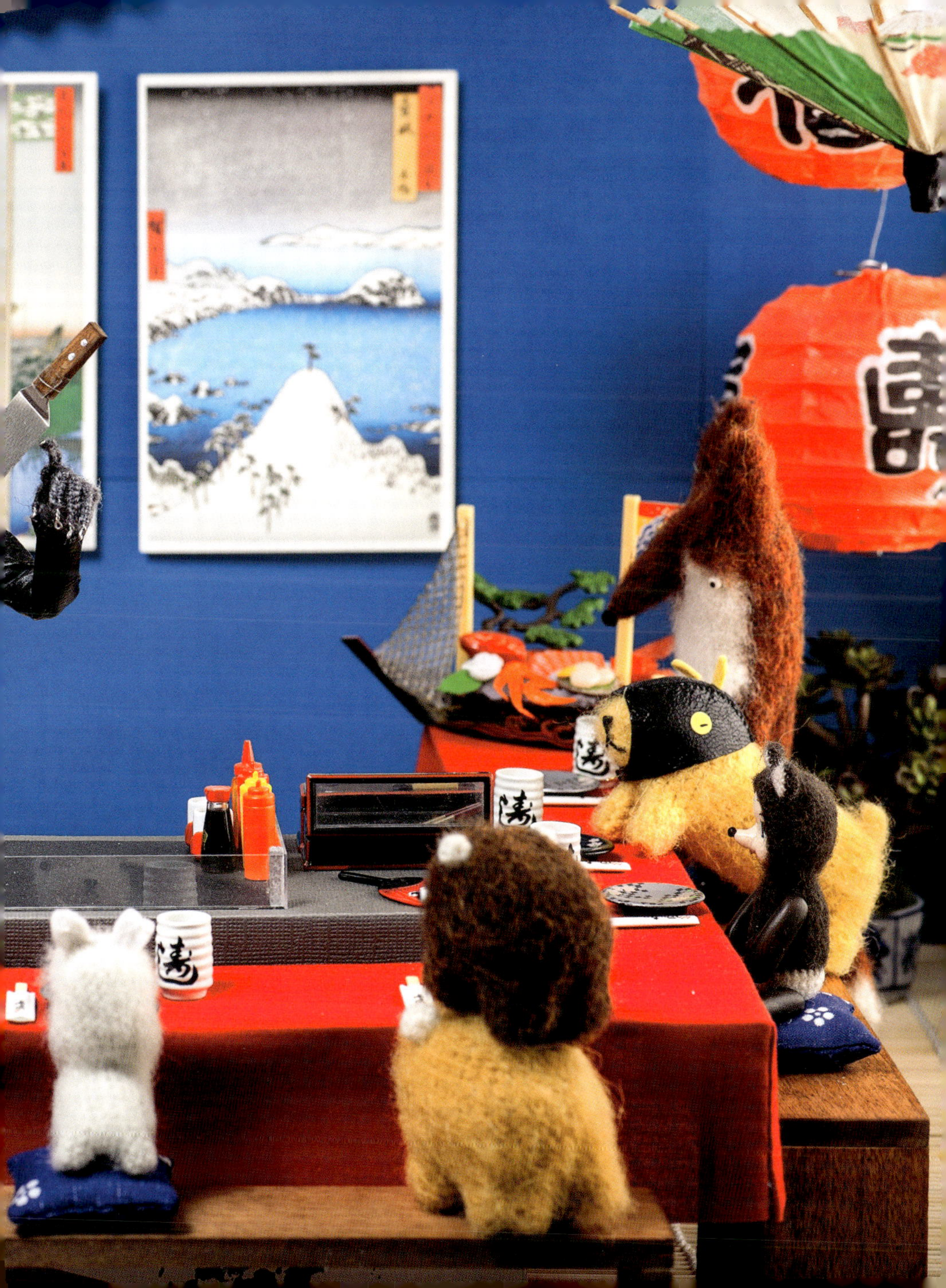

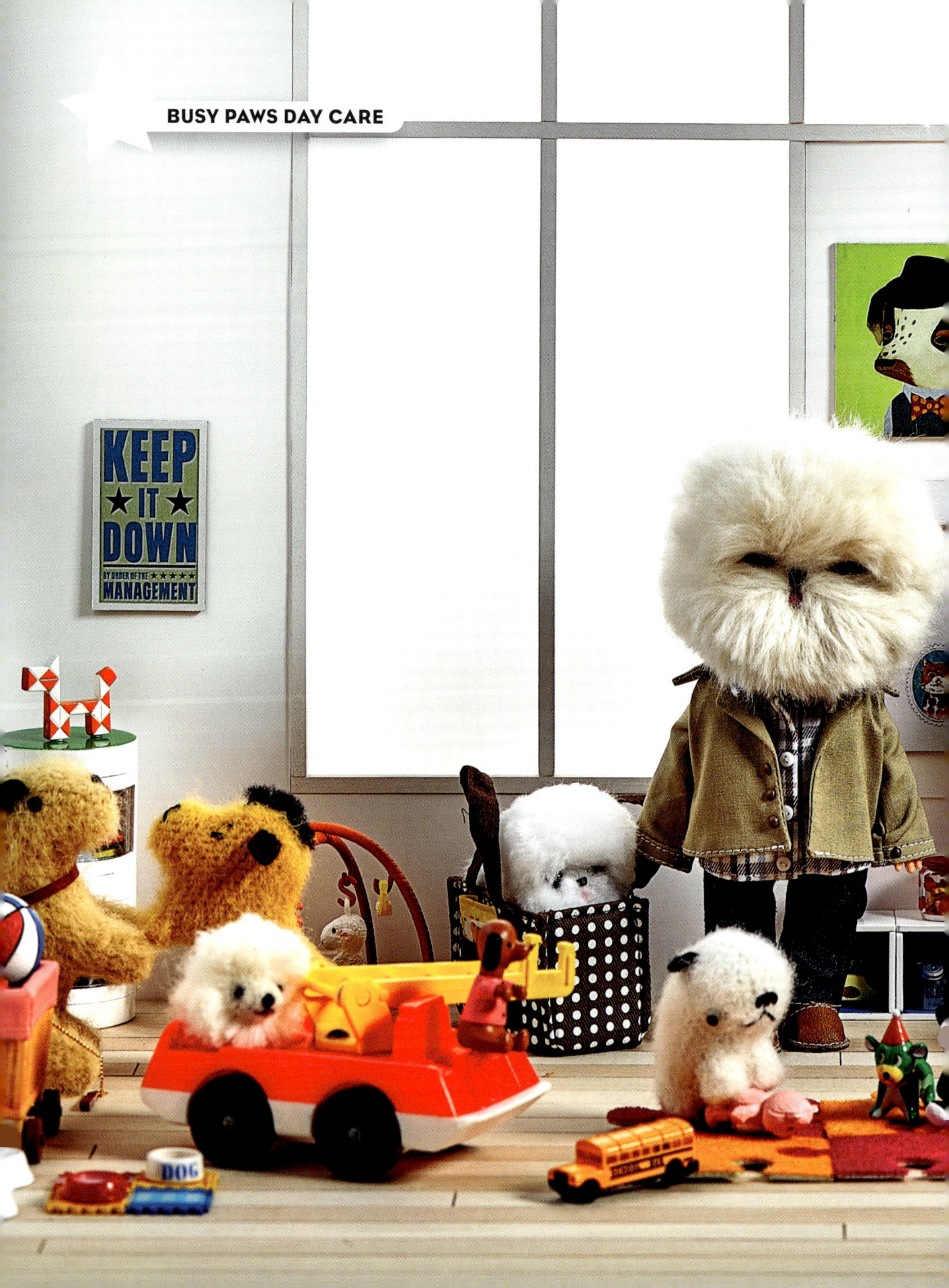

BUSY PAWS DAY CARE
KEEP IT DOWN
BY ORDER OF THE MANAGEMENT
DOG

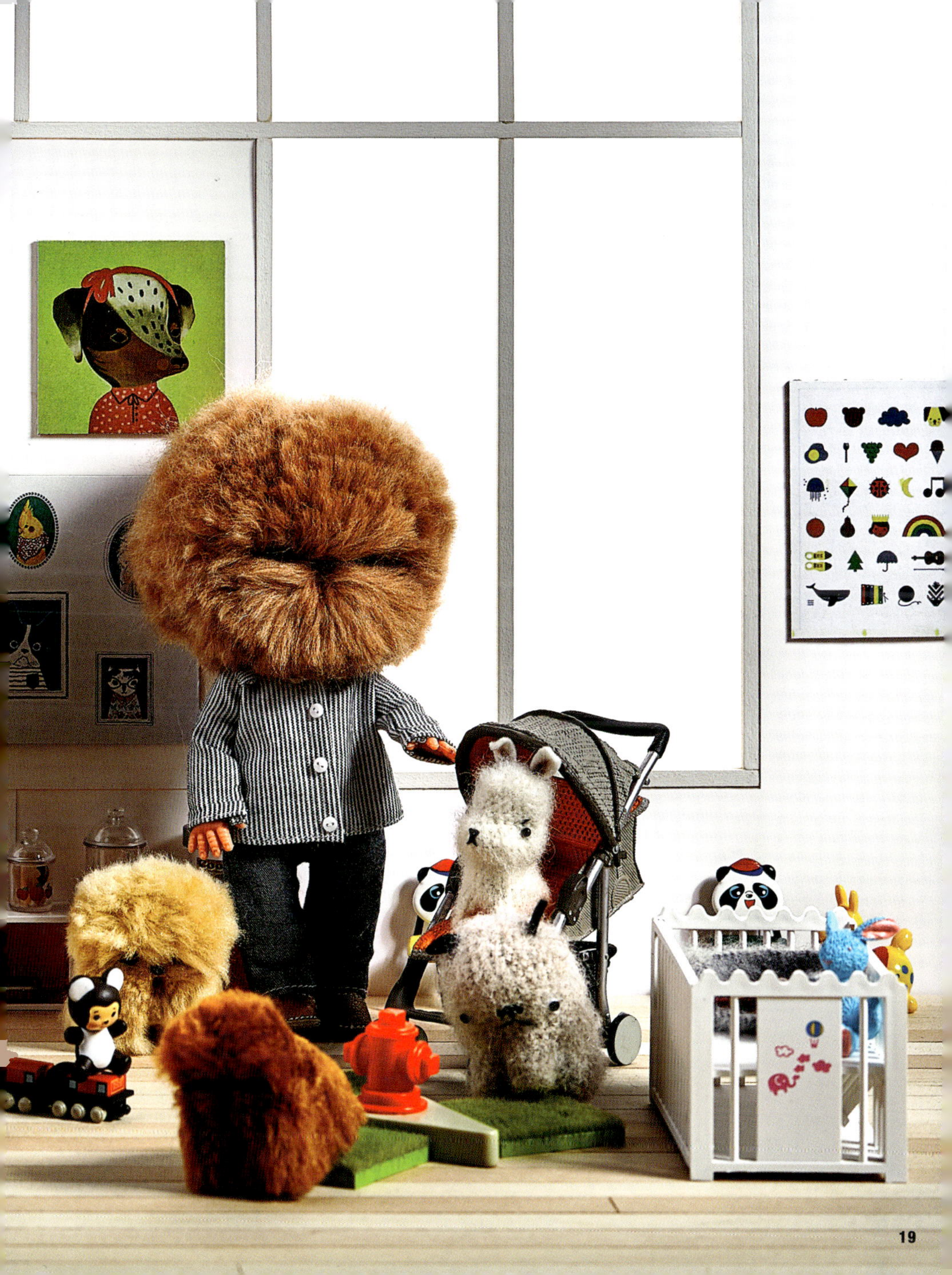

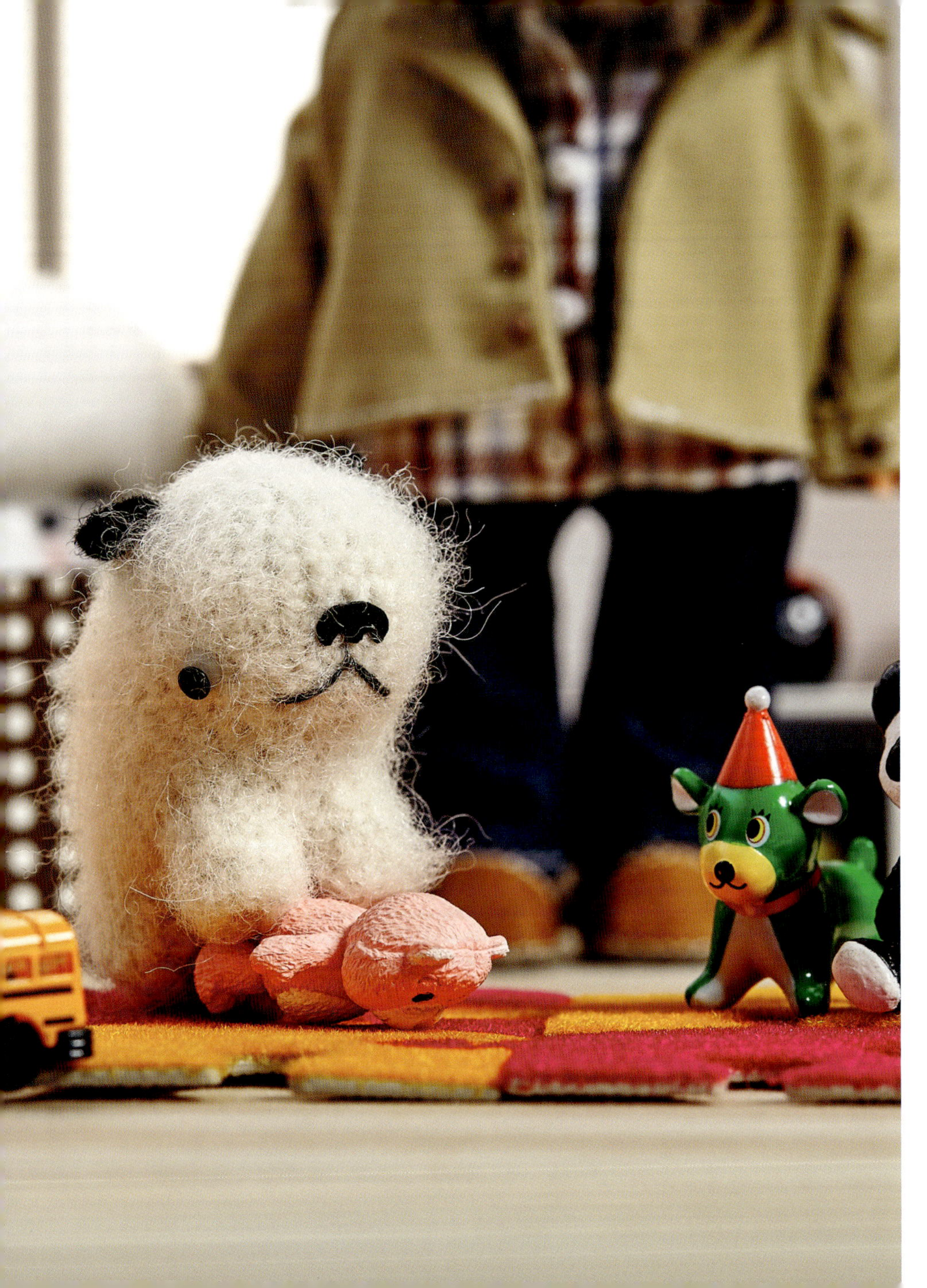

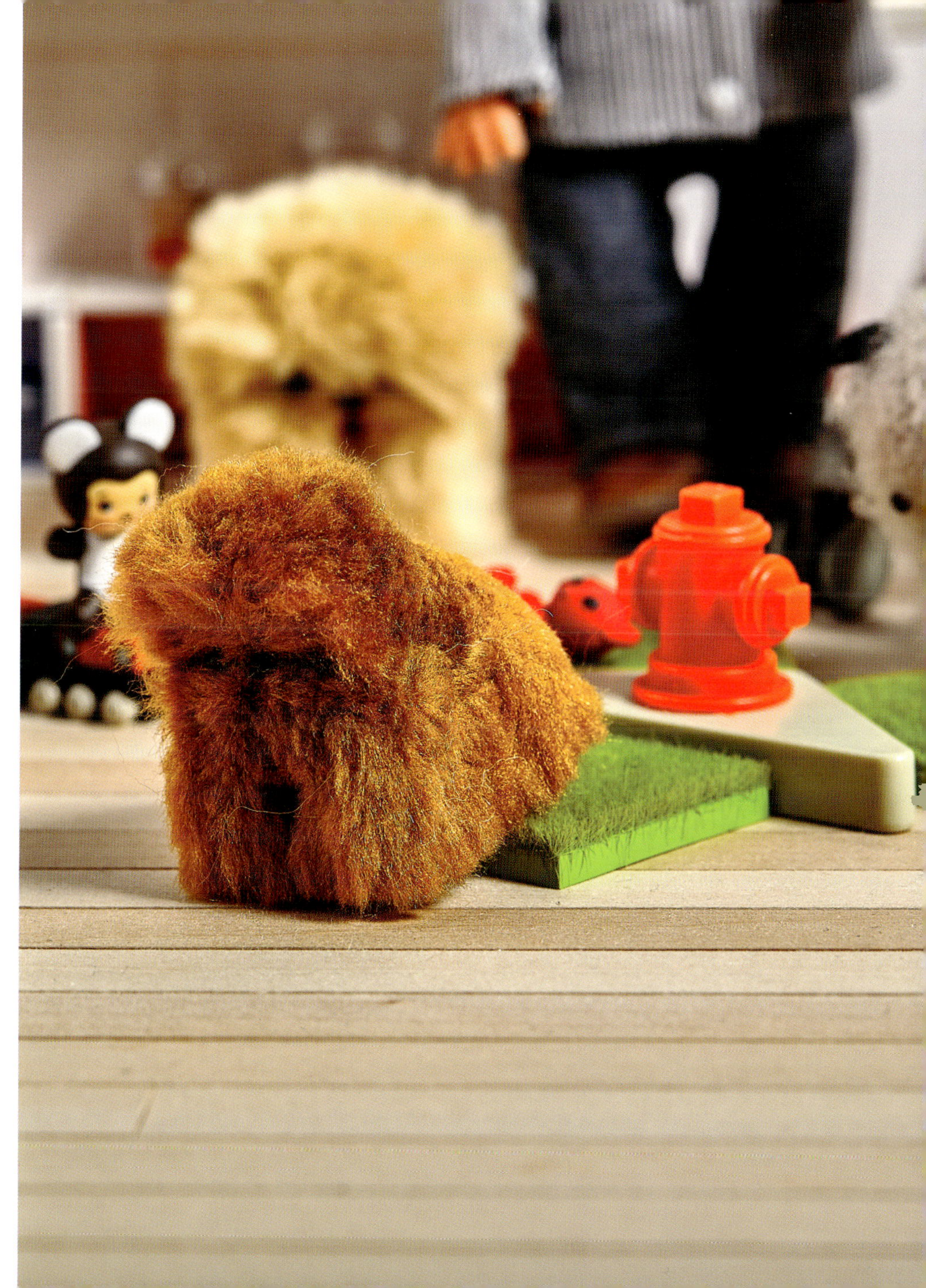

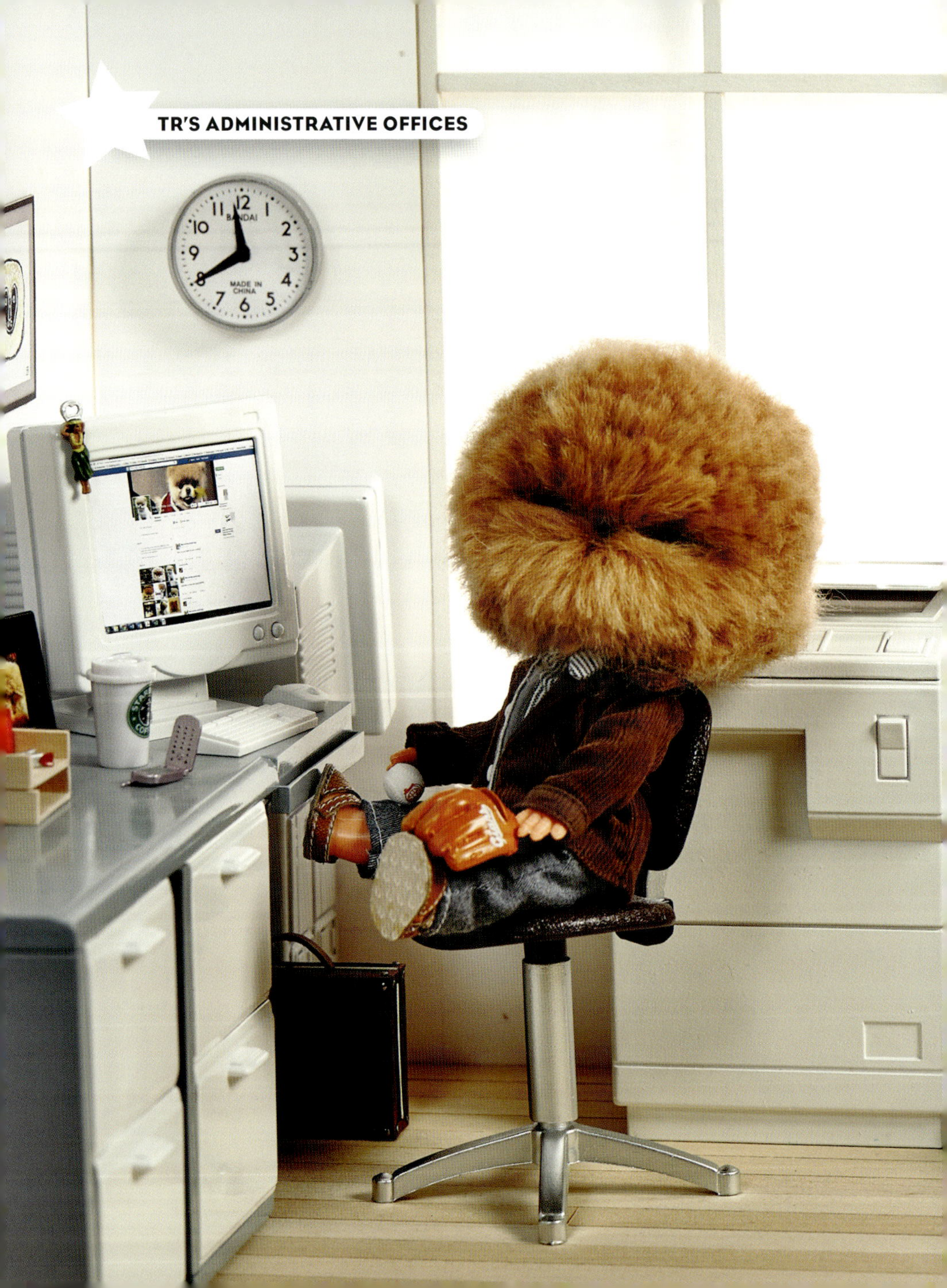
TR'S ADMINISTRATIVE OFFICES
BANDAI
12
11
10
9
8
7
6
5
4
3
2
1
MADE IN
CHINA

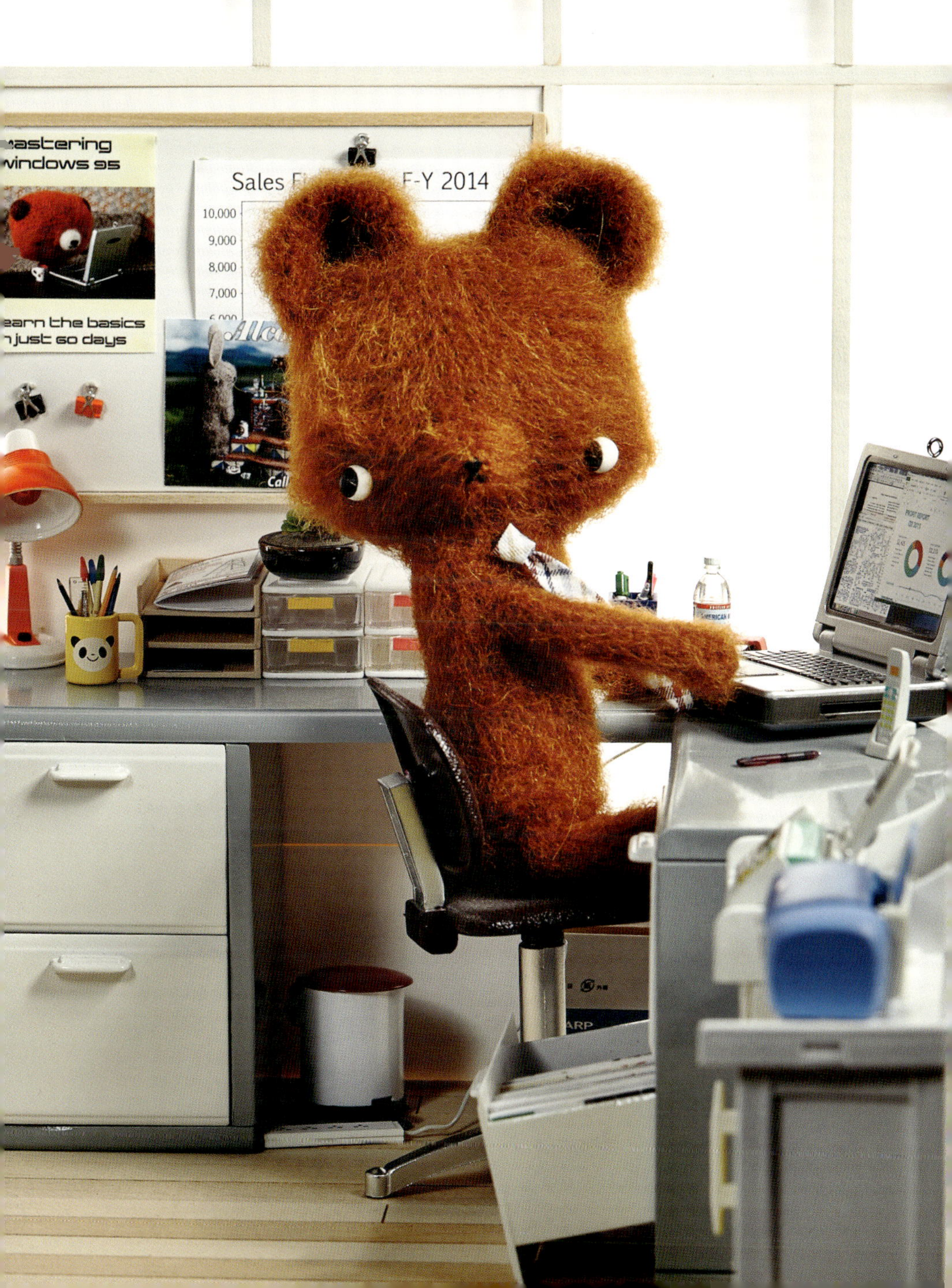

mastering
windows 95
earn the basics
n just 60 days
Sales F   F-Y 2014
10,000
9,000
8,000
7,000
6,000
Alca

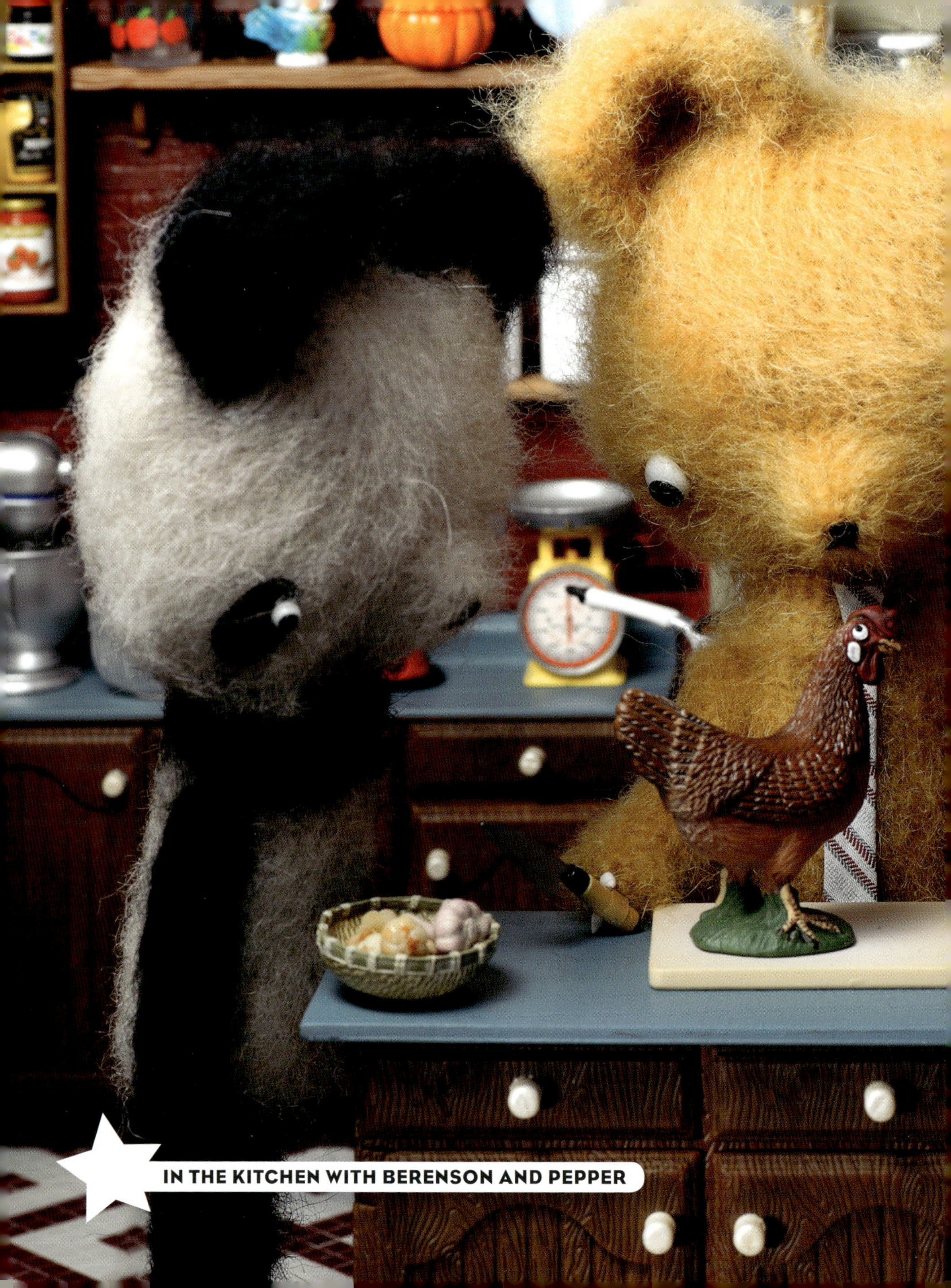

IN THE KITCHEN WITH BERENSON AND PEPPER

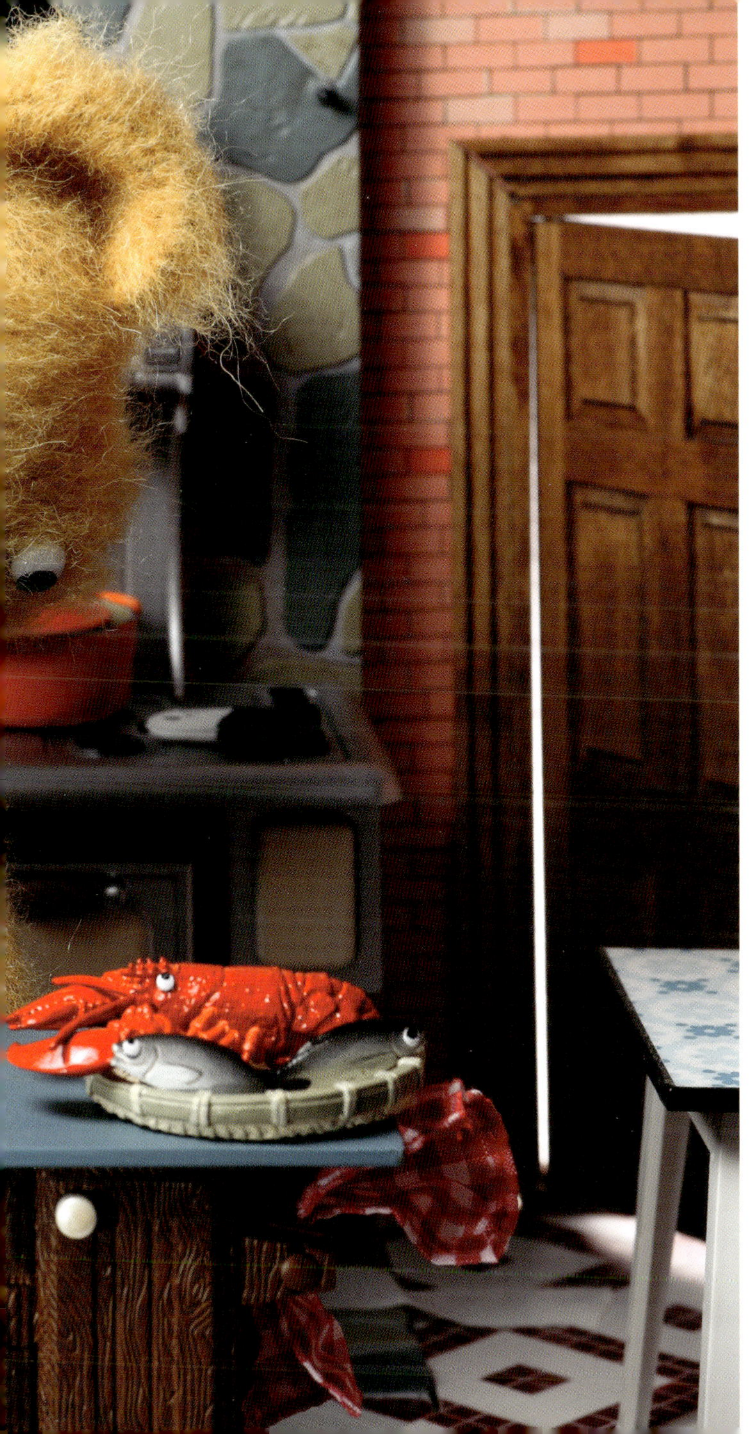

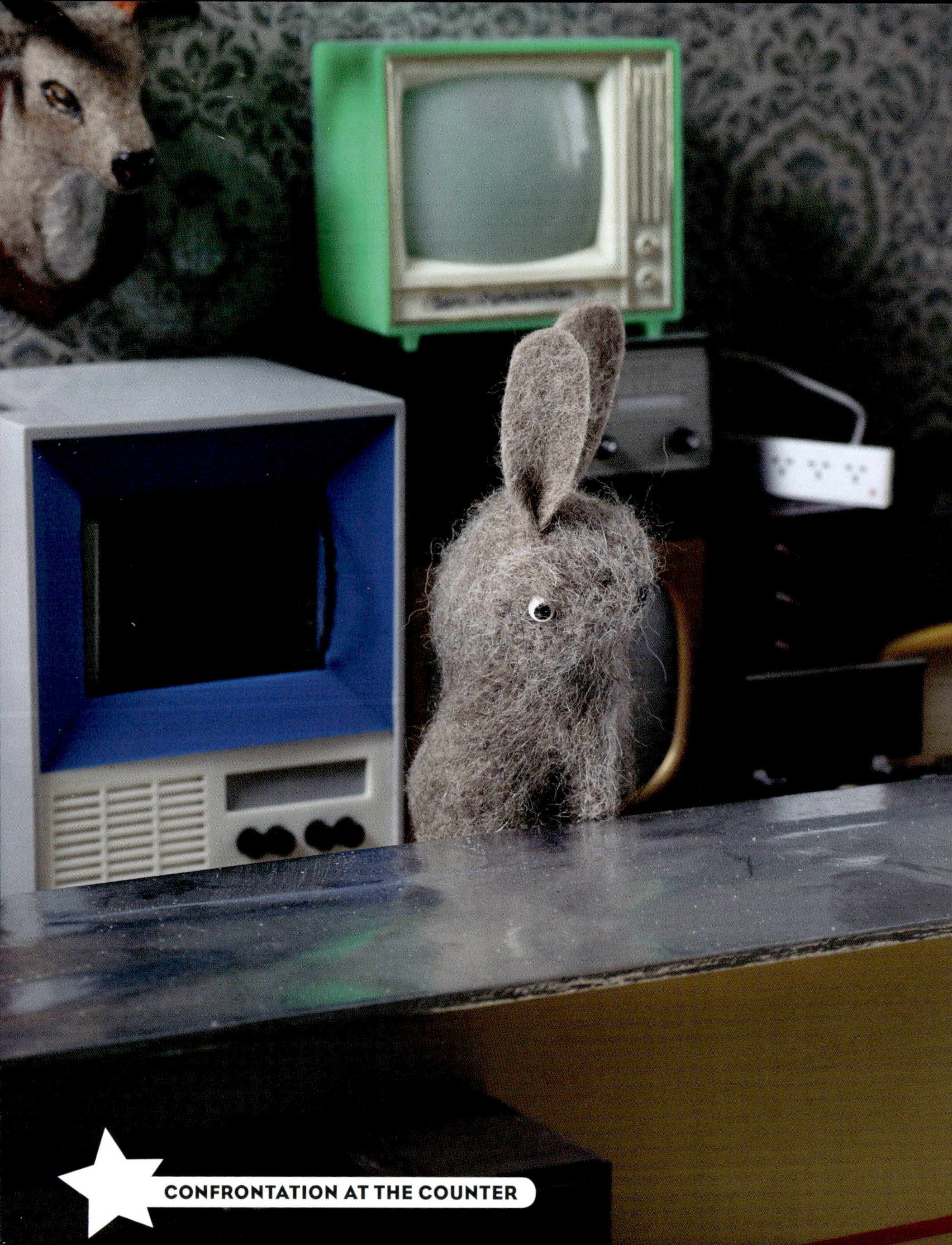
CONFRONTATION AT THE COUNTER

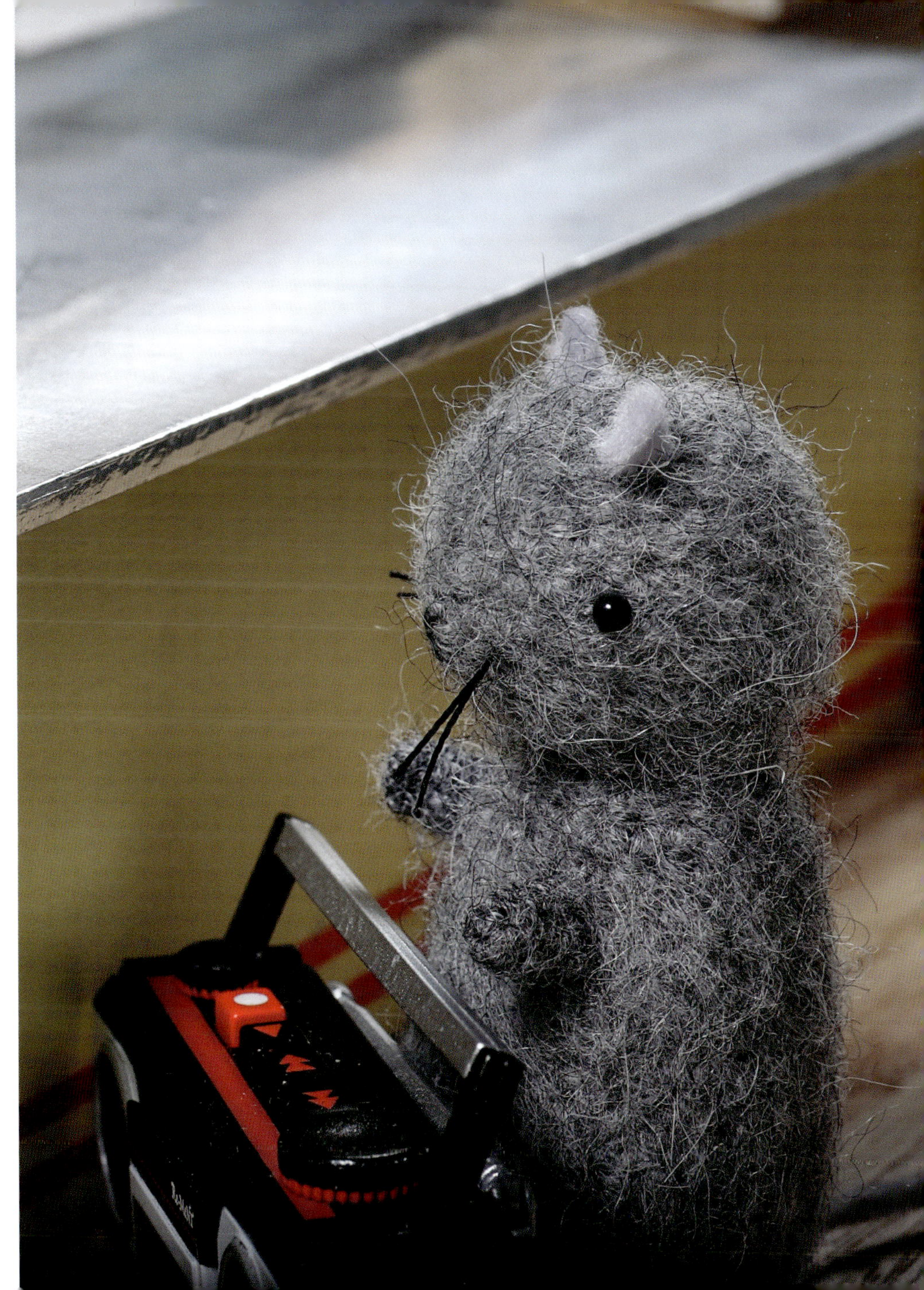

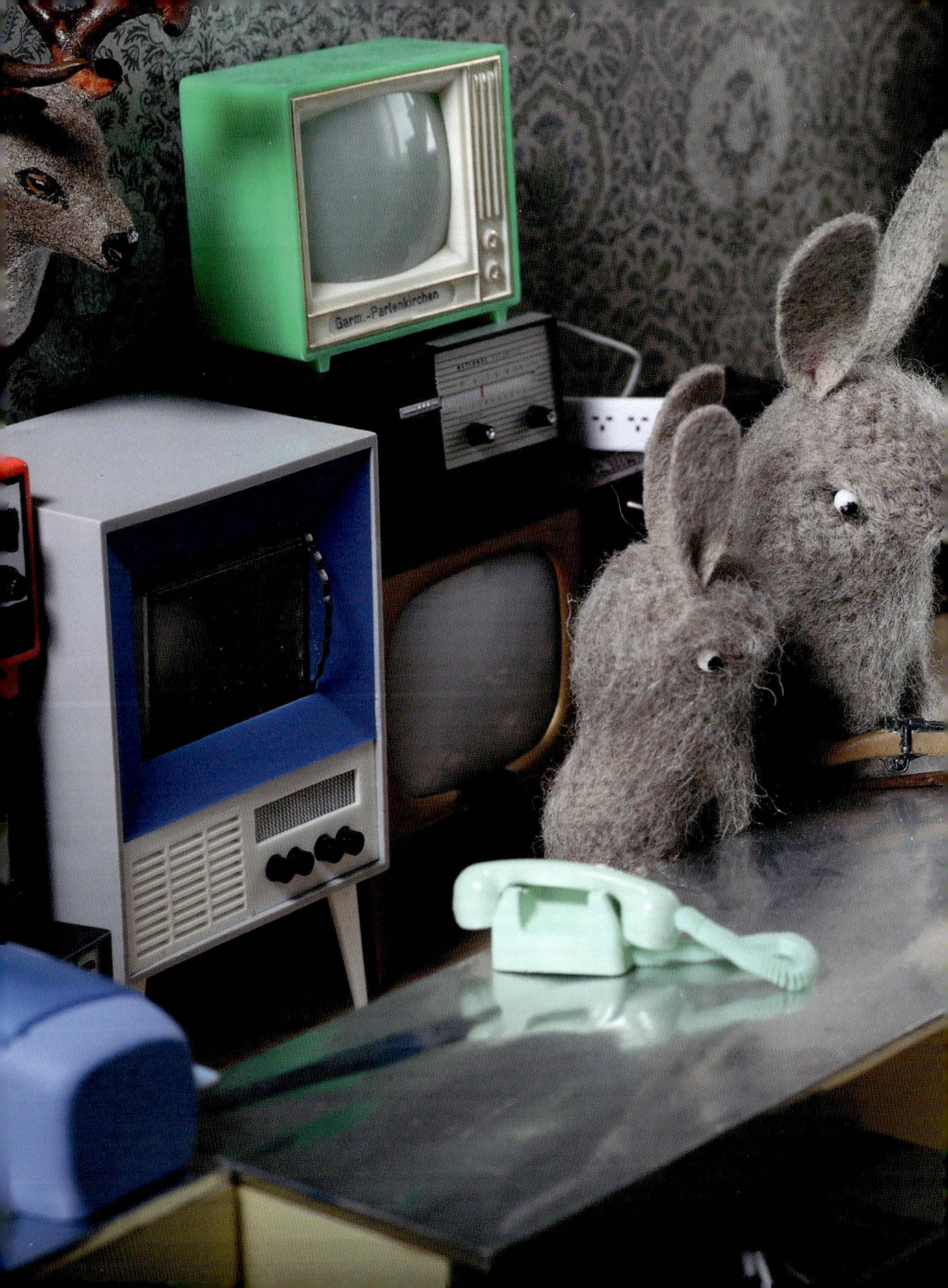
Garm.-Partenkirchen

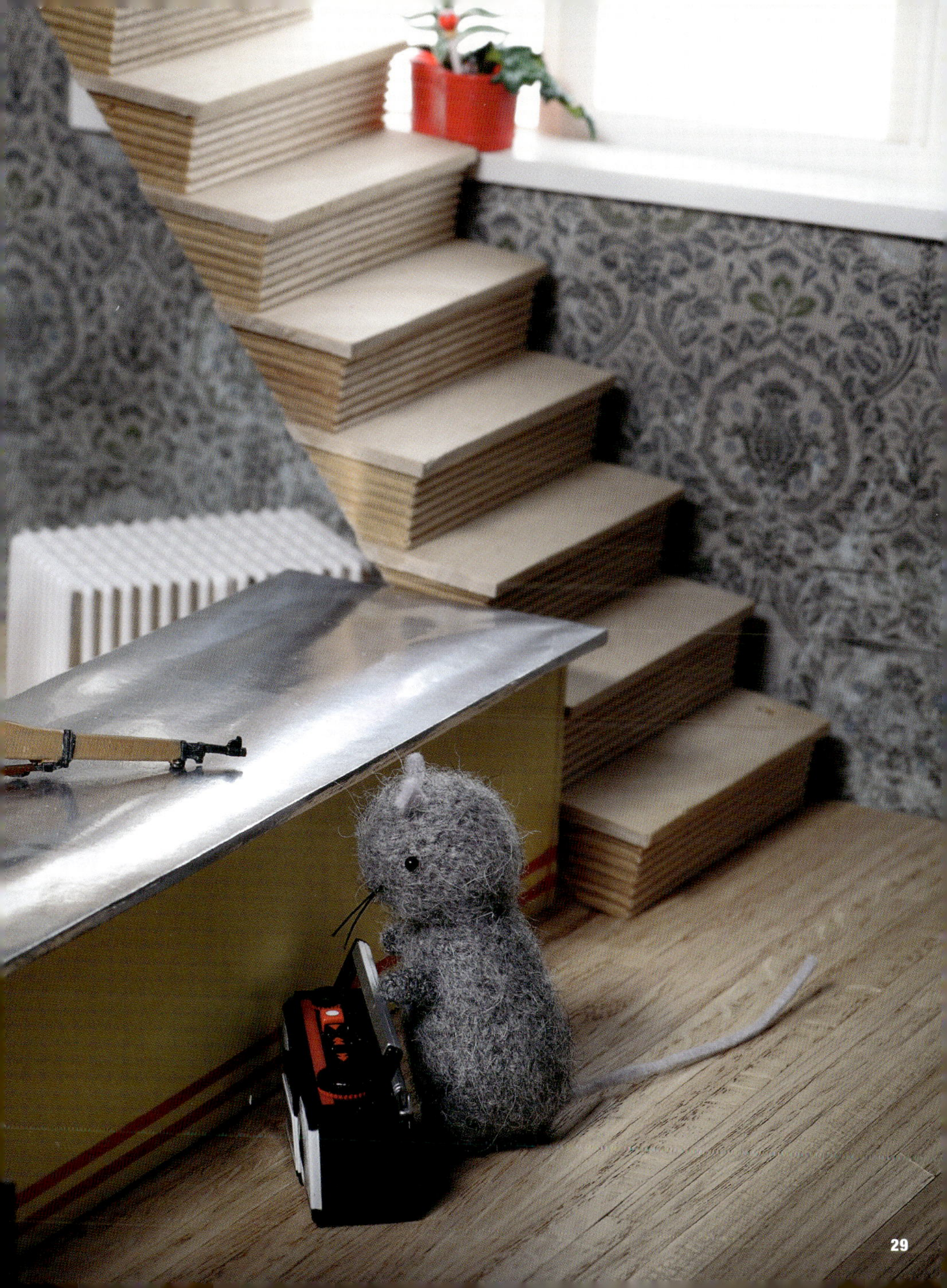

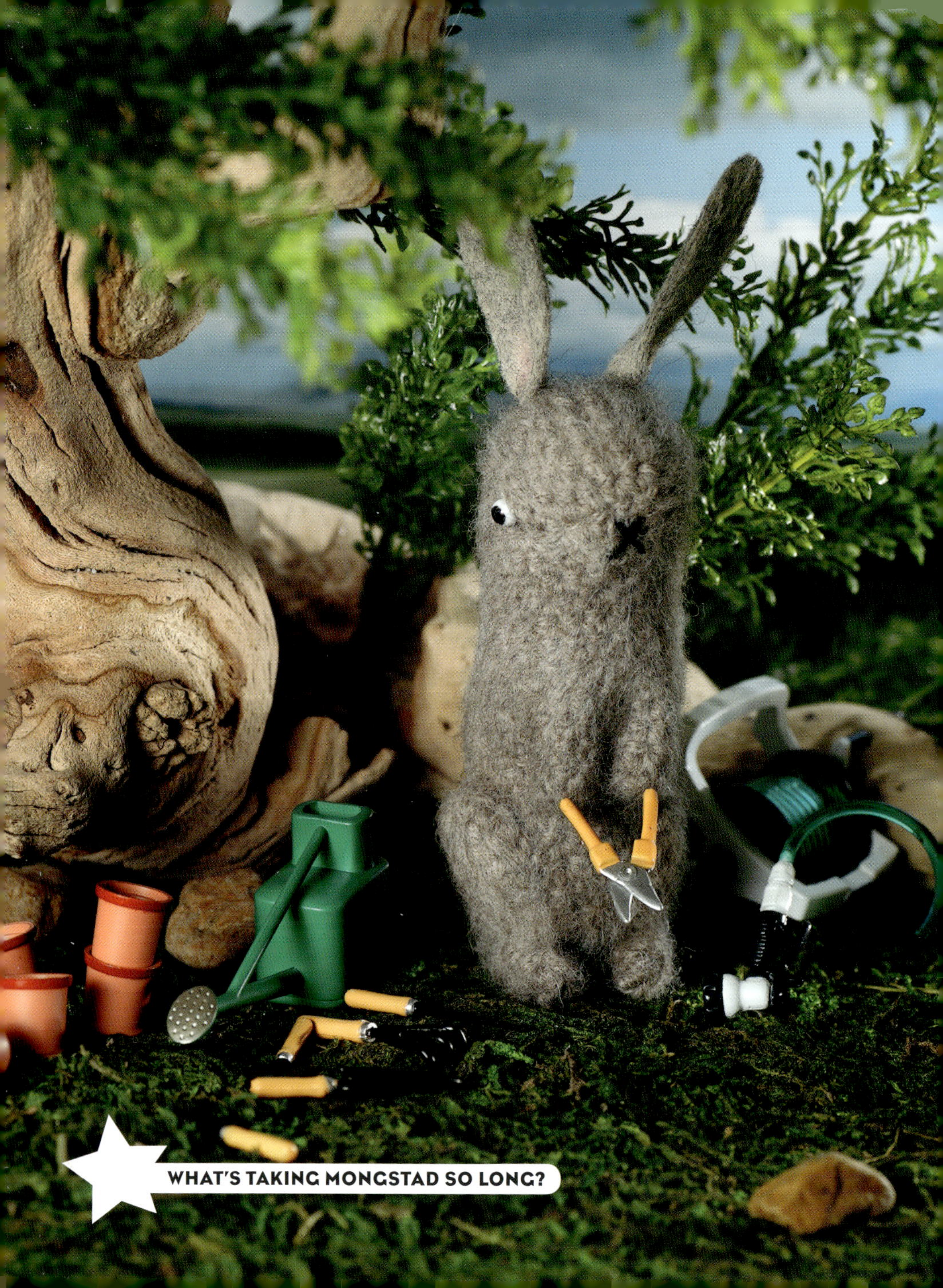
WHAT'S TAKING MONGSTAD SO LONG?

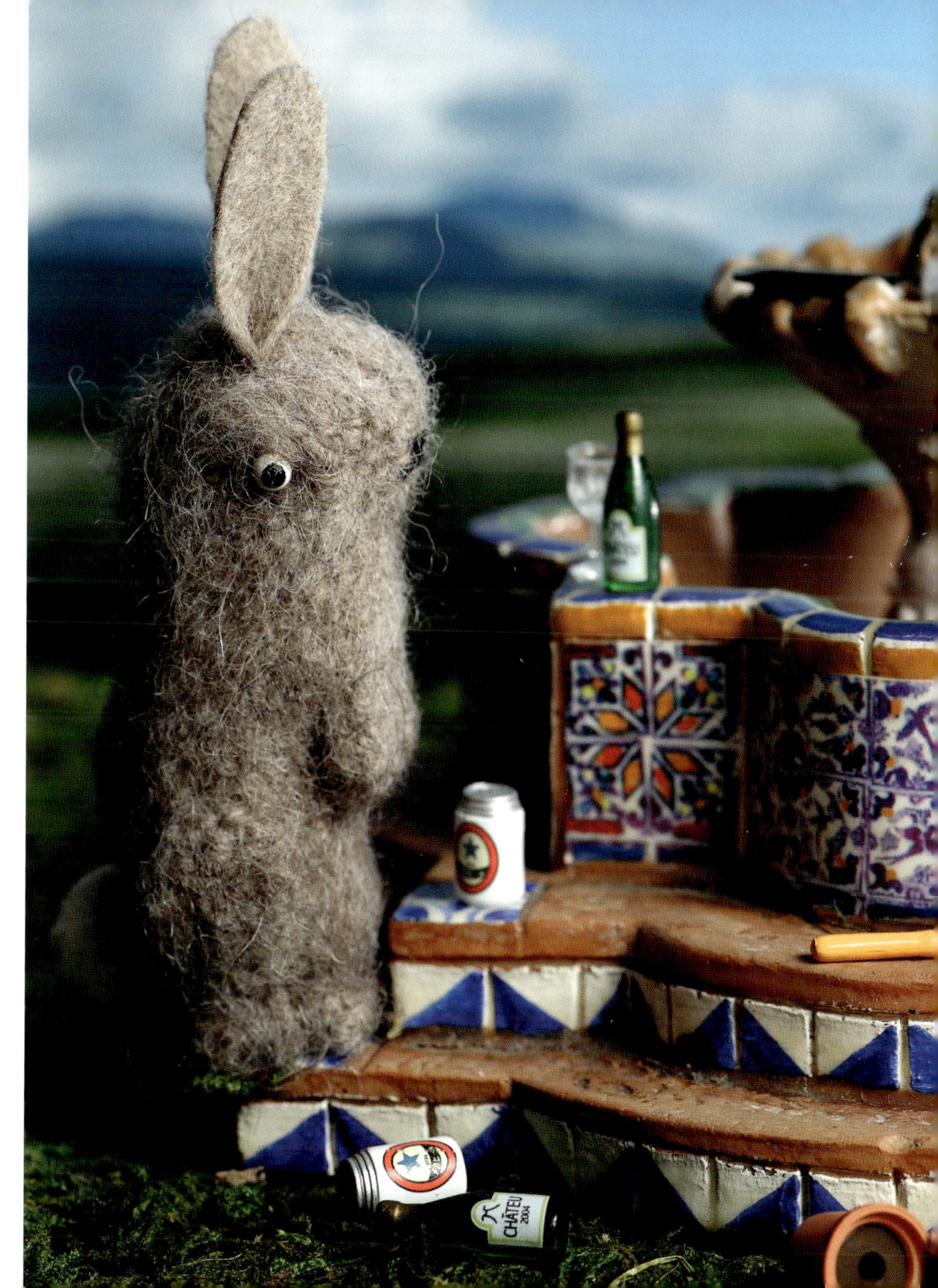

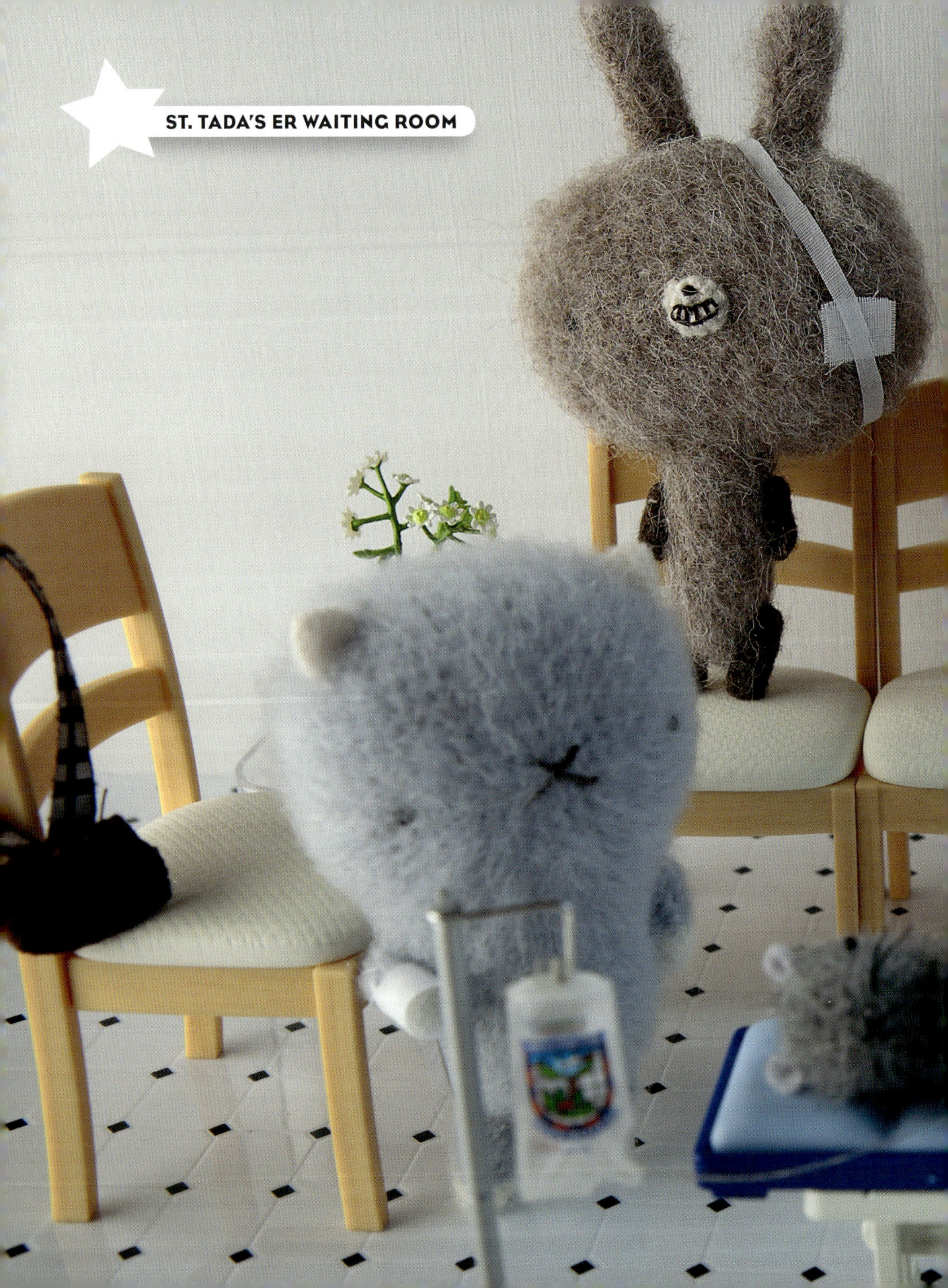
ST. TADA'S ER WAITING ROOM

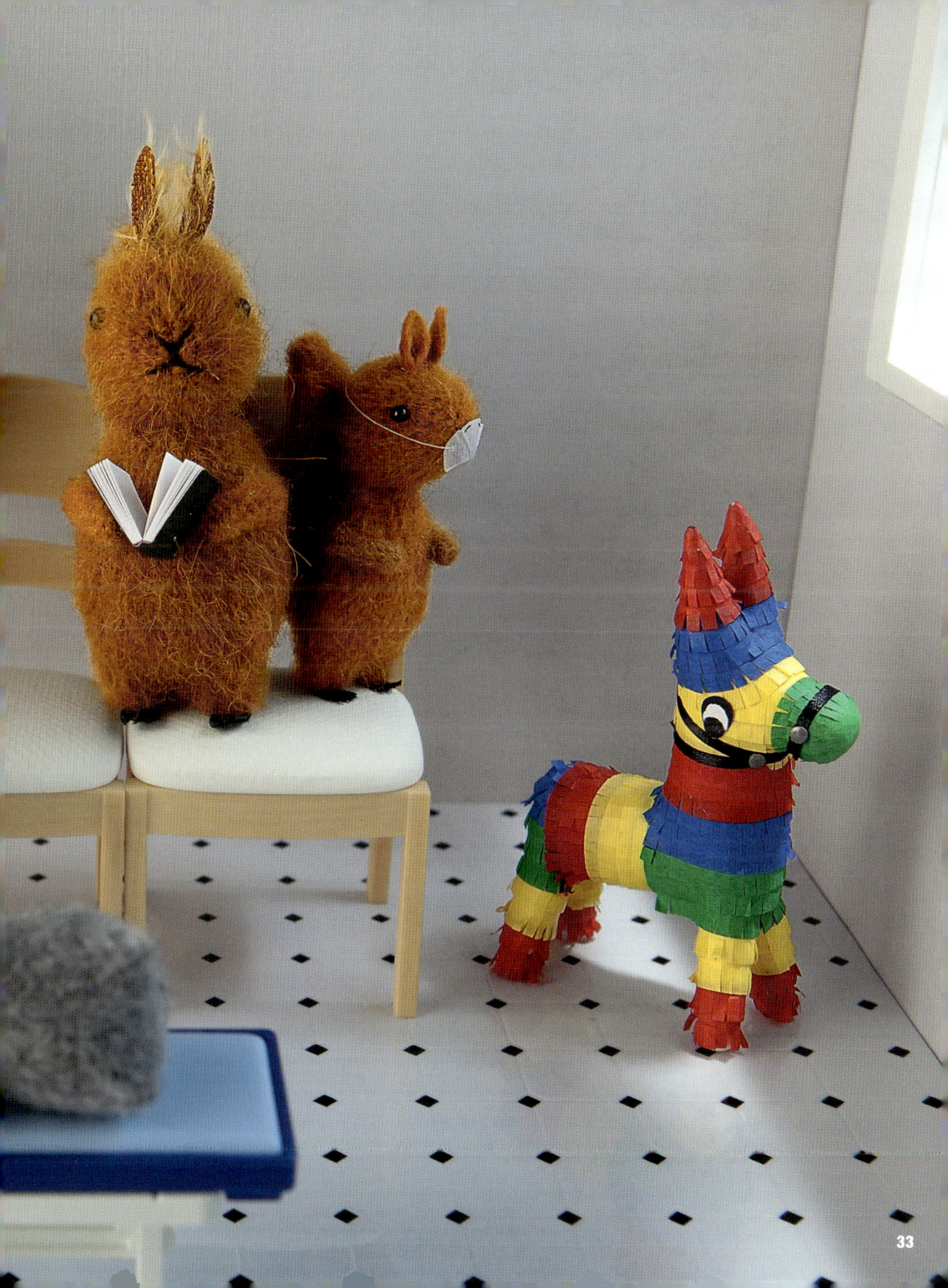

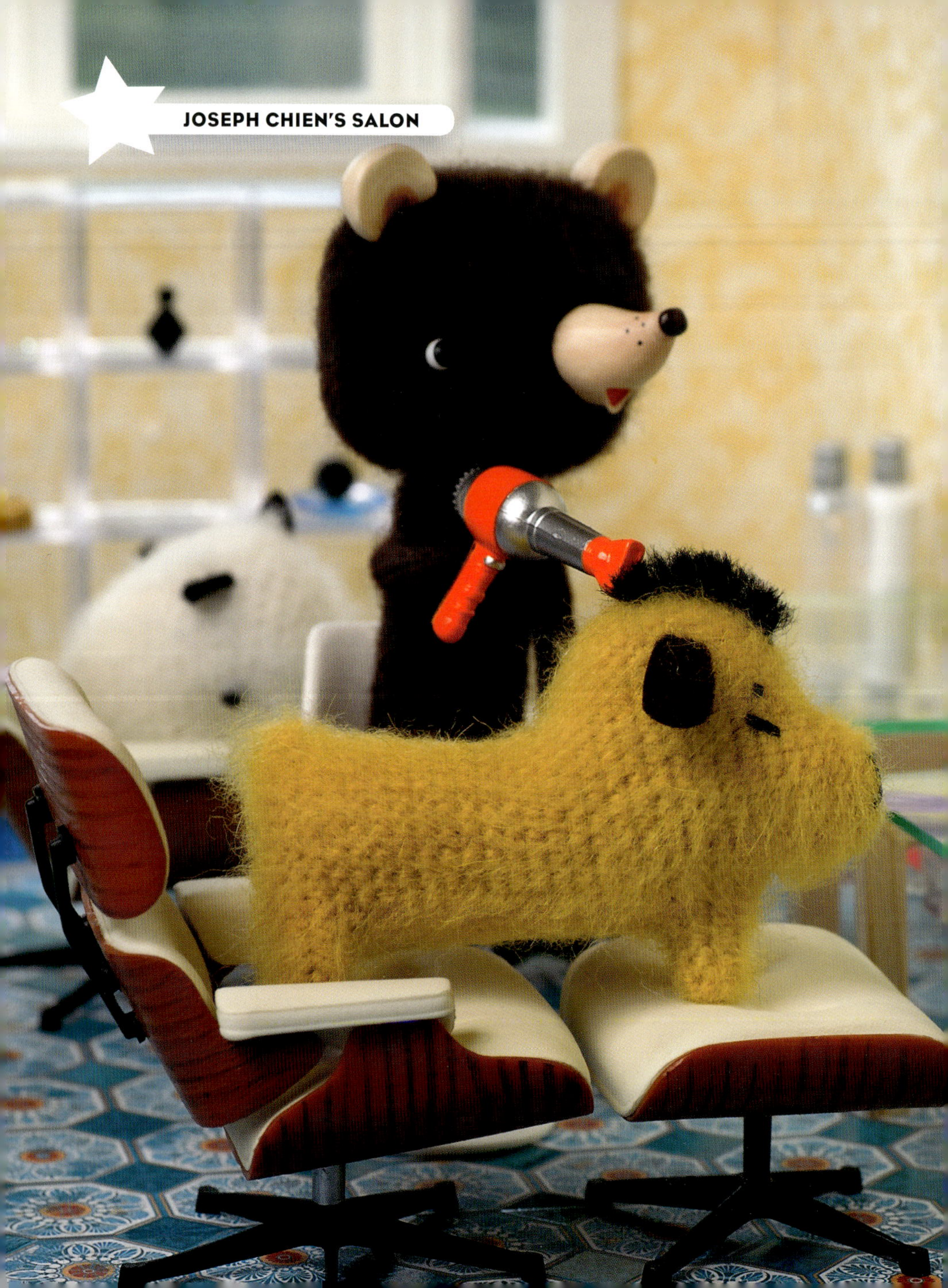
JOSEPH CHIEN'S SALON

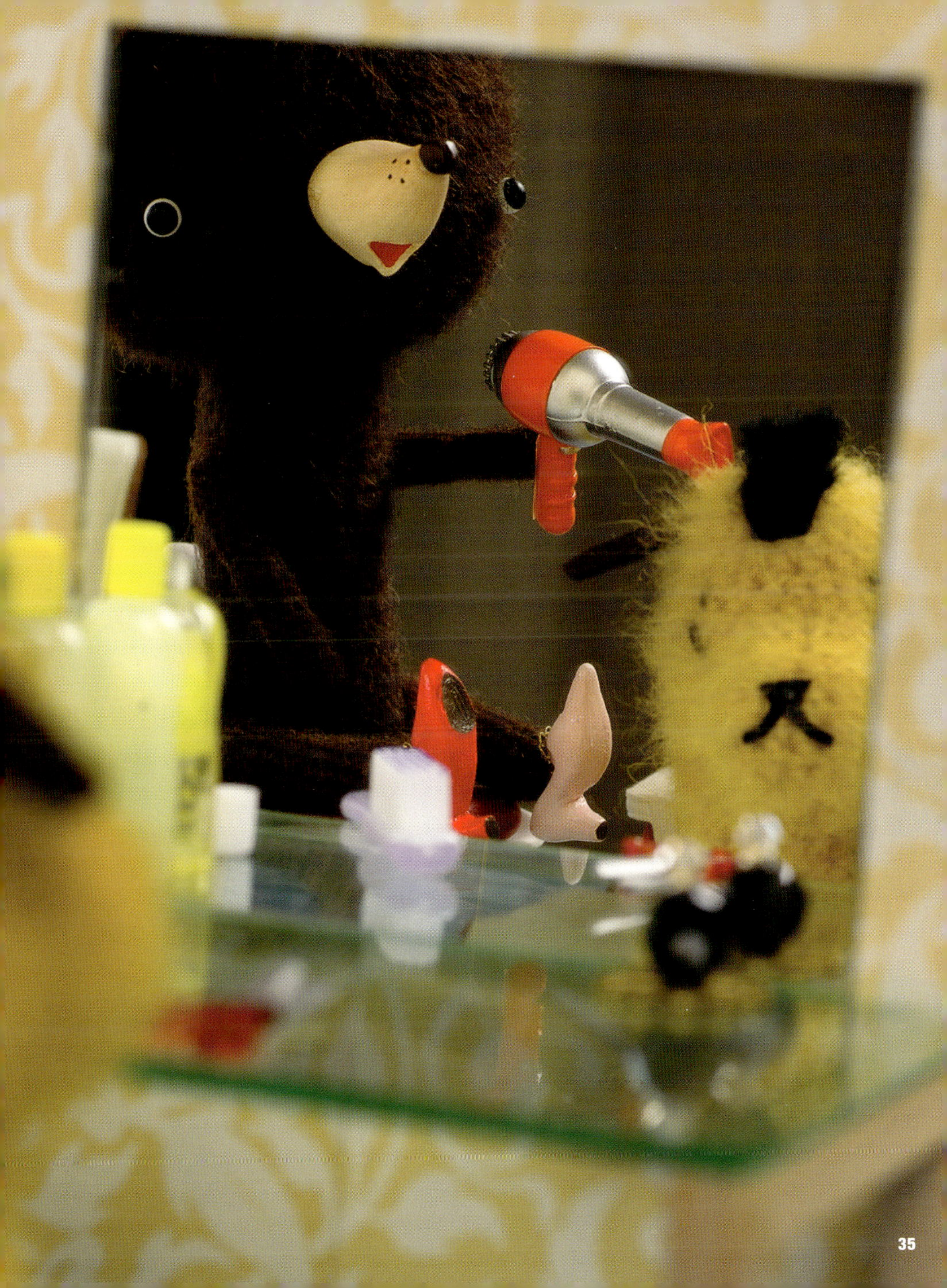

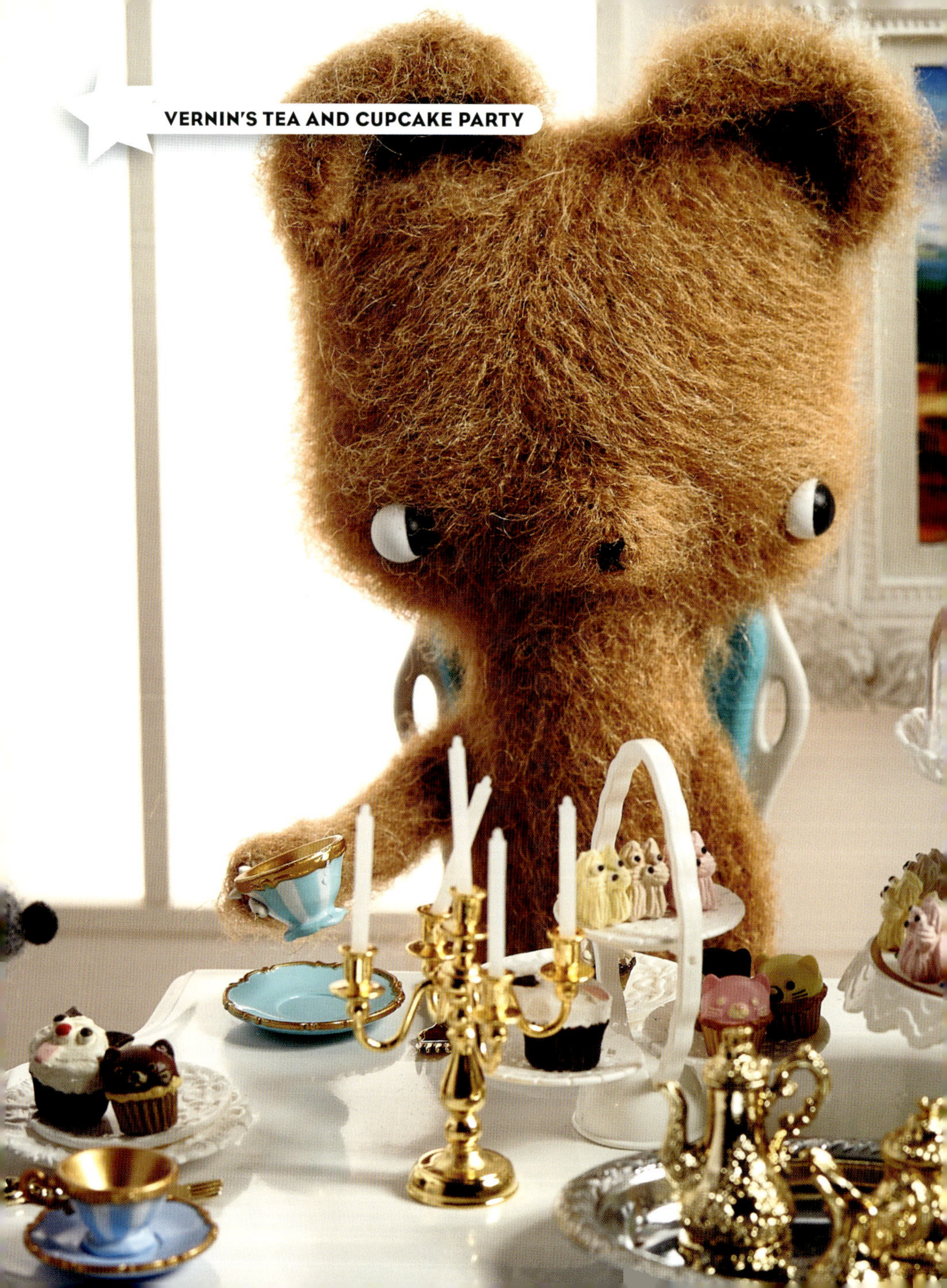
VERNIN'S TEA AND CUPCAKE PARTY

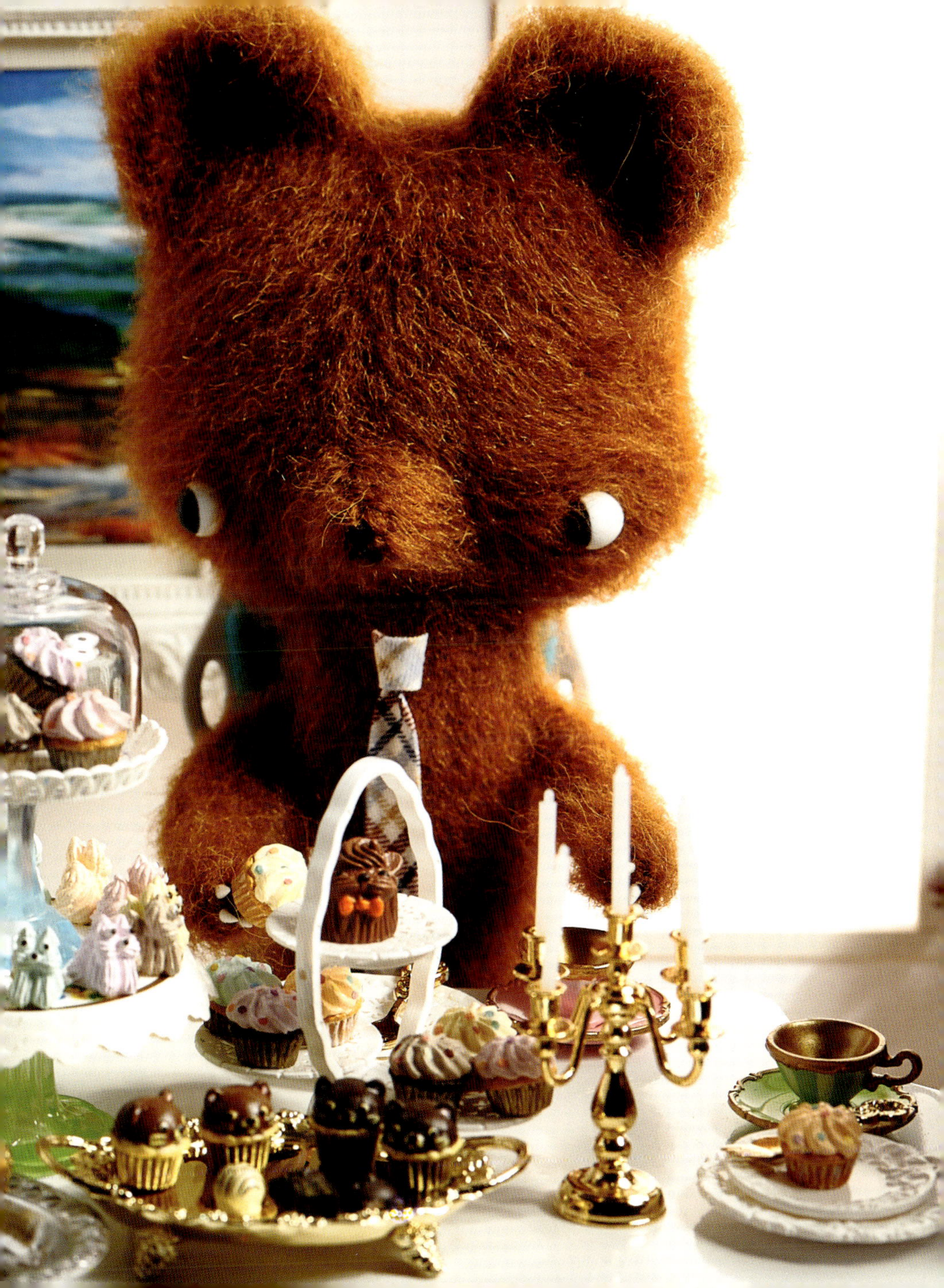

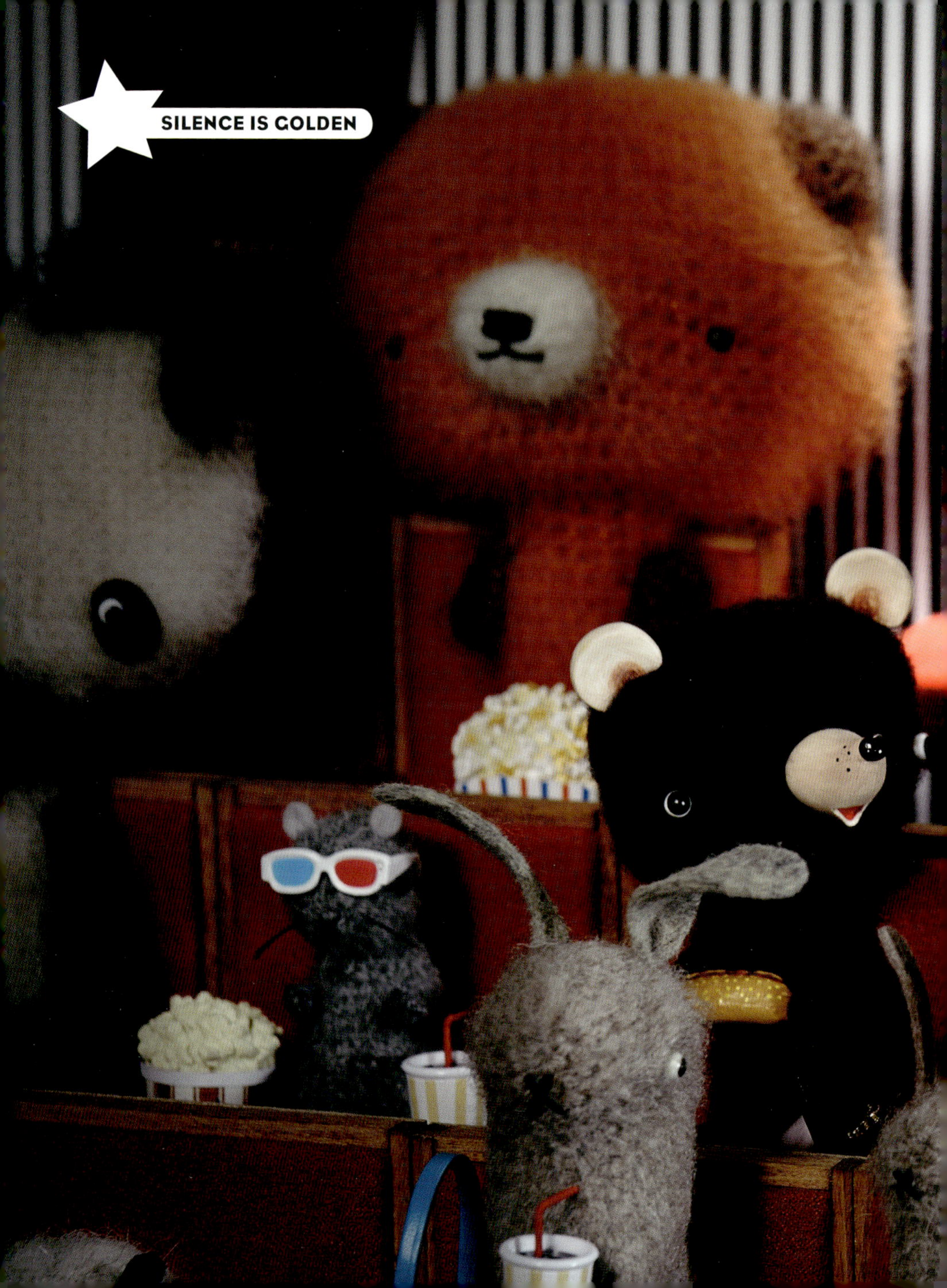

SILENCE IS GOLDEN

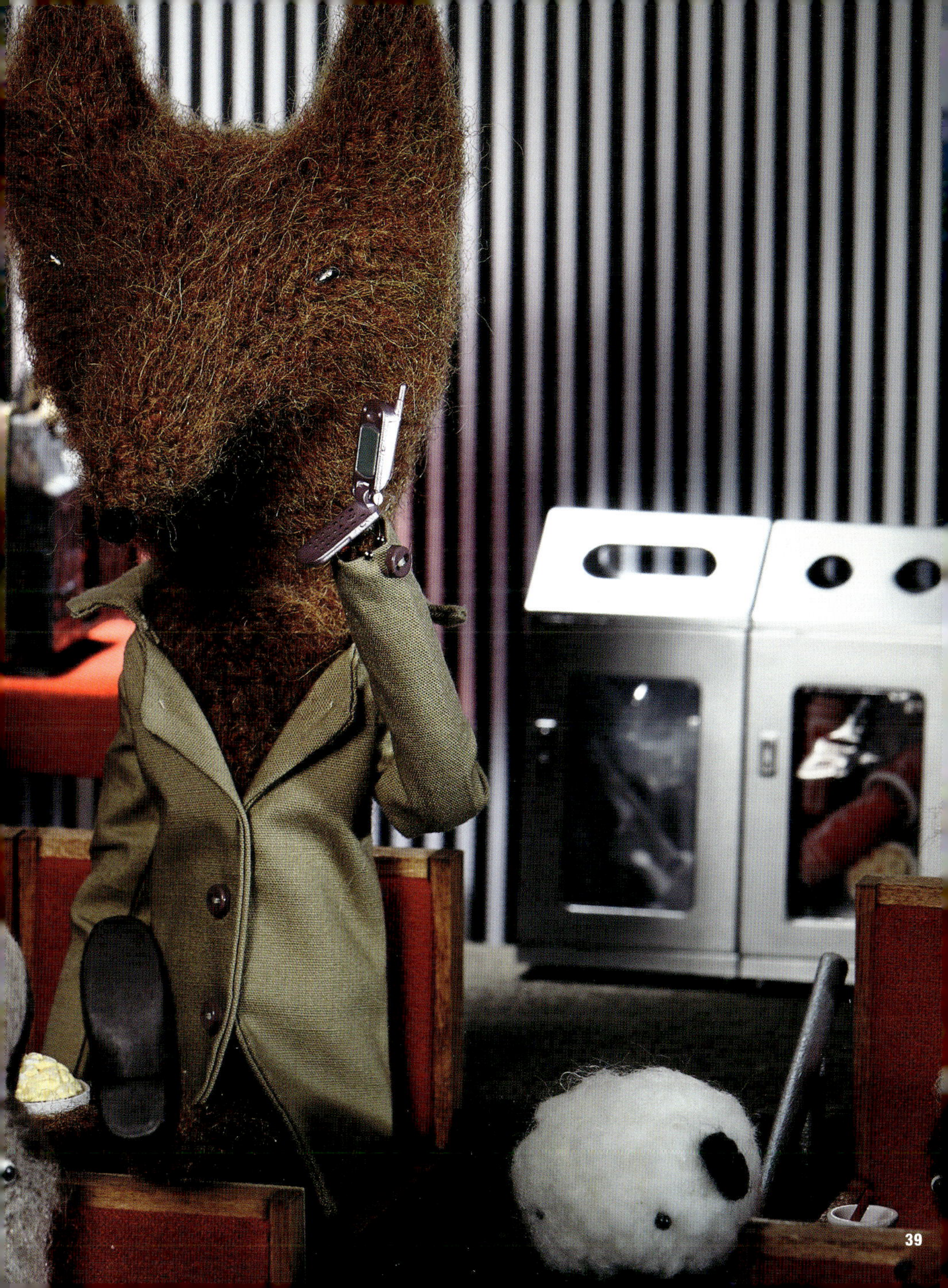

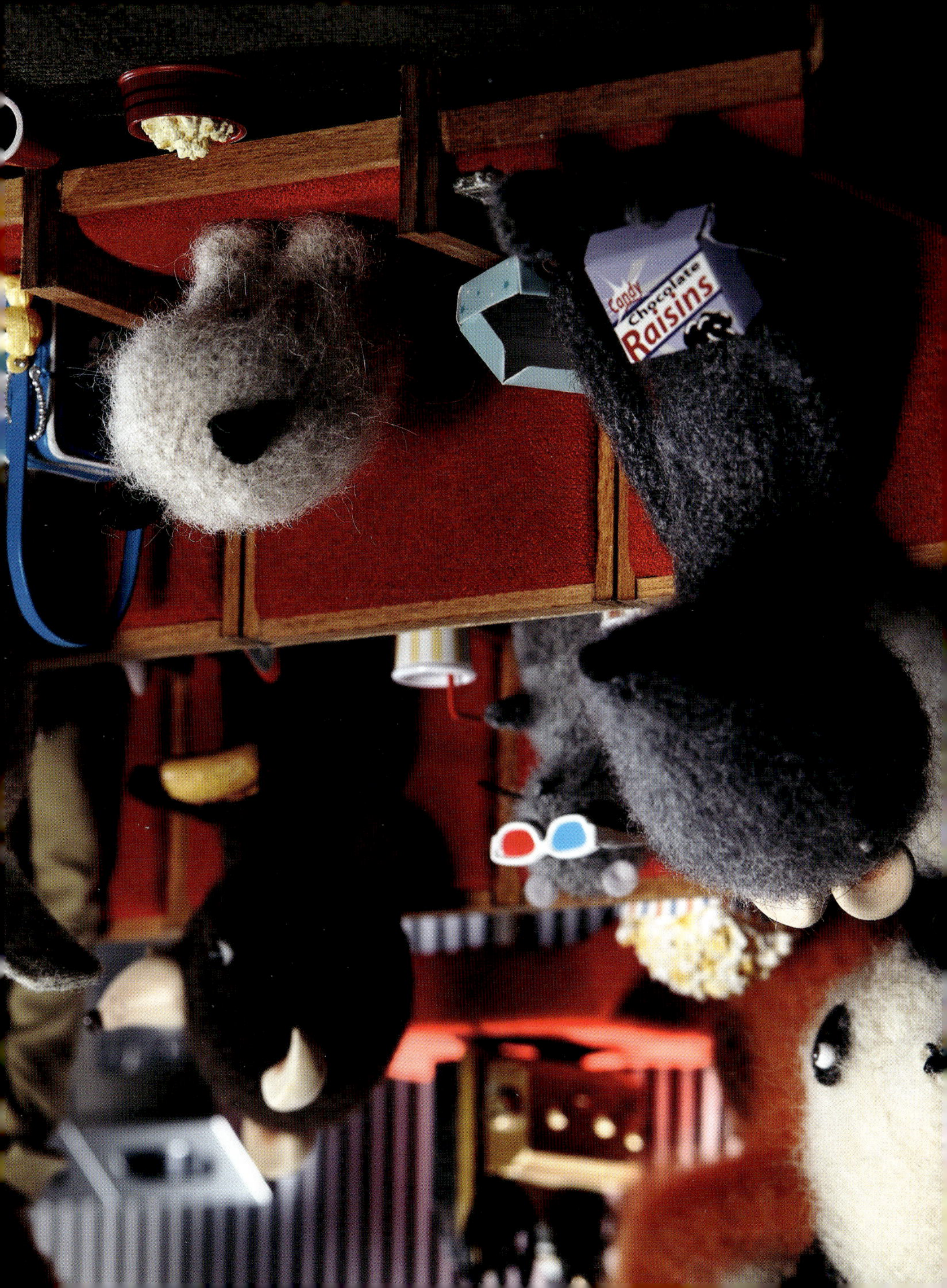

Candy
Chocolate
Raisins

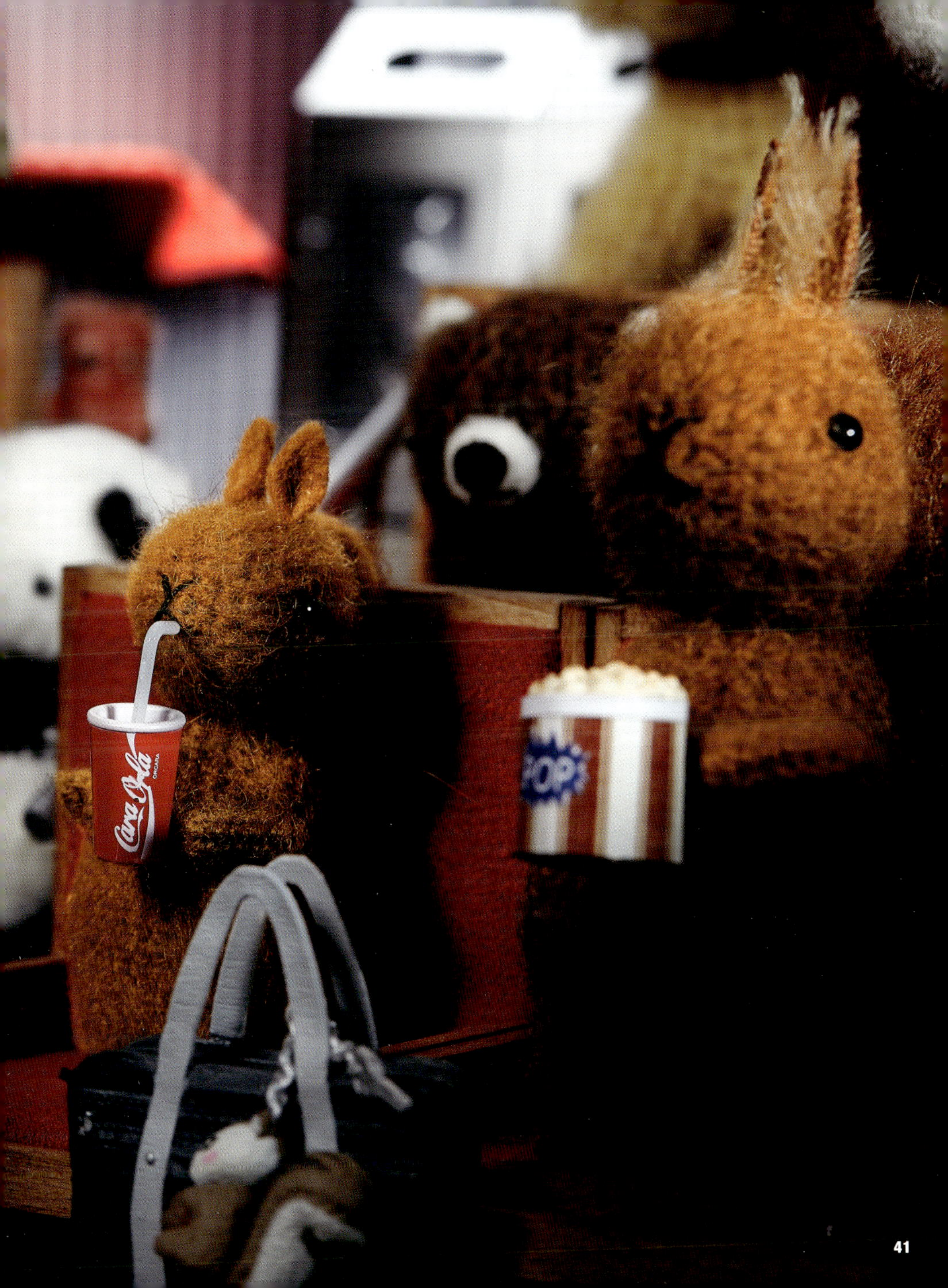

Coca-Cola
POP

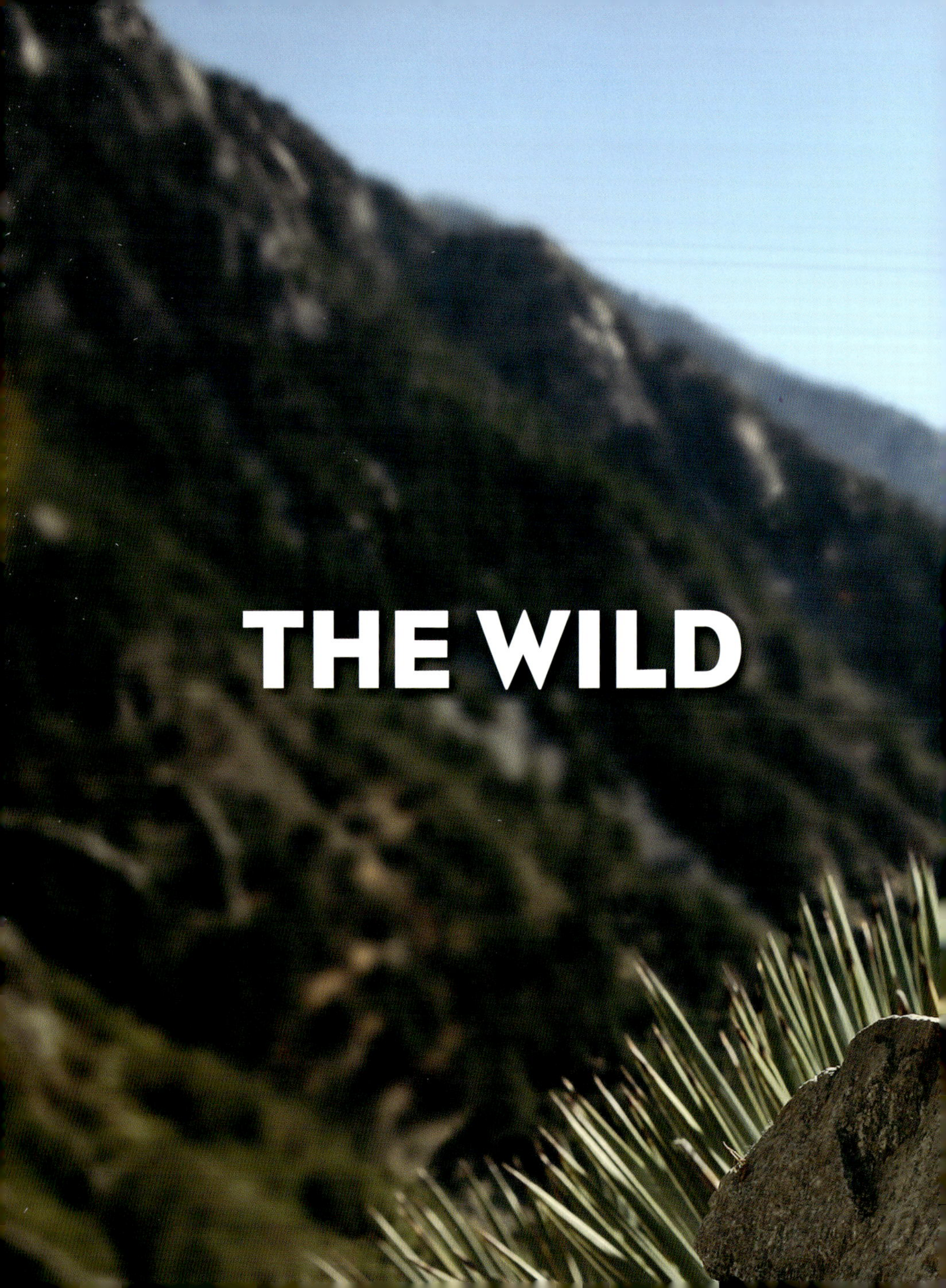

THE WILD

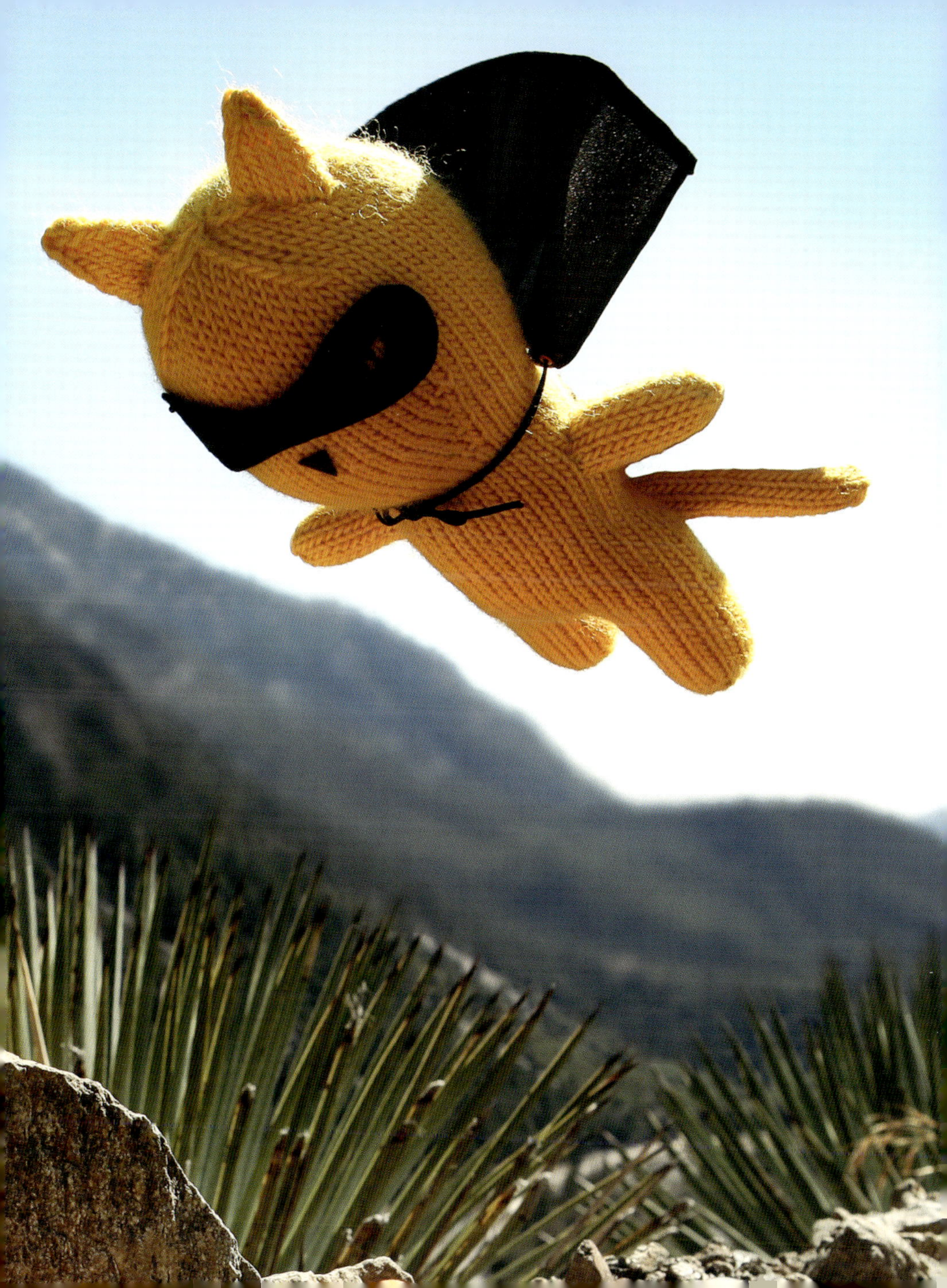

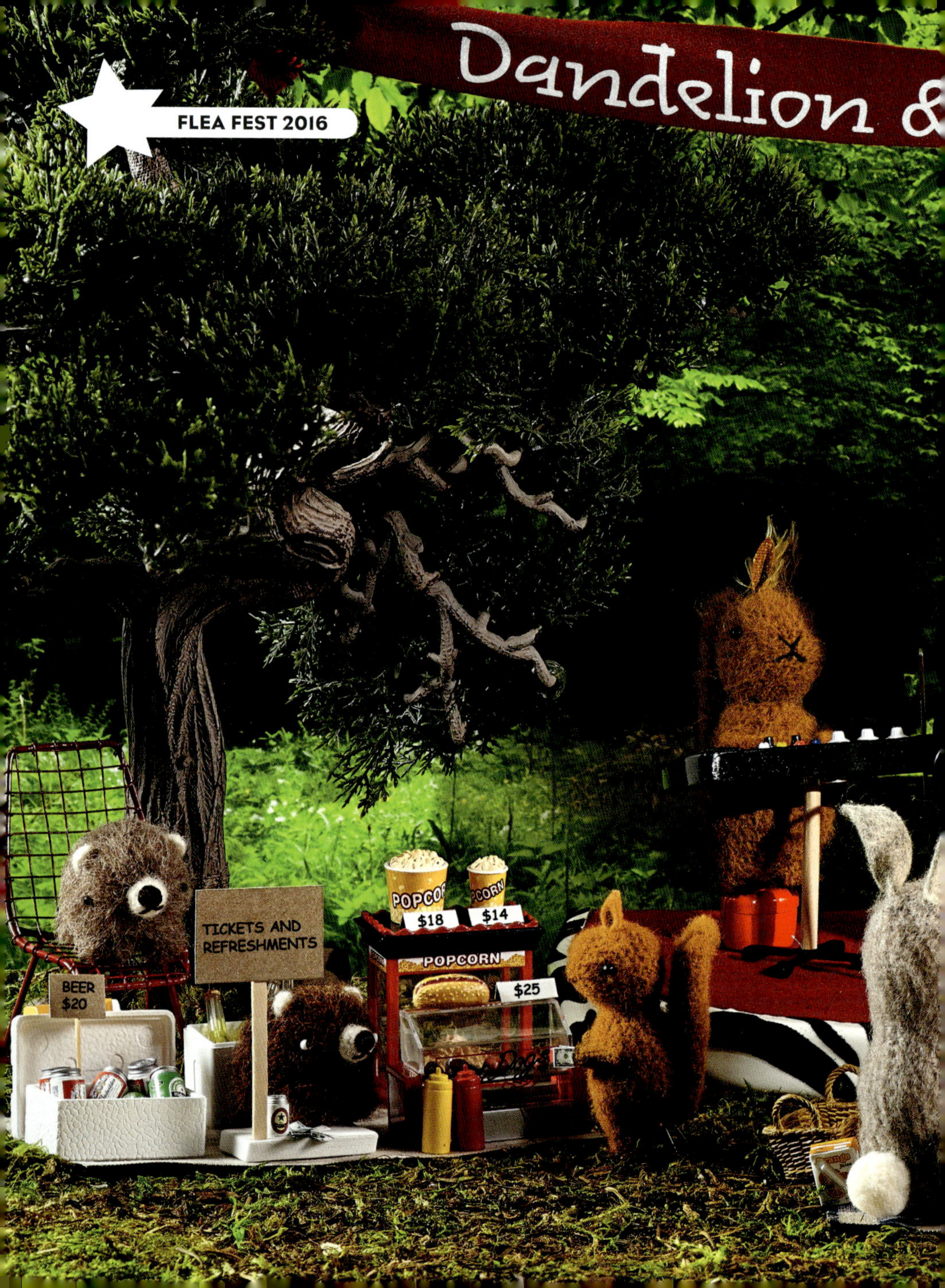
FLEA FEST 2016
Dandelion &
TICKETS AND
REFRESHMENTS
POPCORN
POPCORN
$18
$14
POPCORN
$25
BEER
$20

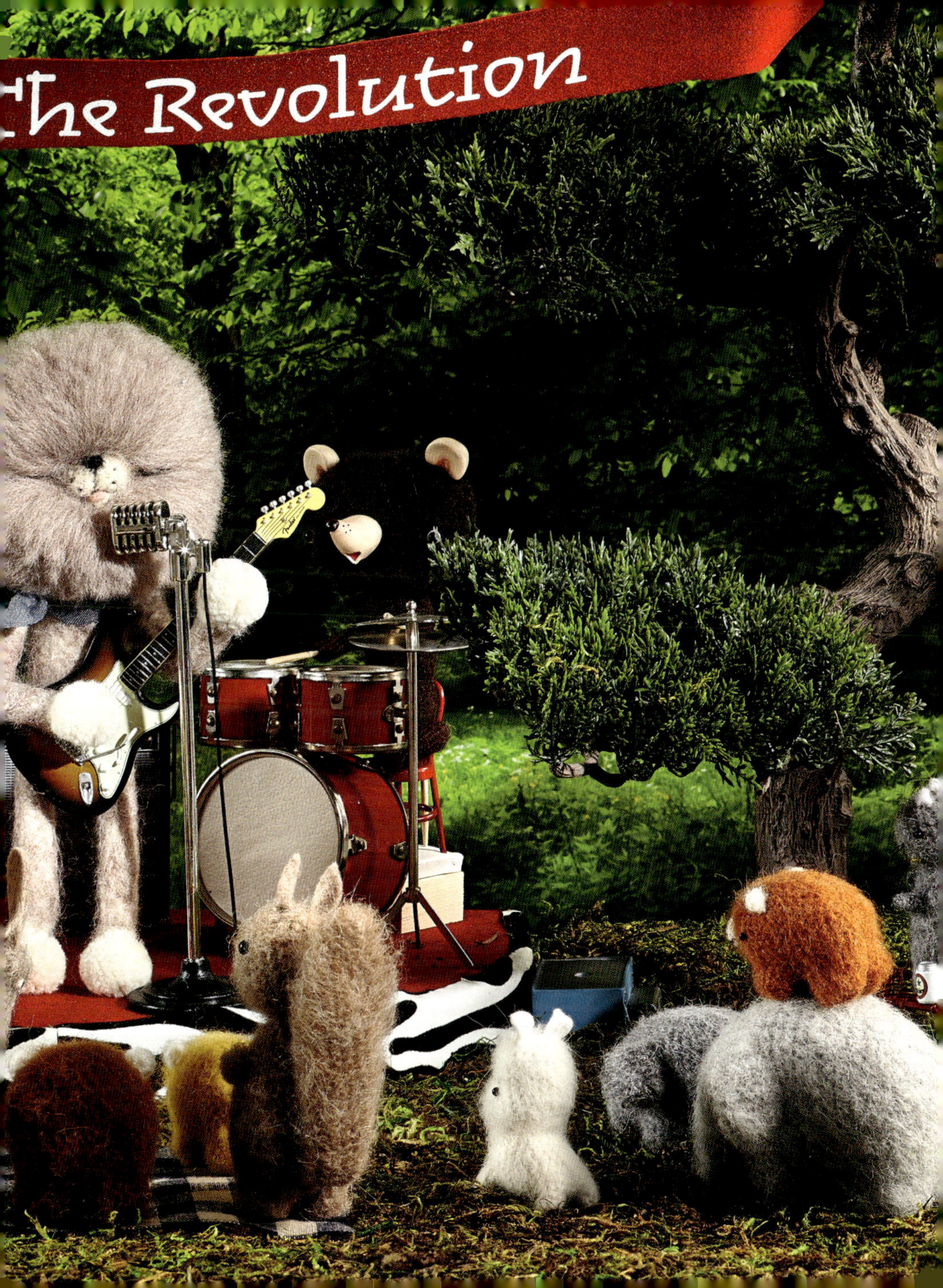
The Revolution

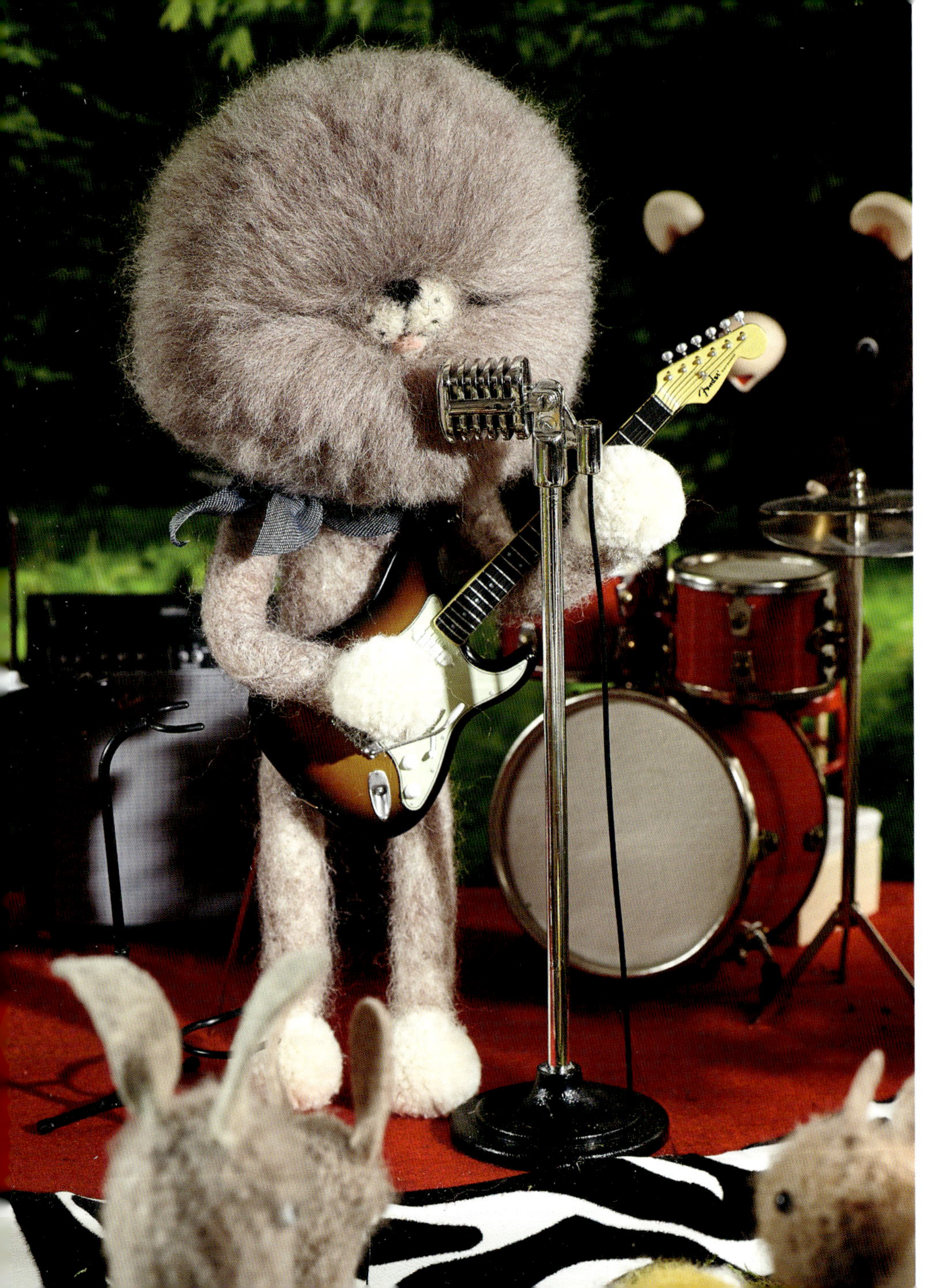

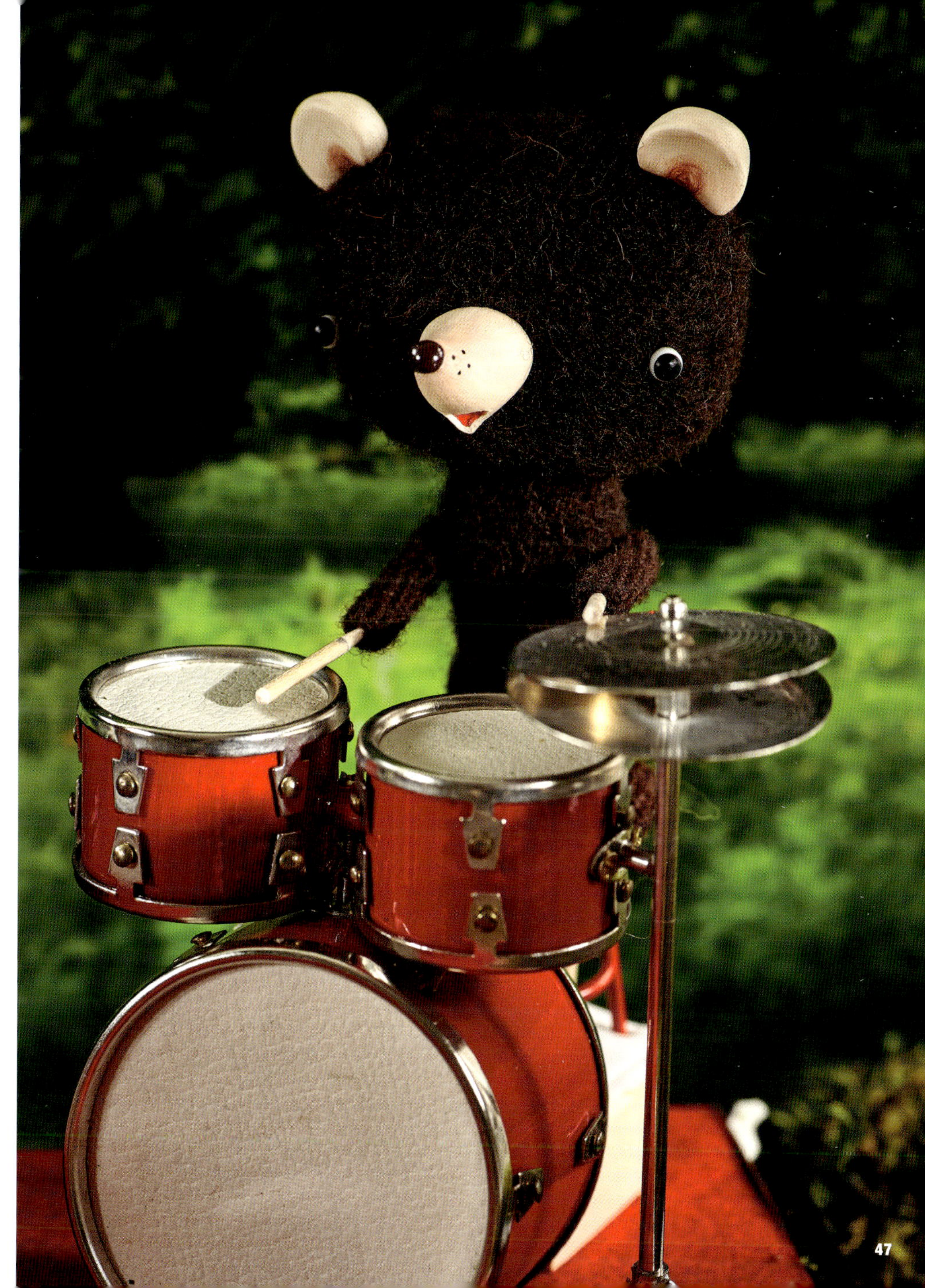

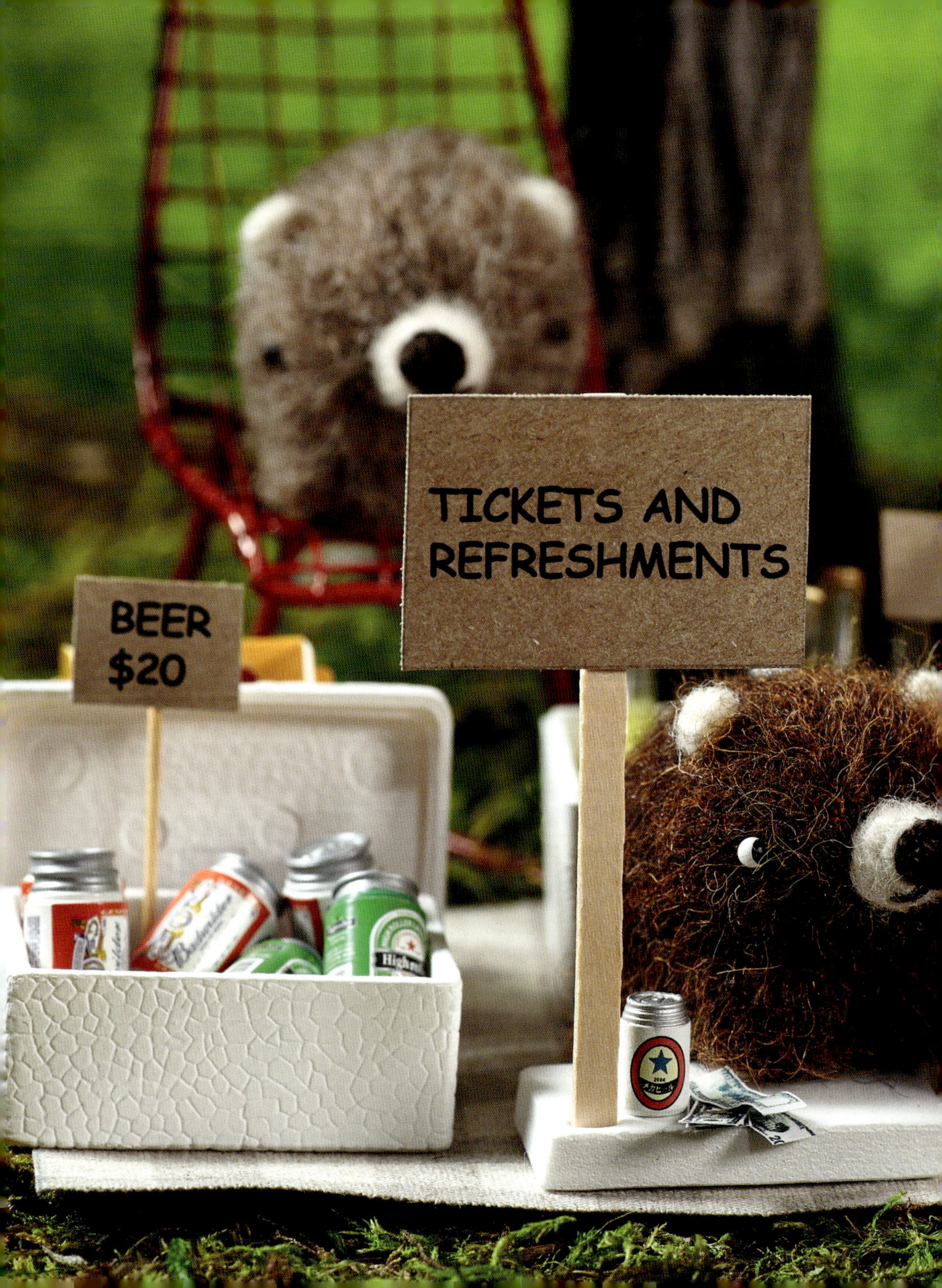
TICKETS AND
REFRESHMENTS
BEER
$20

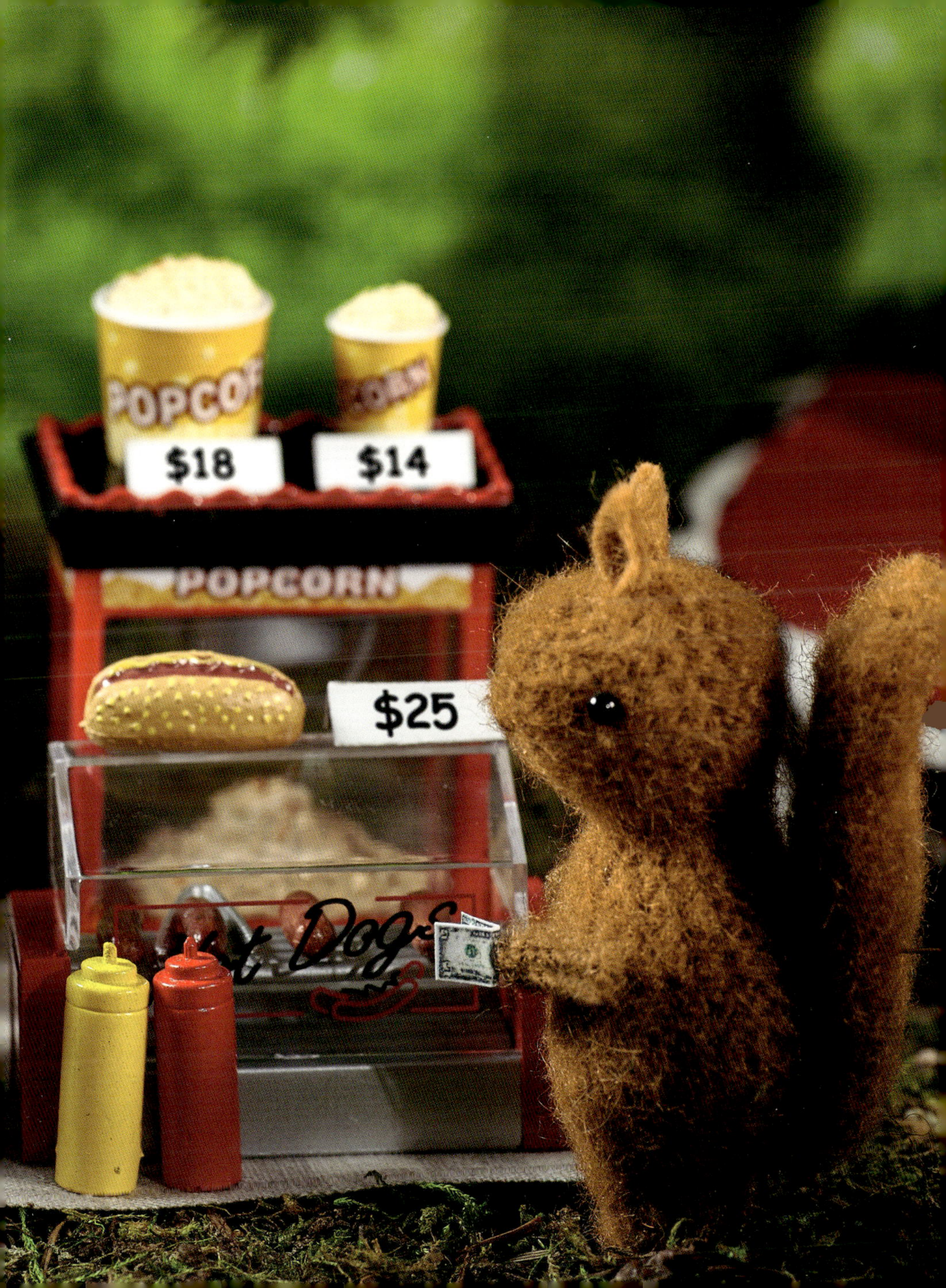

POPCOR
POPC
$18
$14
POPCORN
$25
Dogs

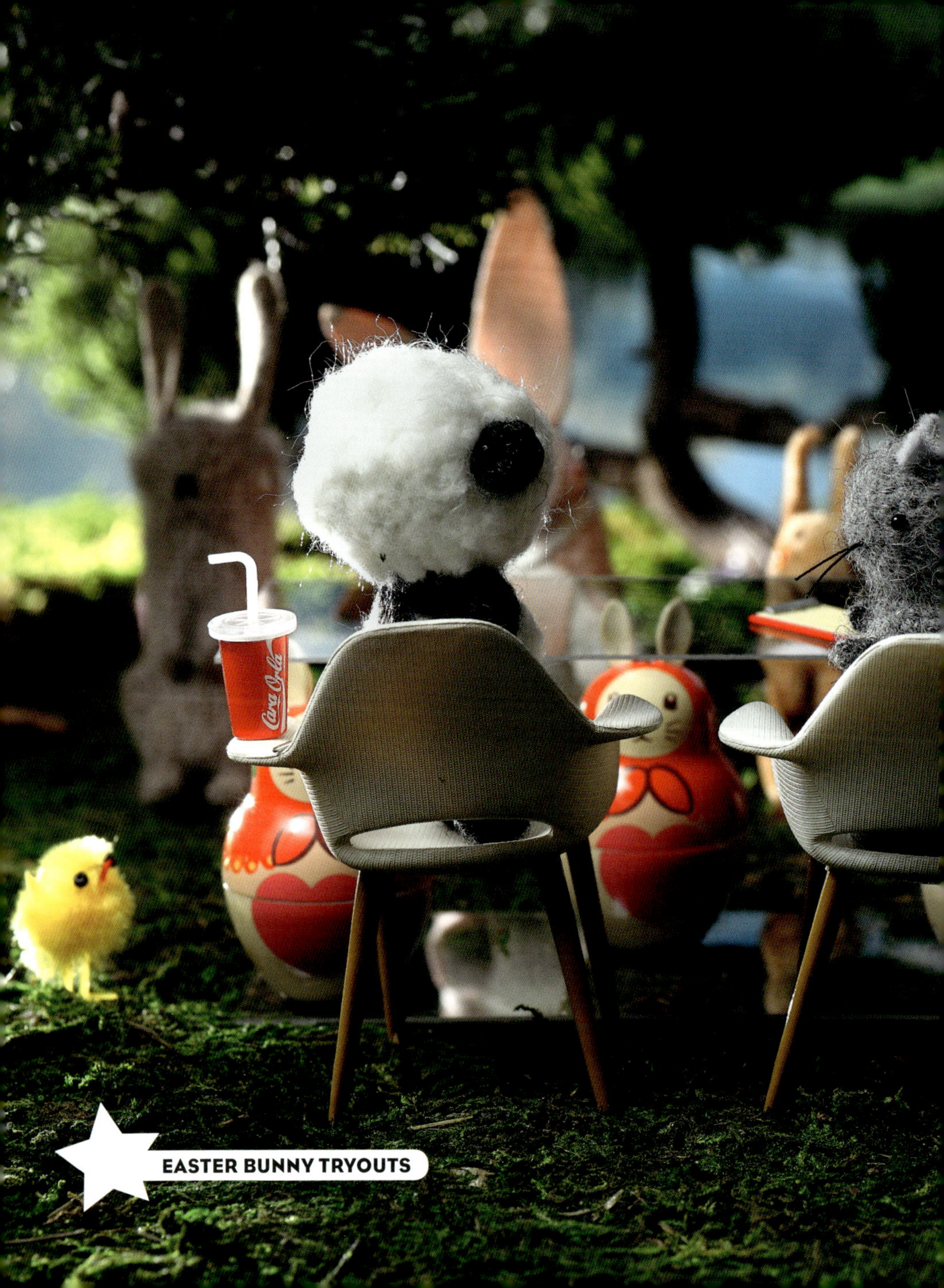

EASTER BUNNY TRYOUTS

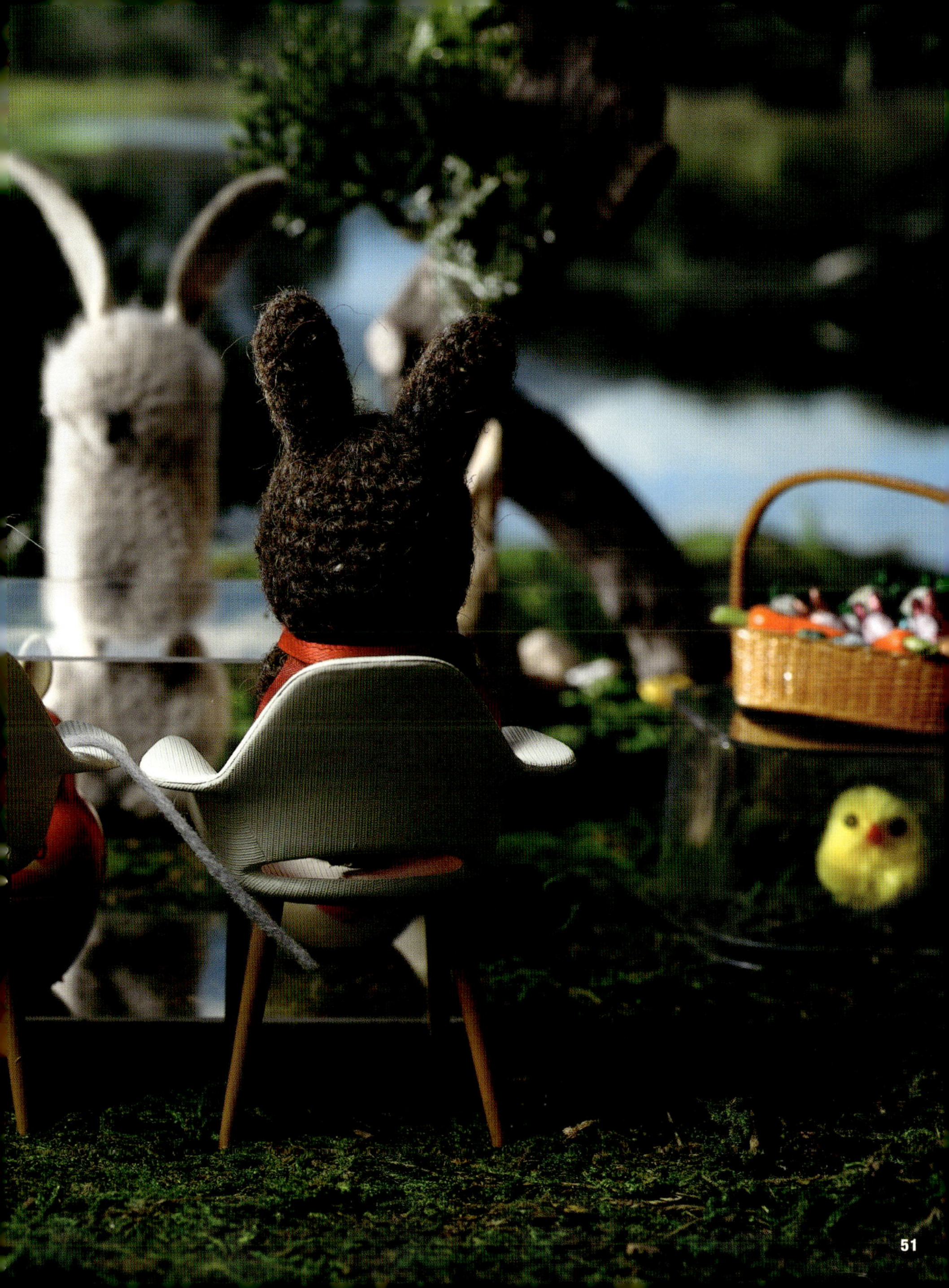

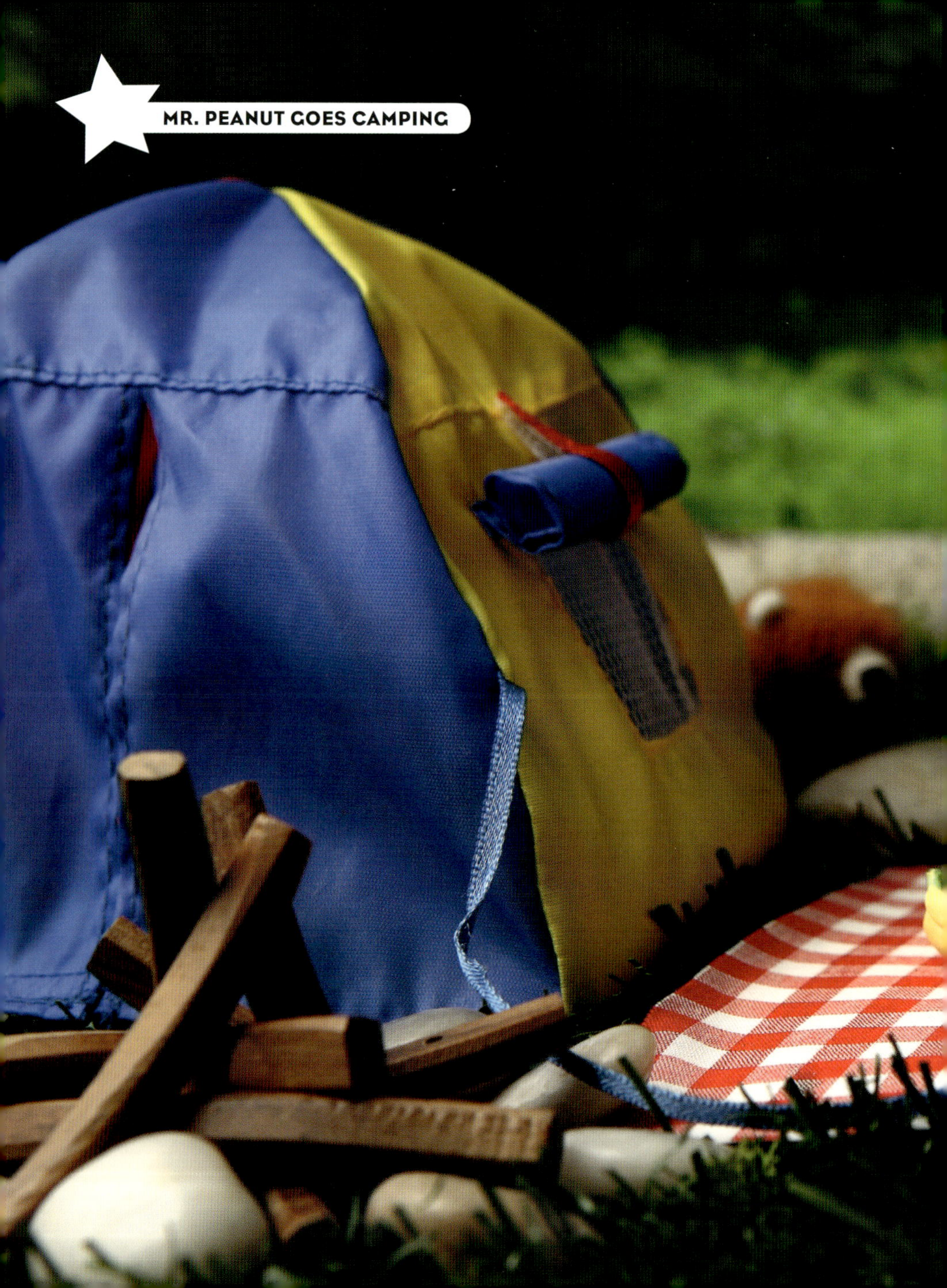
MR. PEANUT GOES CAMPING

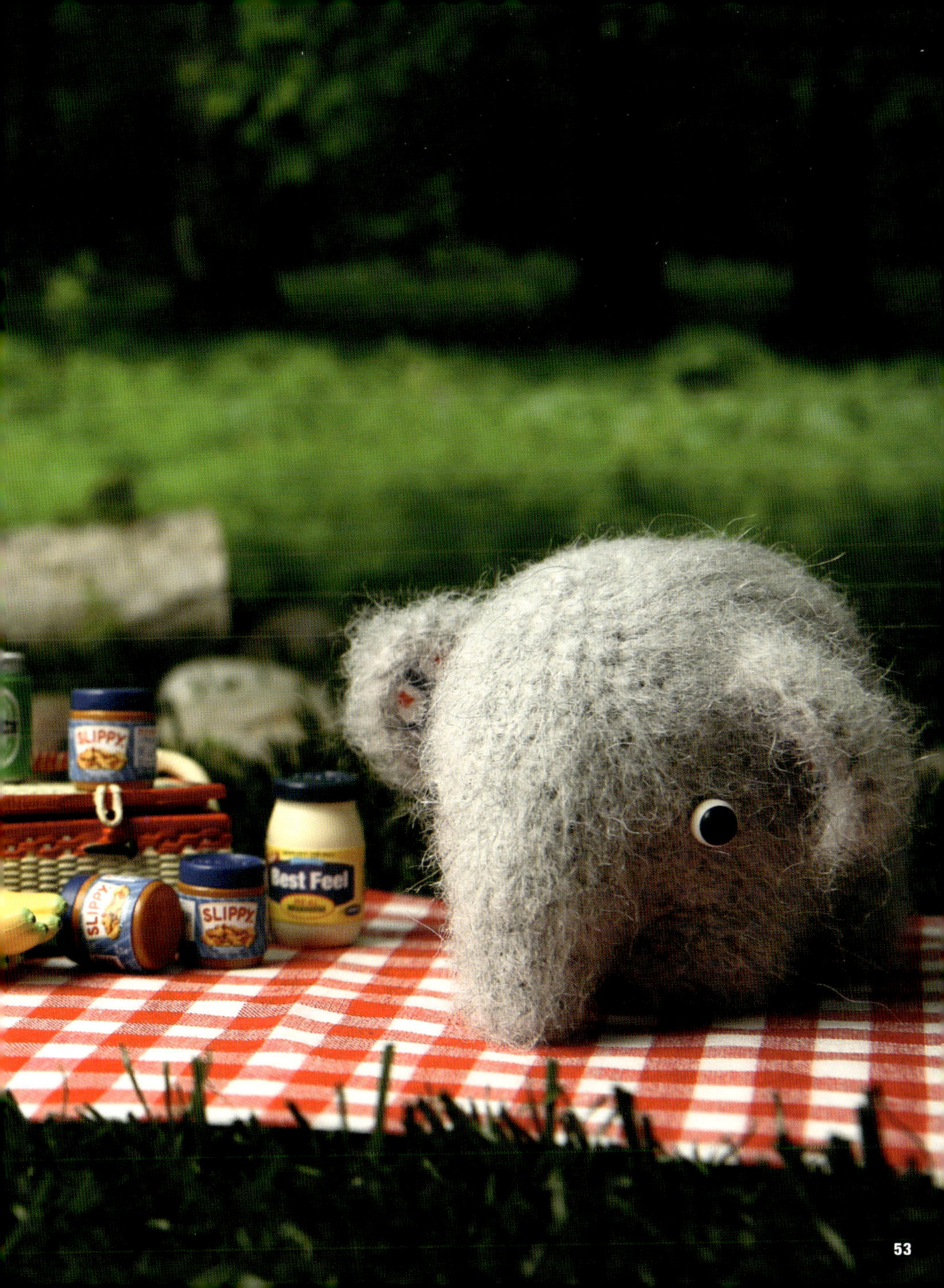
SLIPPY
Best Feel
SLIPPY
SLIPPY

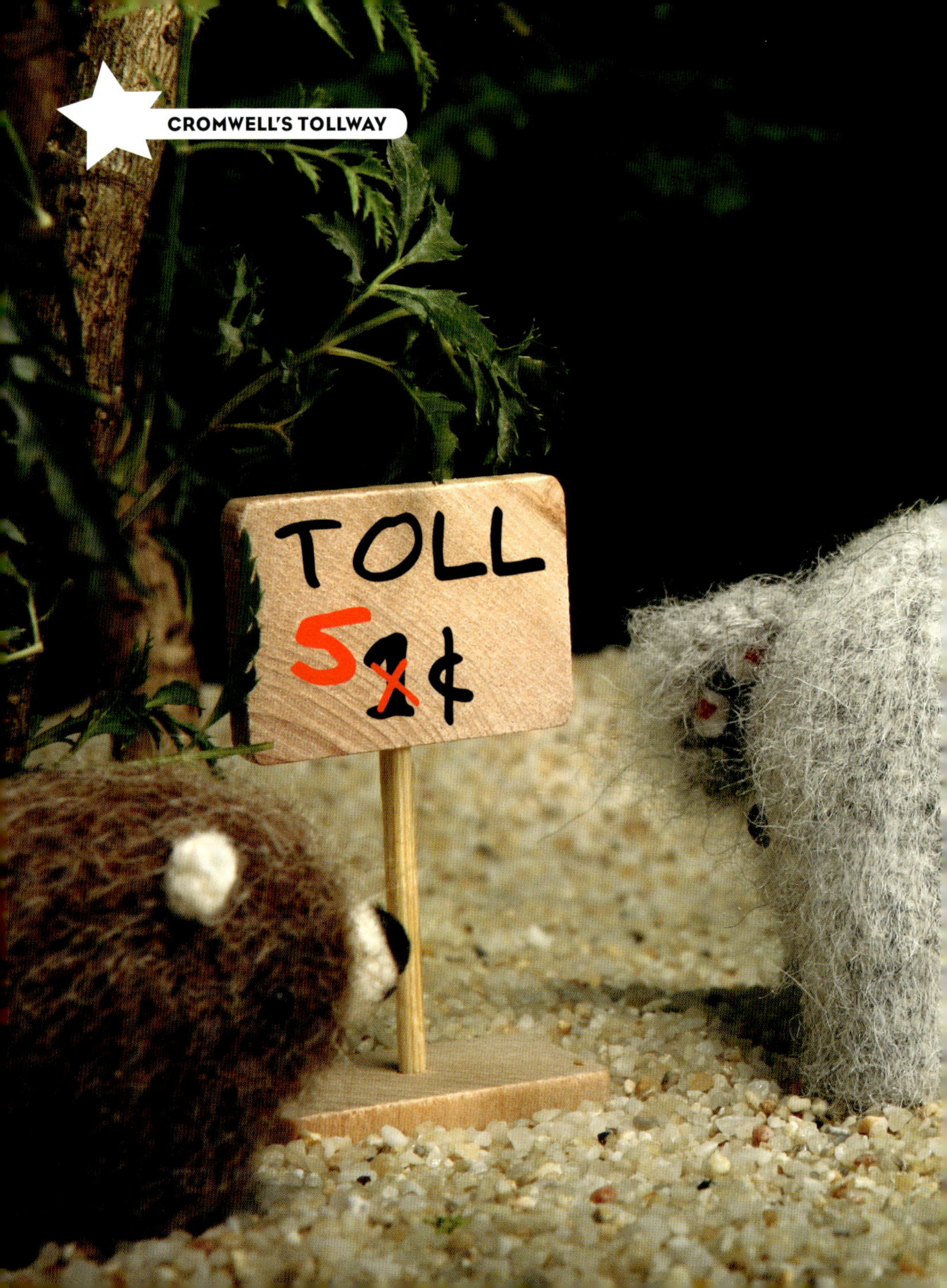
TOLL
5 X̶ ¢

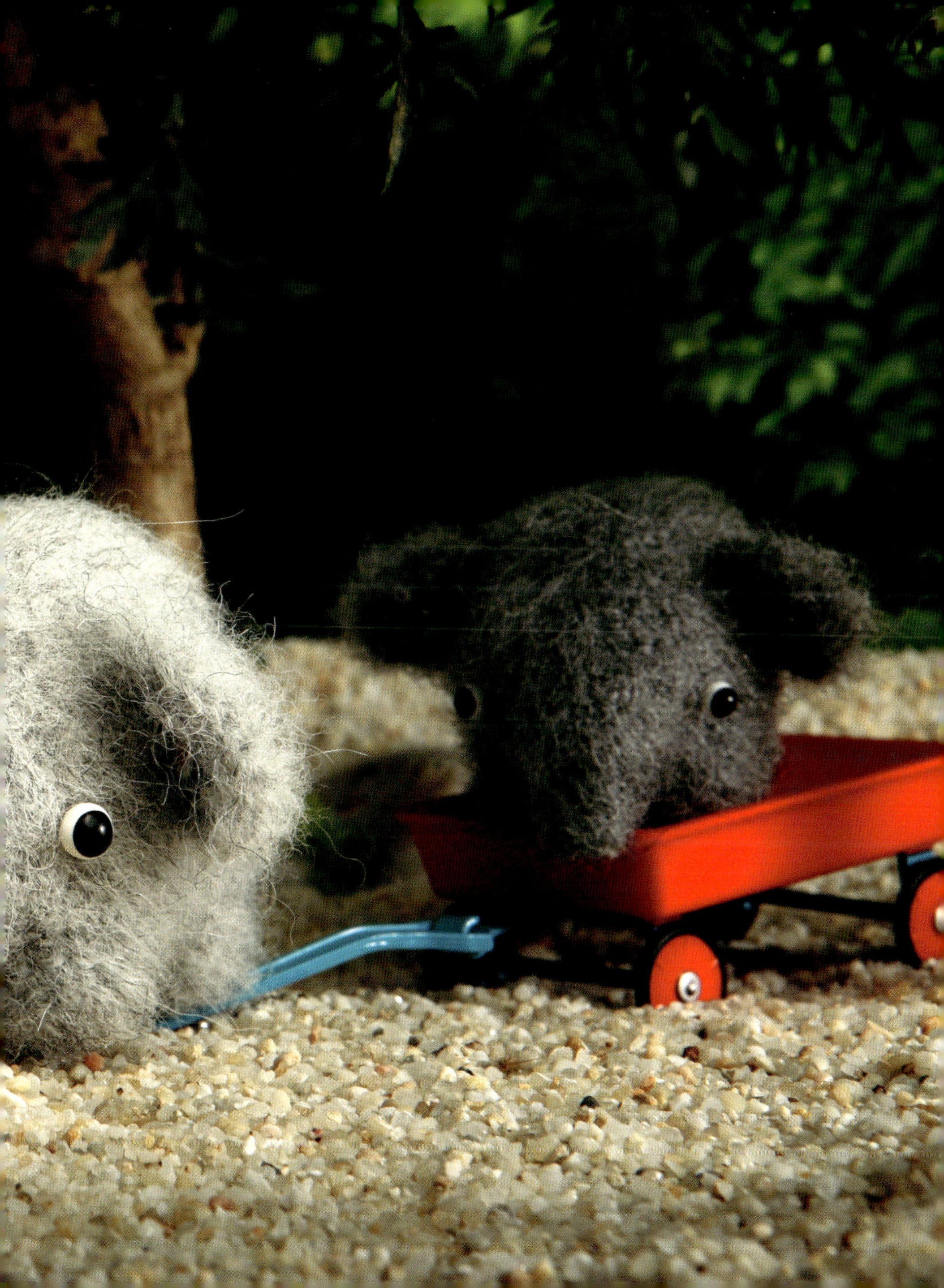

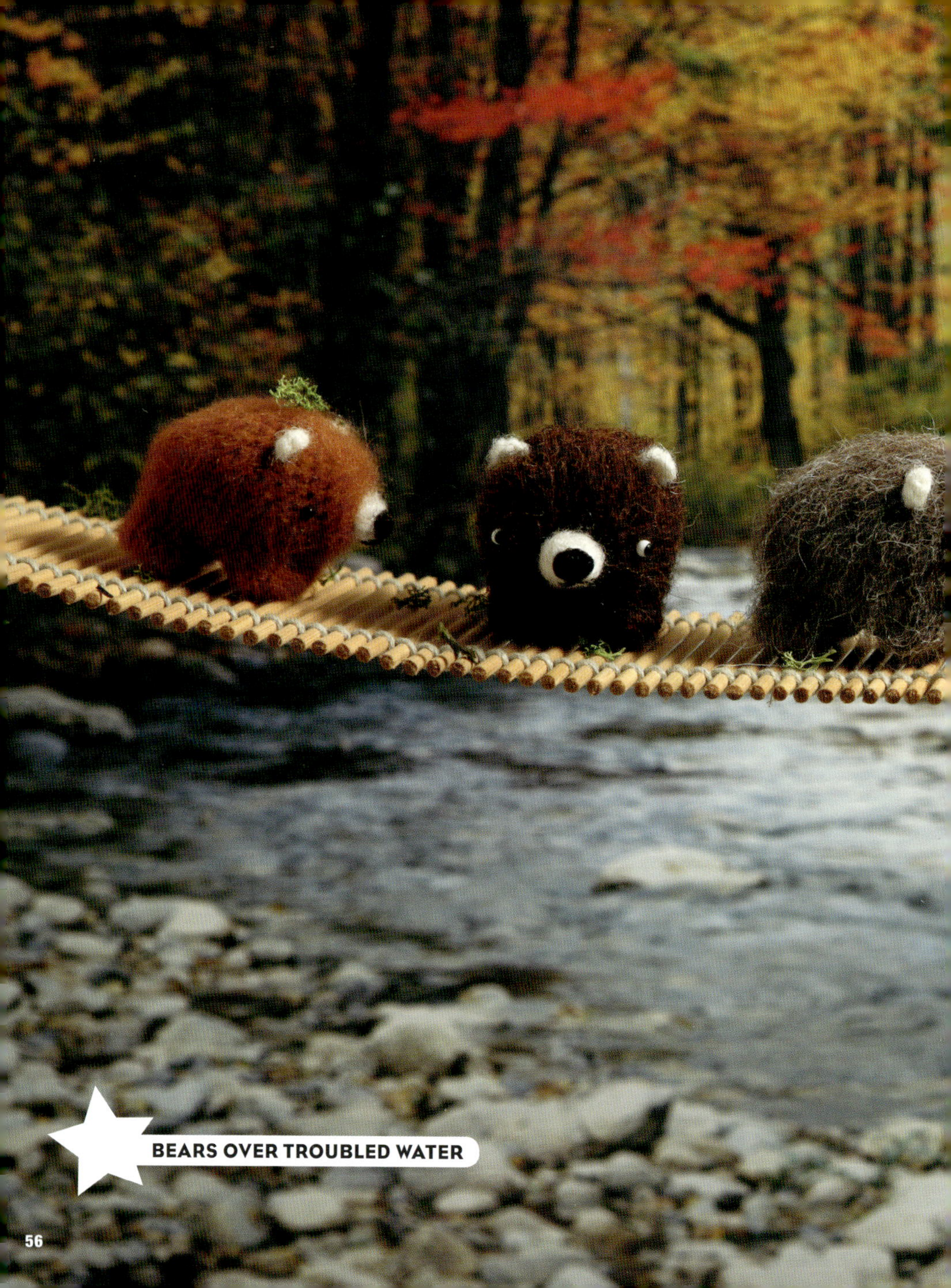
BEARS OVER TROUBLED WATER

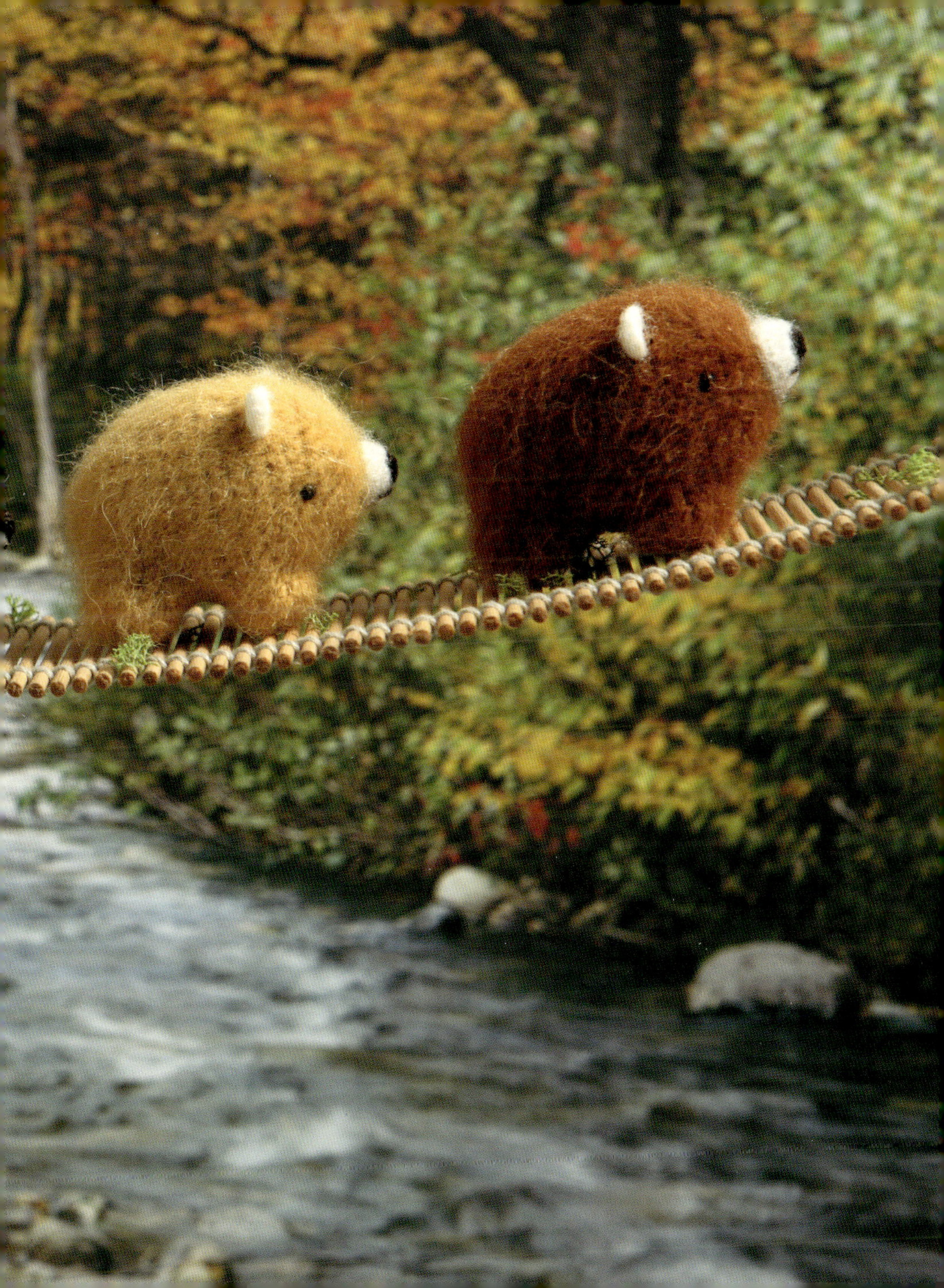

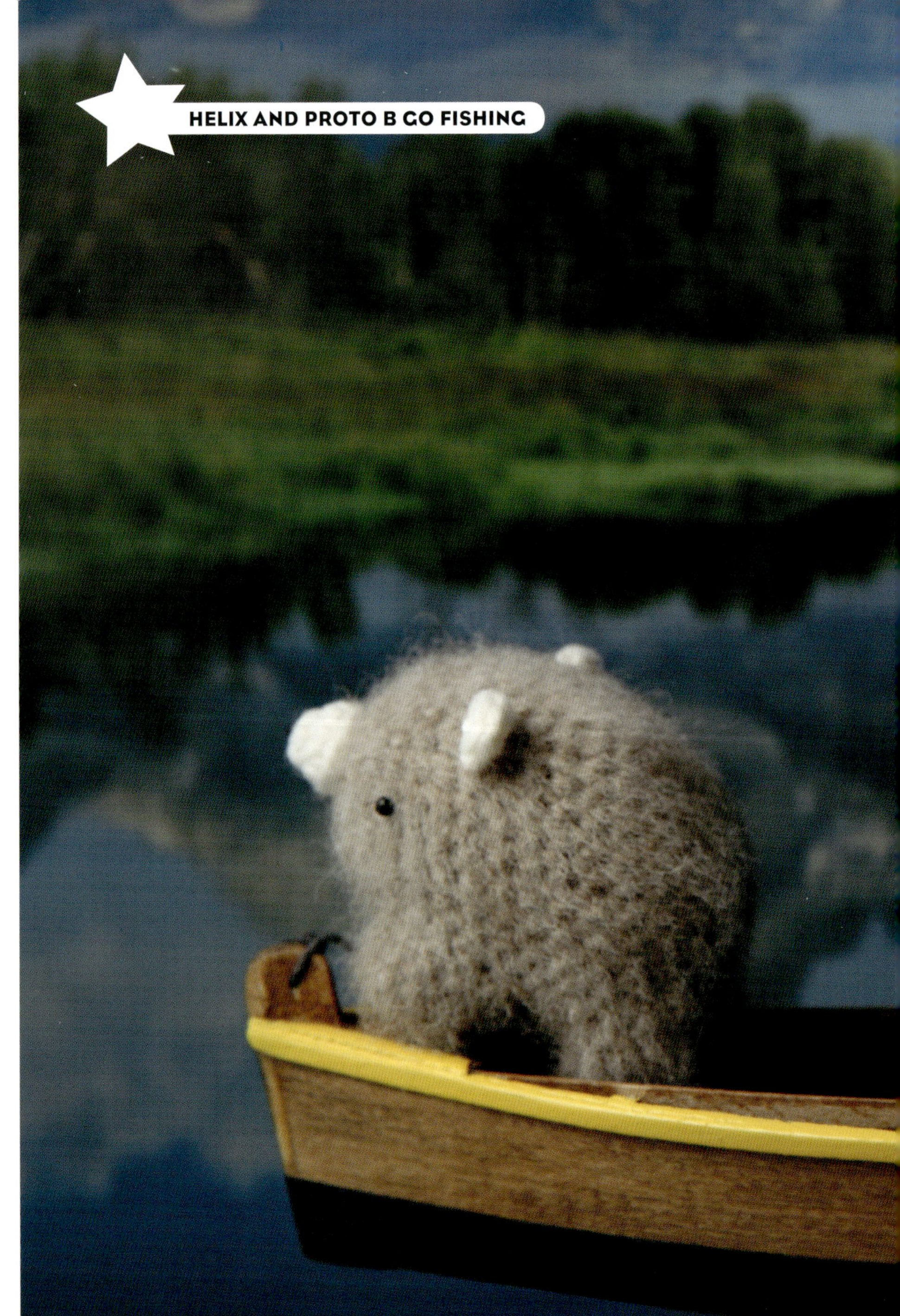
HELIX AND PROTO B GO FISHING

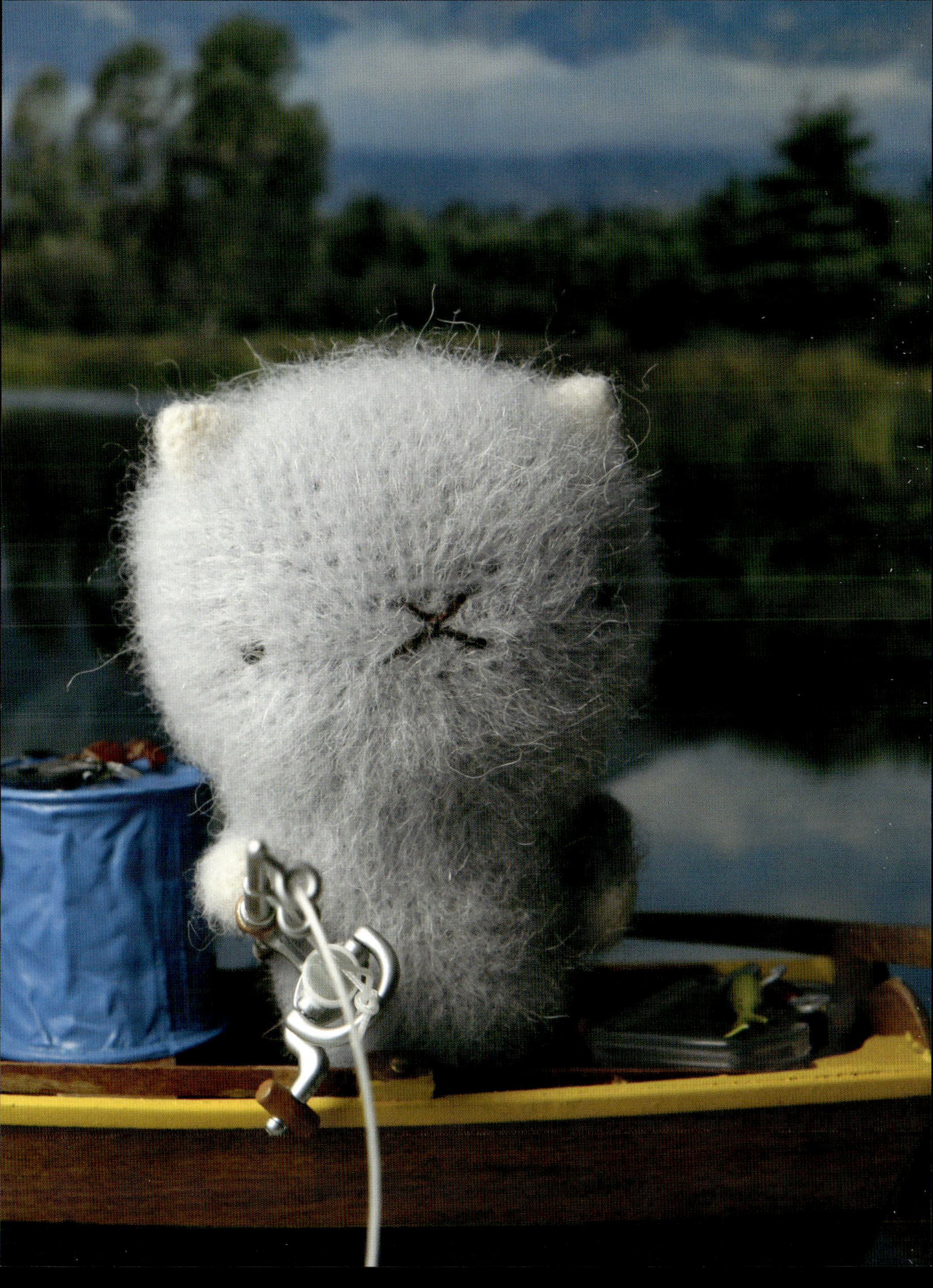

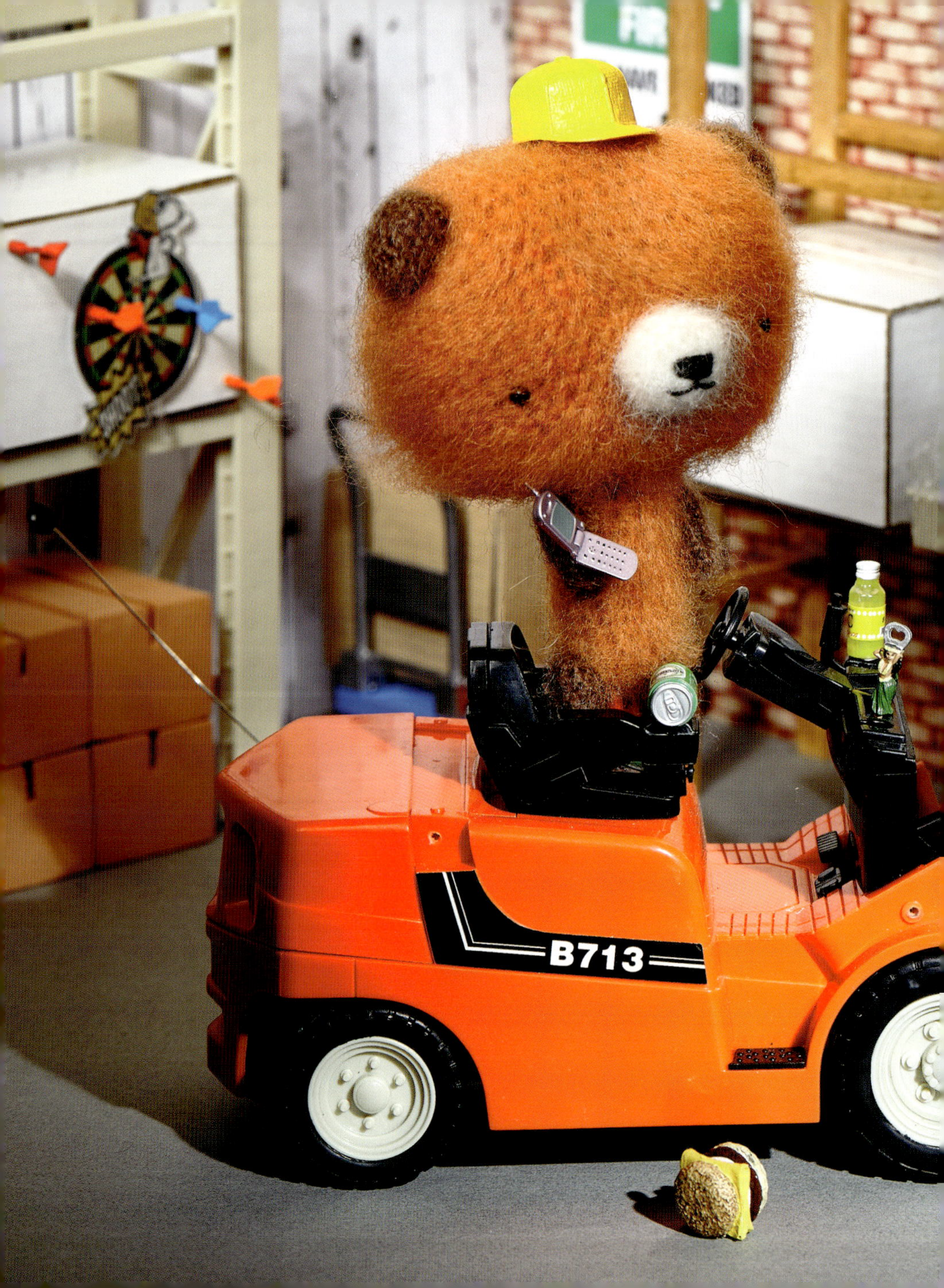
B713

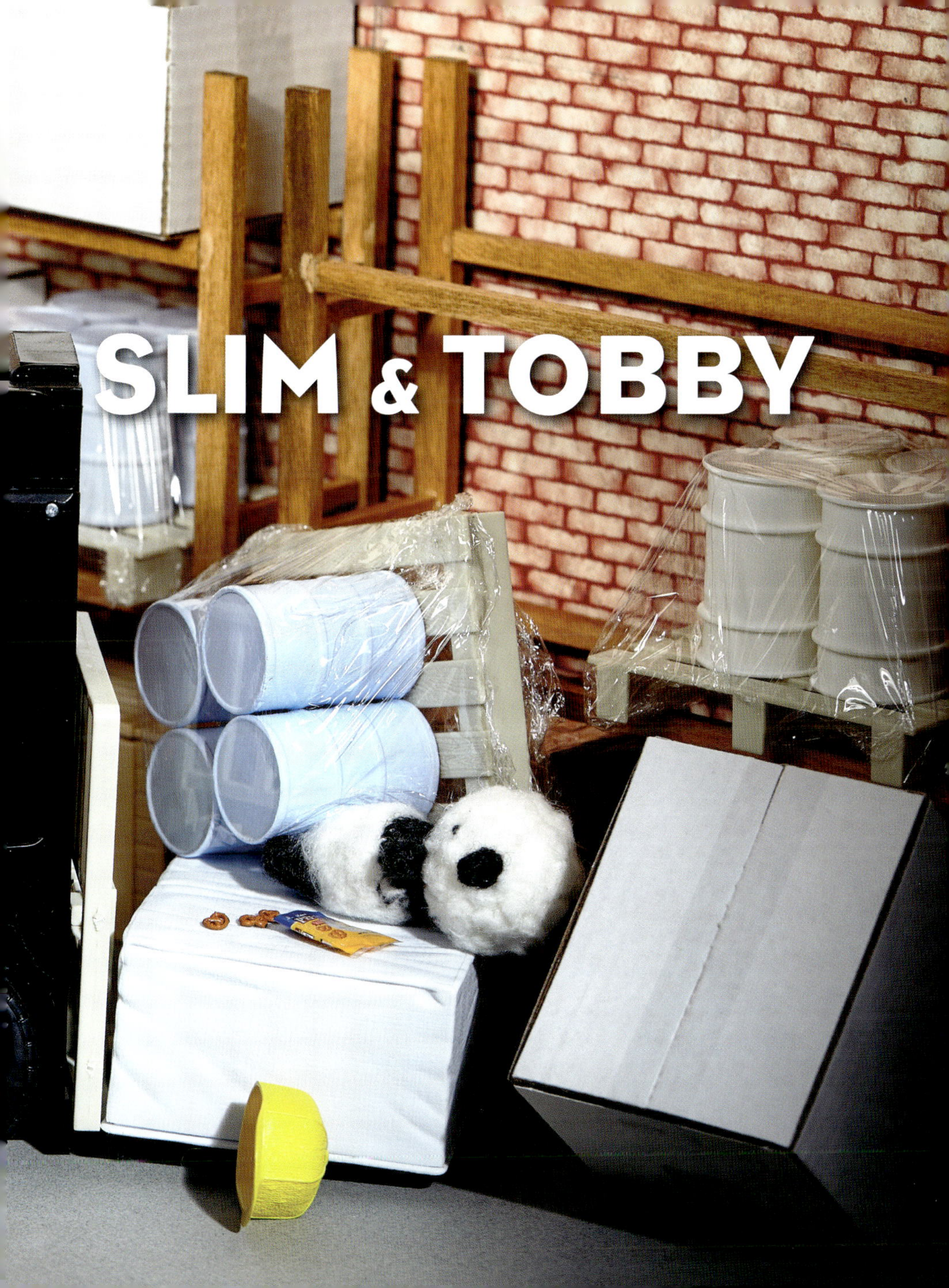
SLIM & TOBBY

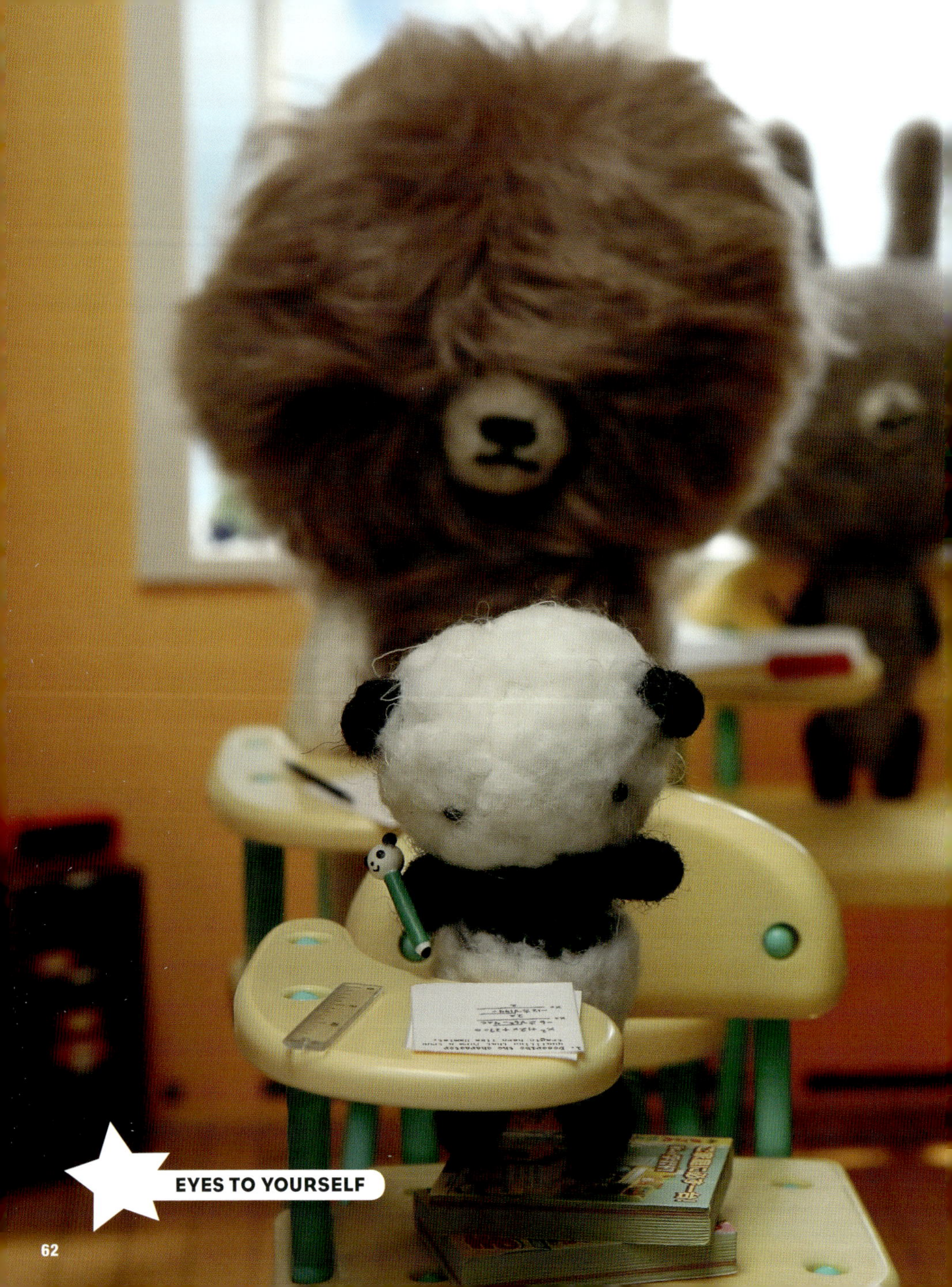

EYES TO YOURSELF

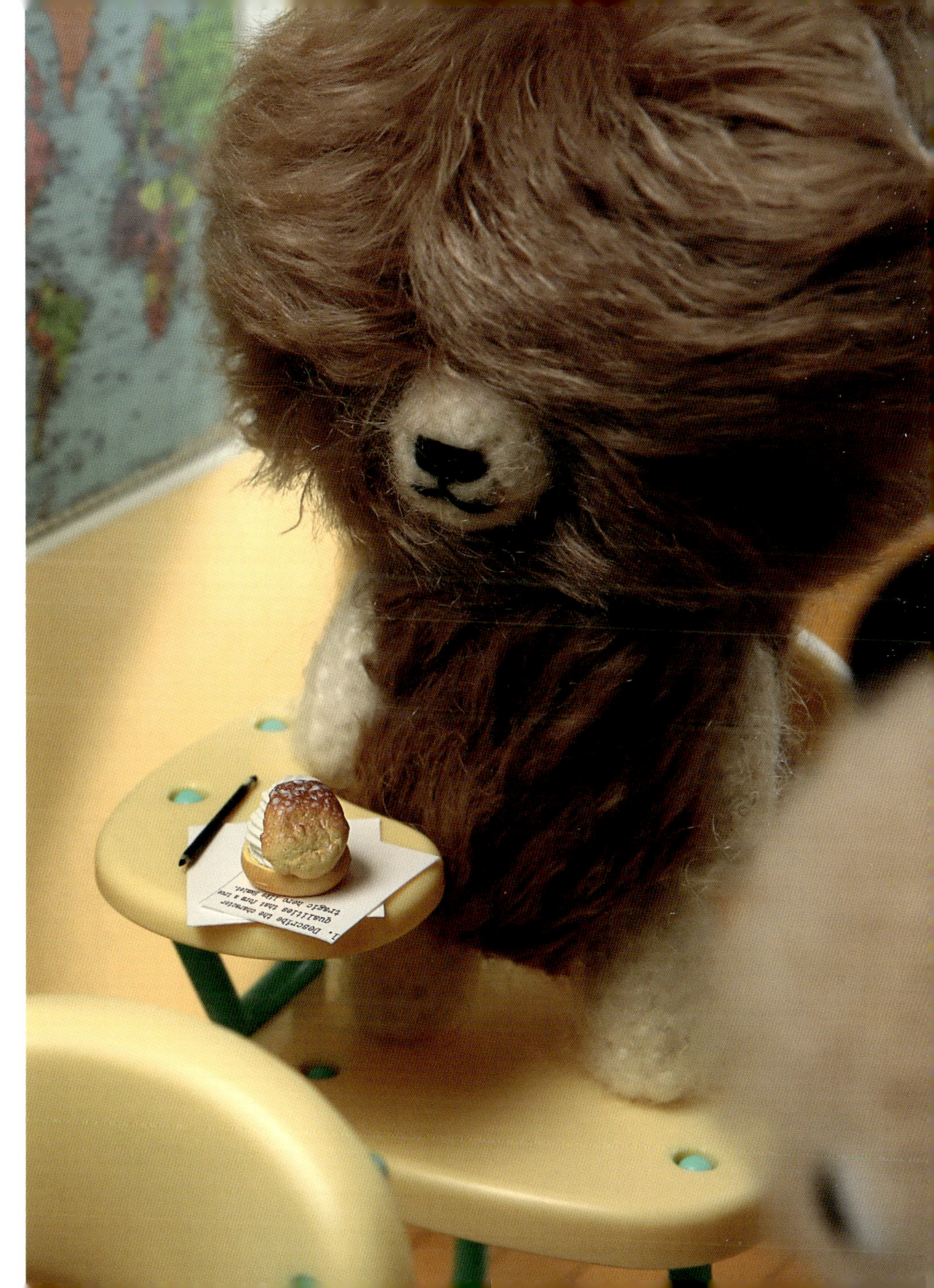

1. Describe the qualities that form a true
tragic hero like Hamlet.

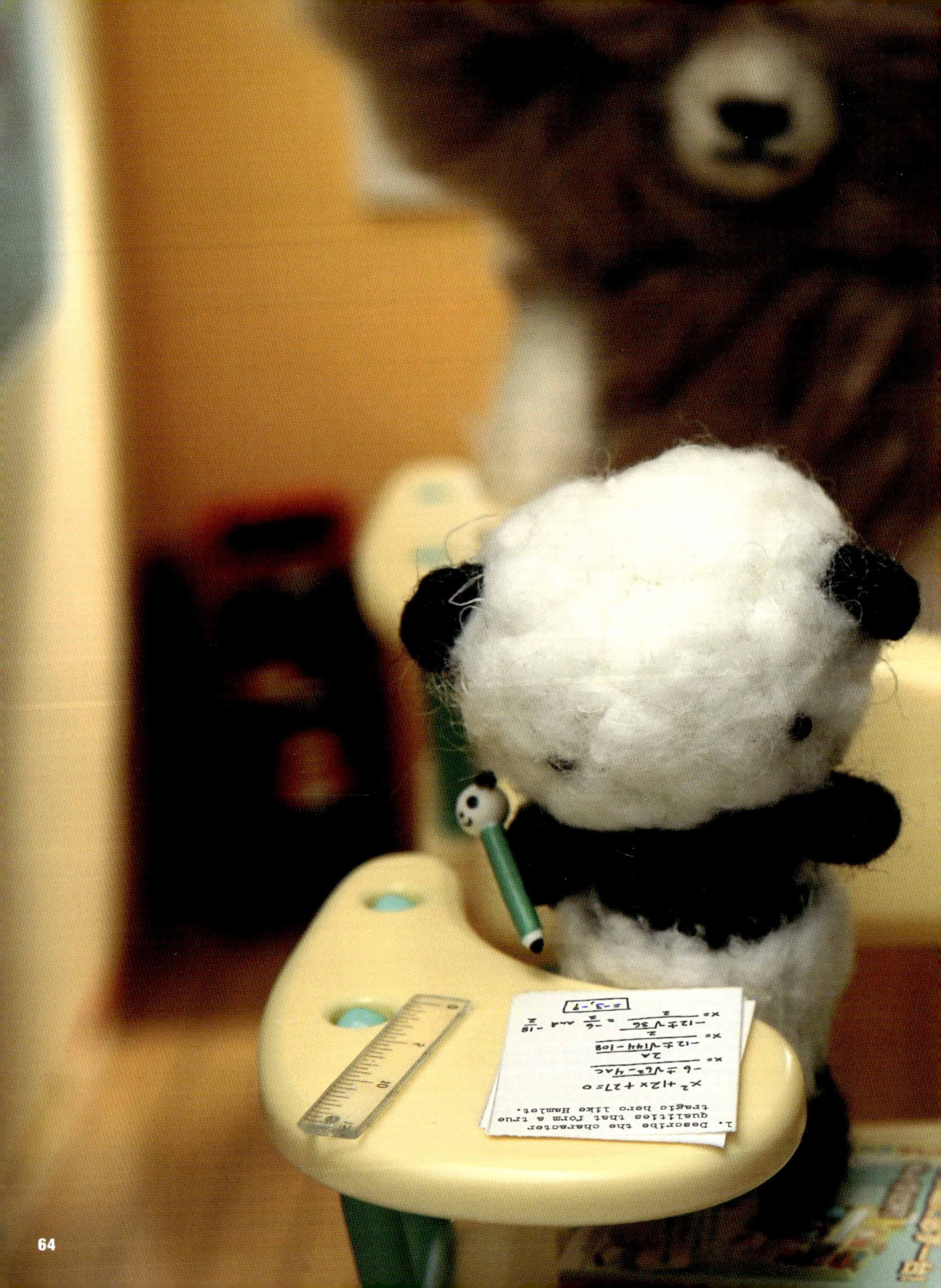

1. Describe the character qualities that form a true tragic hero like Hamlet.
x² + 12x + 27 = 0
x = (-6 ± √(6² - 4AC)) / 2A
x = (-12 ± √(144 - 108)) / 2
x = (-12 ± √36) / 2 = -6/2 and -18/2
= -3, -9

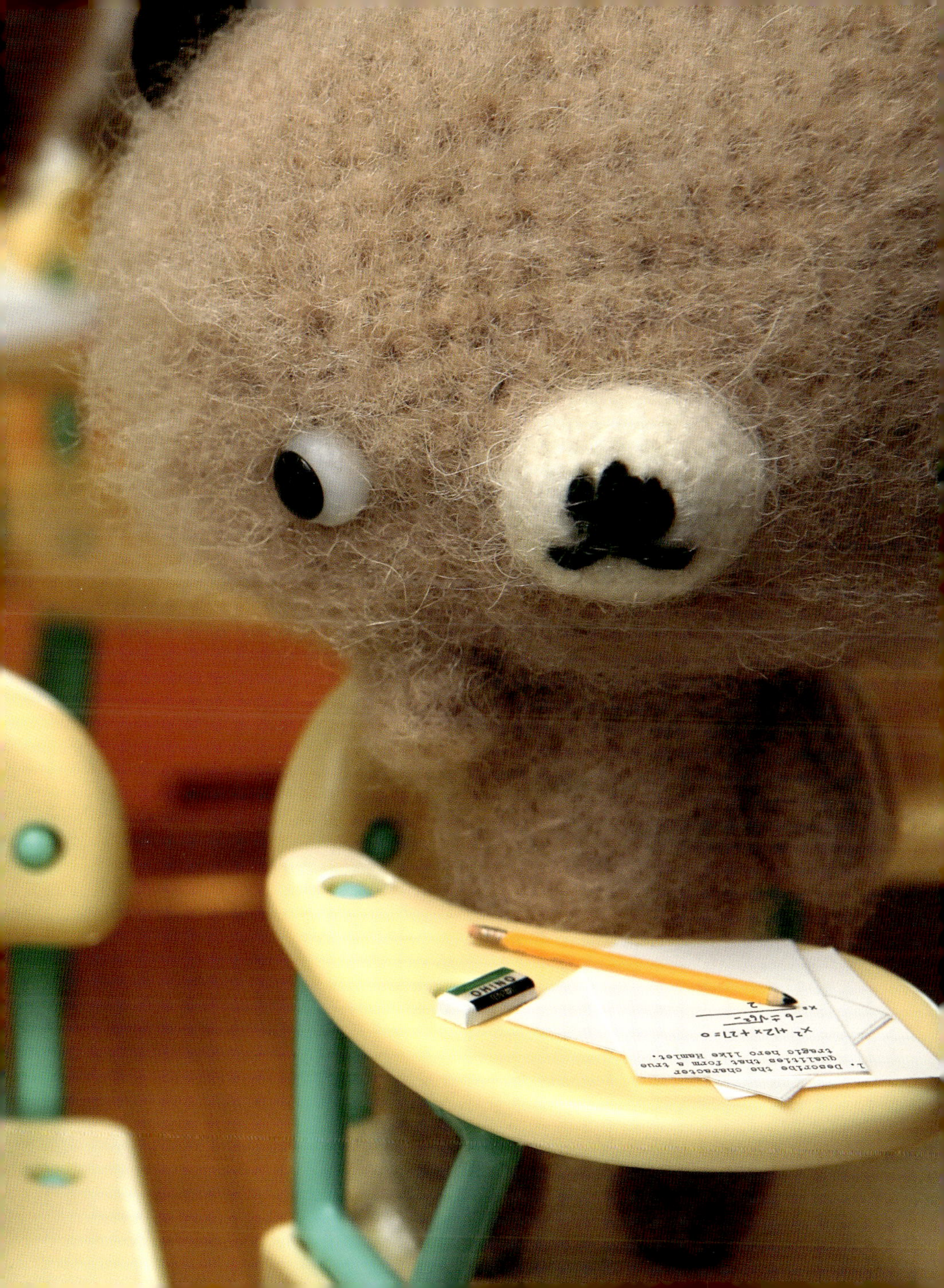

1. Describe the character qualities that form a true tragic hero like Hamlet.
x² +12x +21 = 0
x = (-b ± √b²-...) / 2

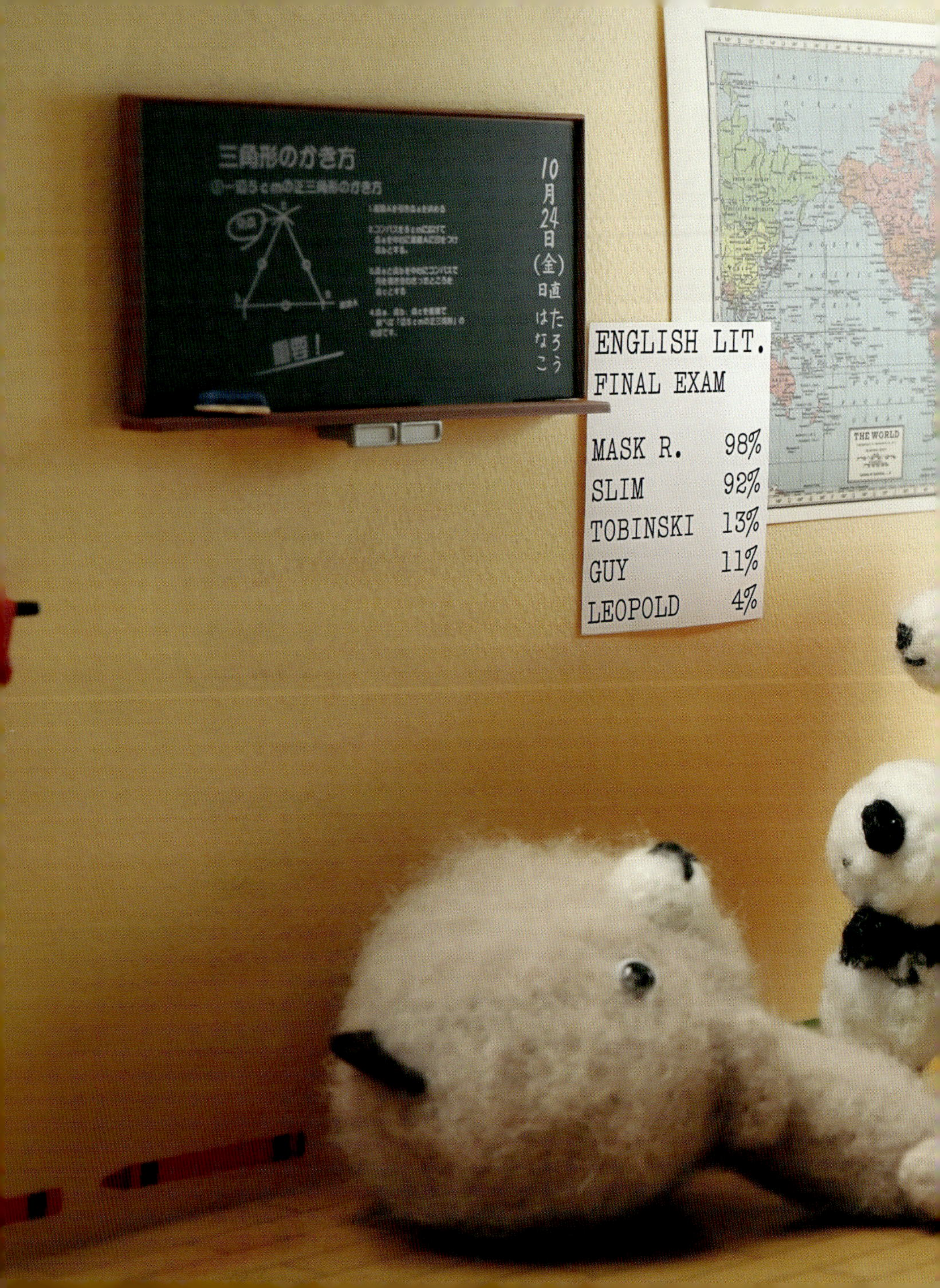
三角形のかき方
①―辺とその両はしの角で三角形のかき方
10月24日（金）
日直
たろう
はなこ
重習！

ENGLISH LIT.
FINAL EXAM

MASK R.   98%
SLIM   92%
TOBINSKI   13%
GUY   11%
LEOPOLD   4%

THE WORLD

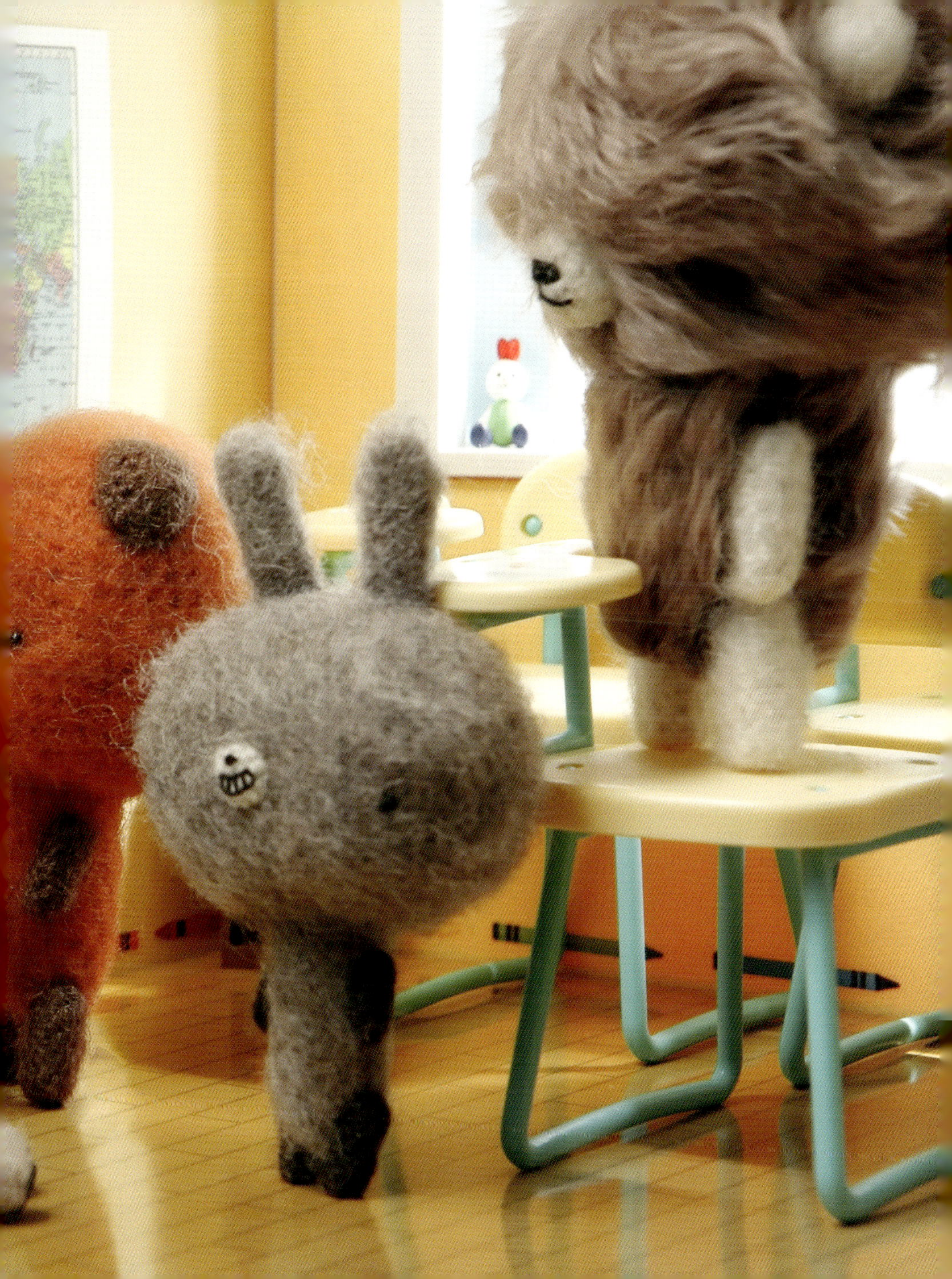

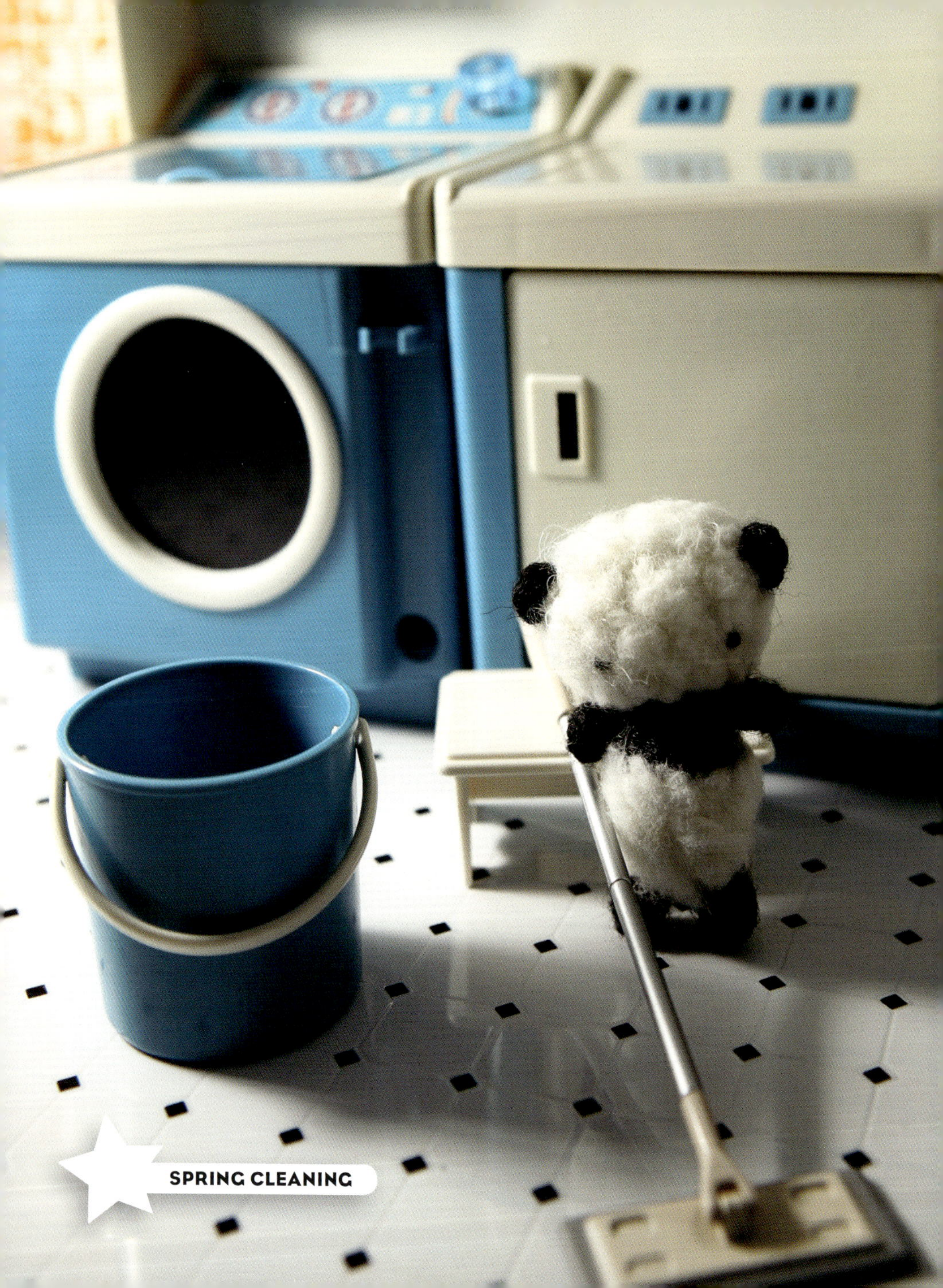

SPRING CLEANING

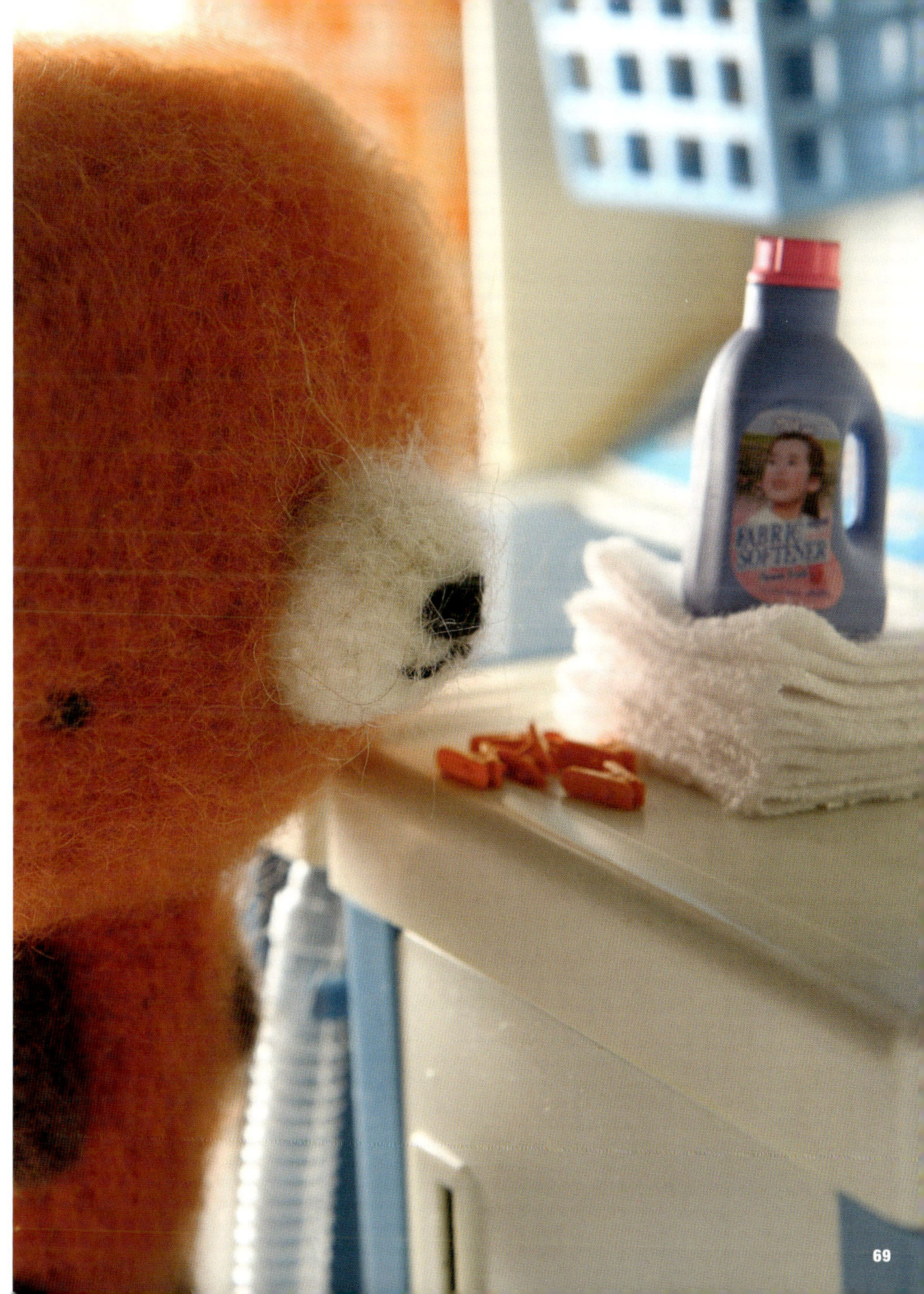
FABRIC
SOFTENER

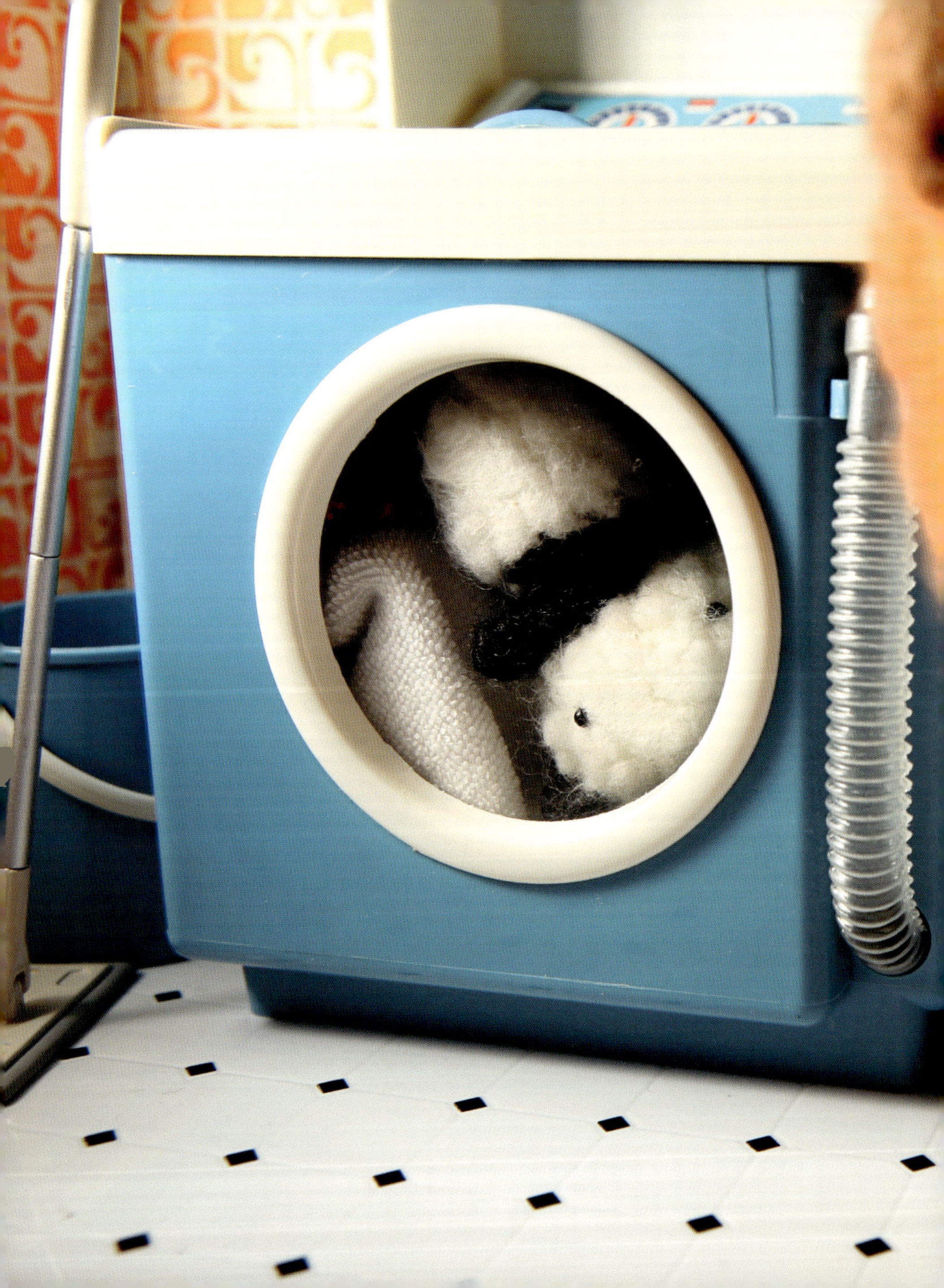

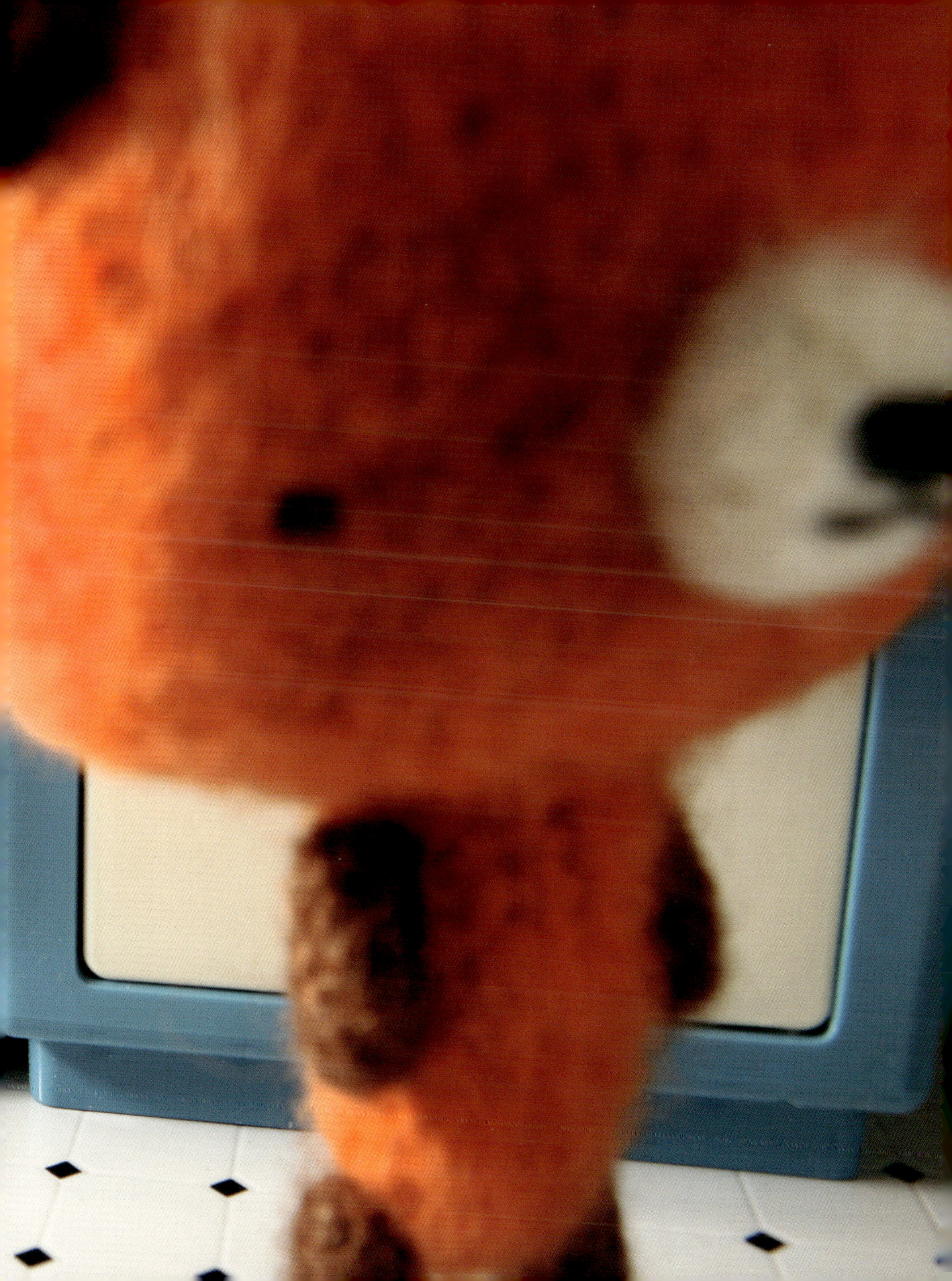

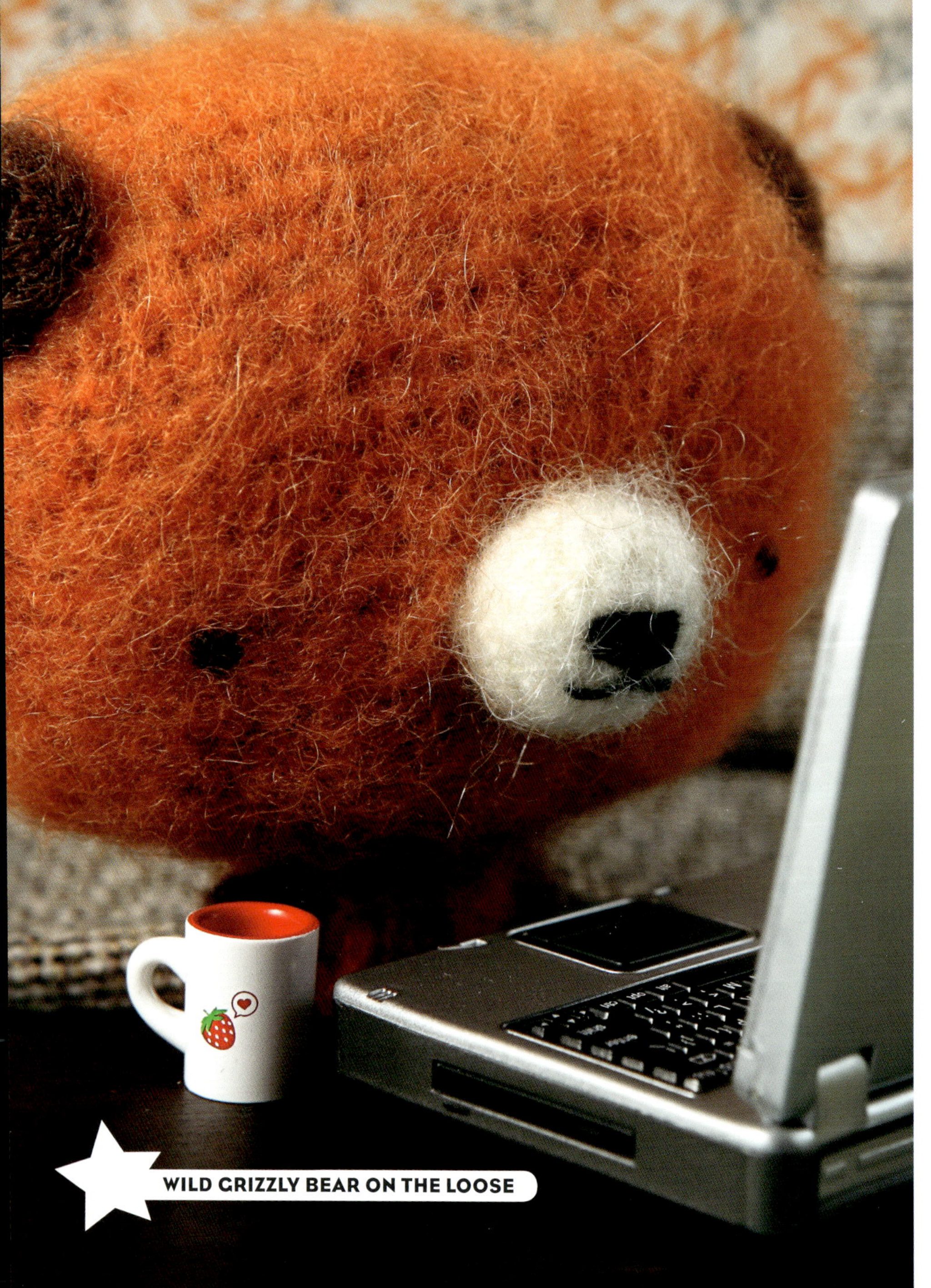

WILD GRIZZLY BEAR ON THE LOOSE

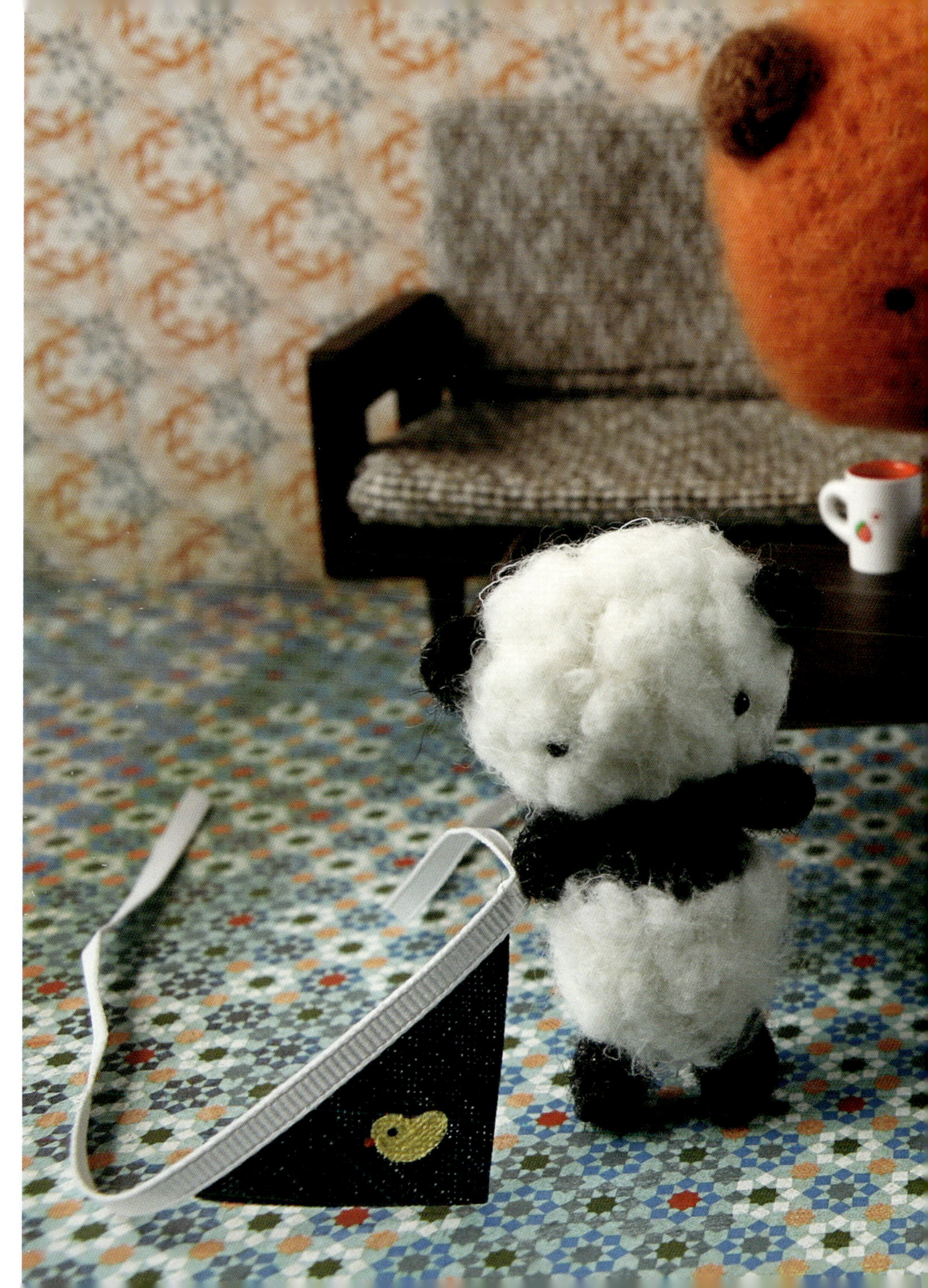

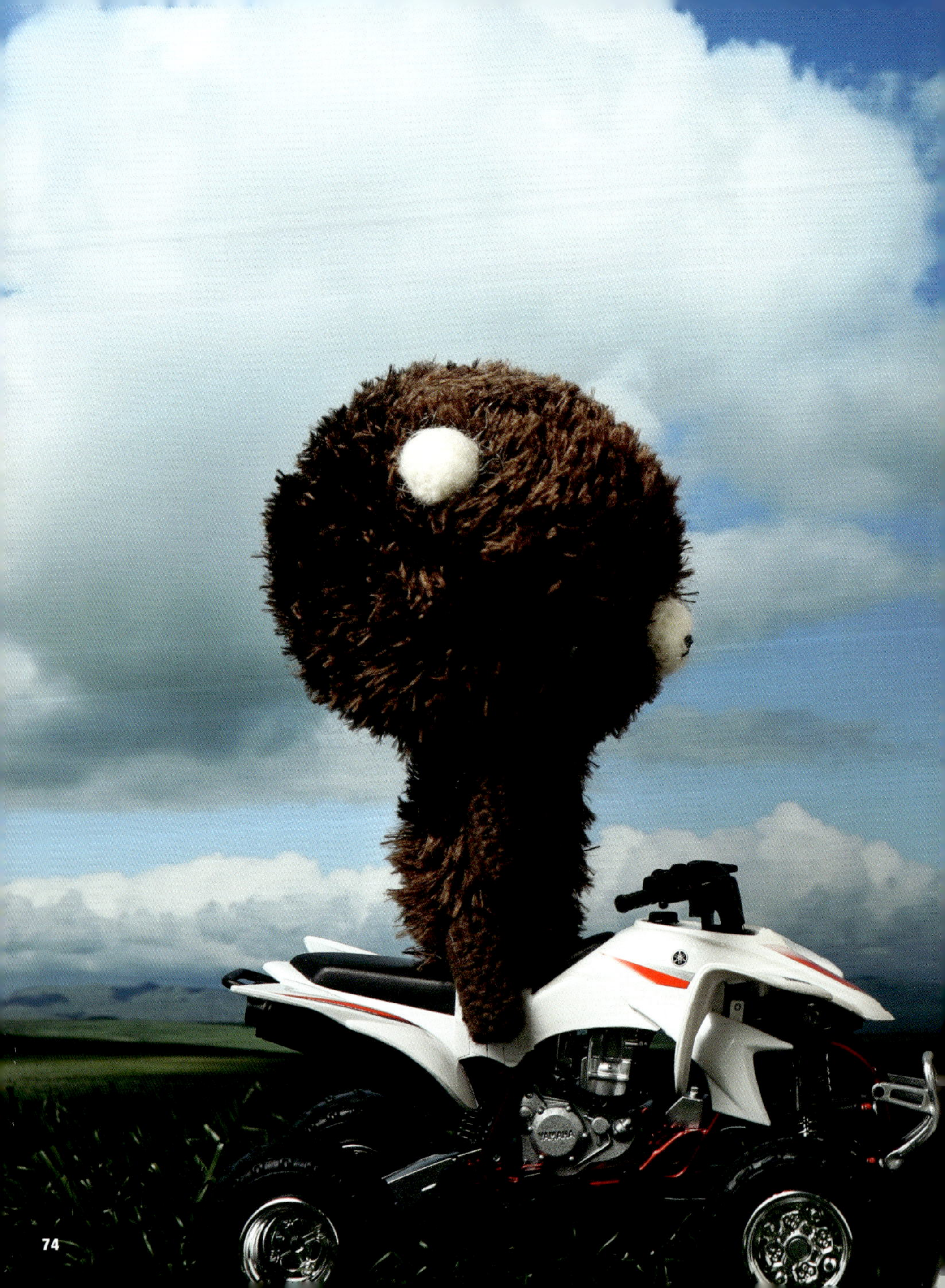

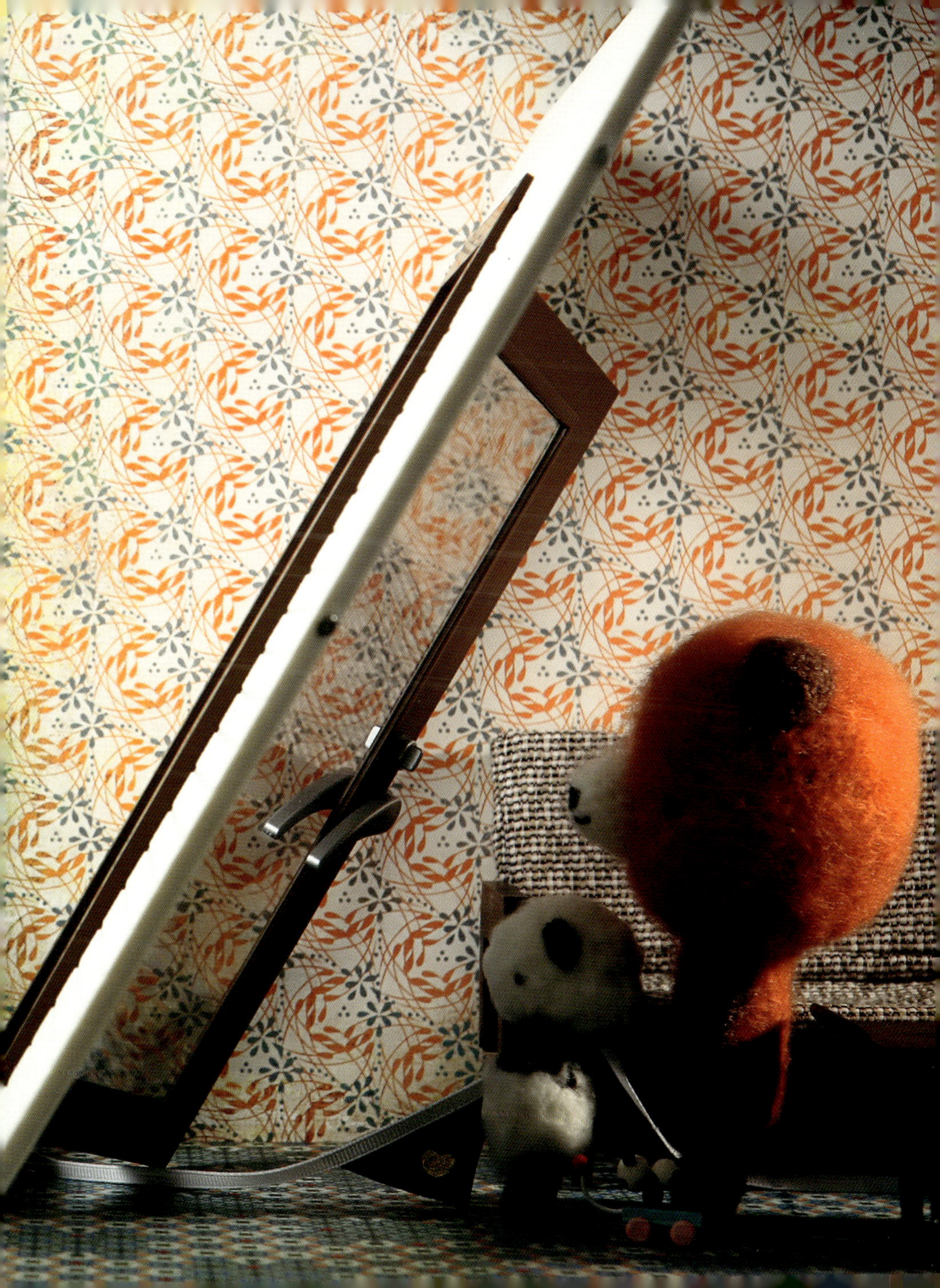

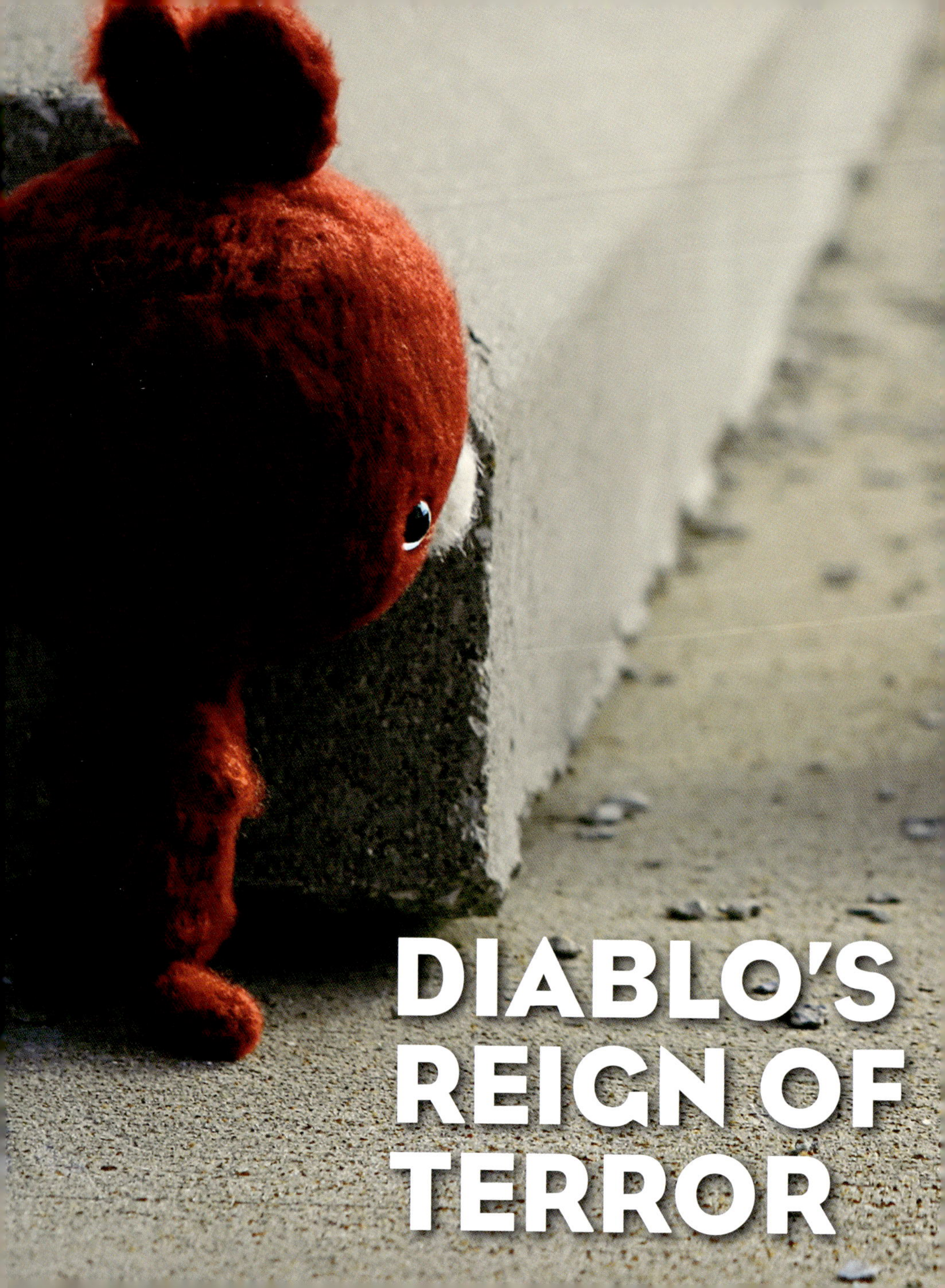
DIABLO'S
REIGN OF
TERROR

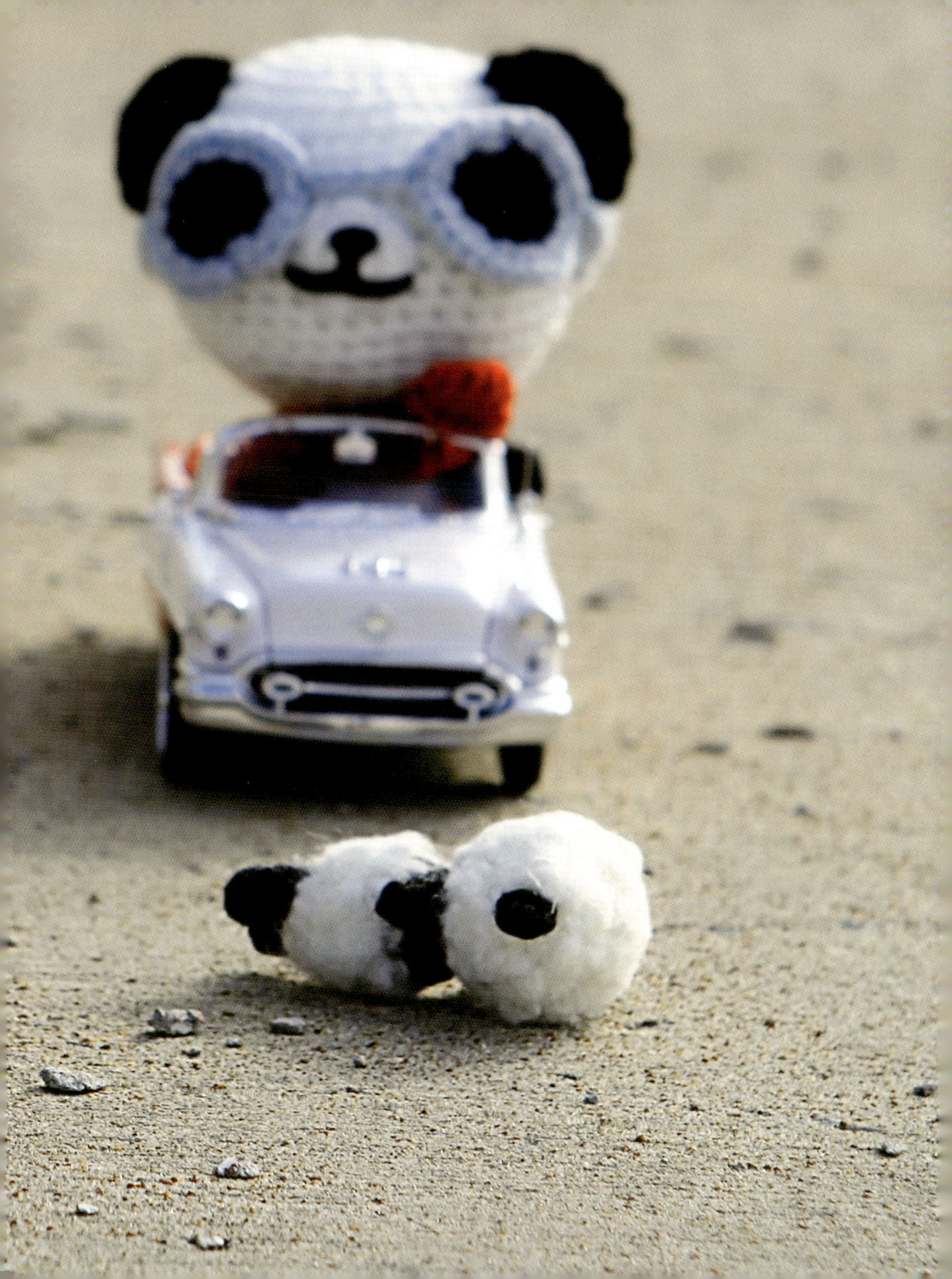

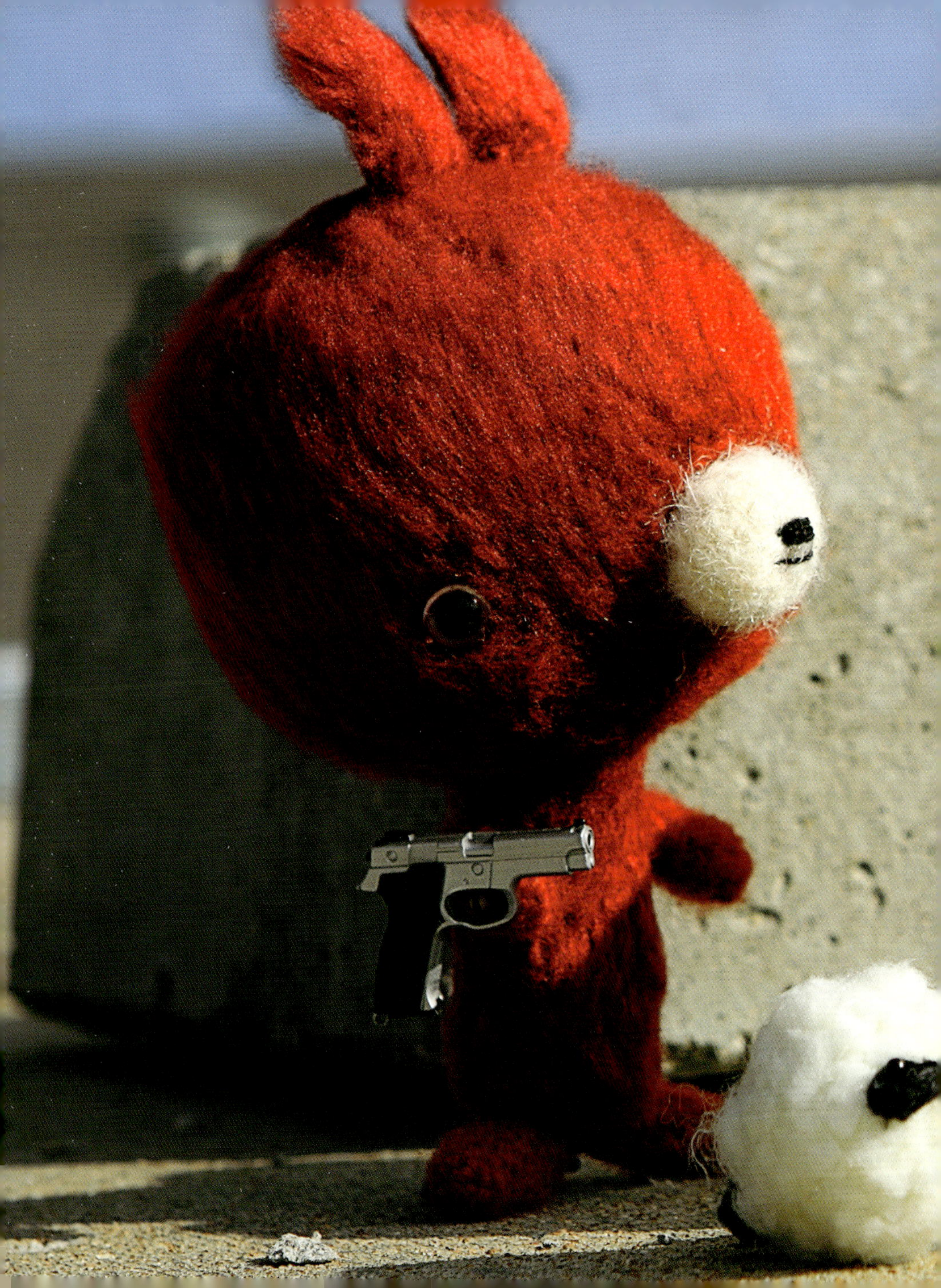

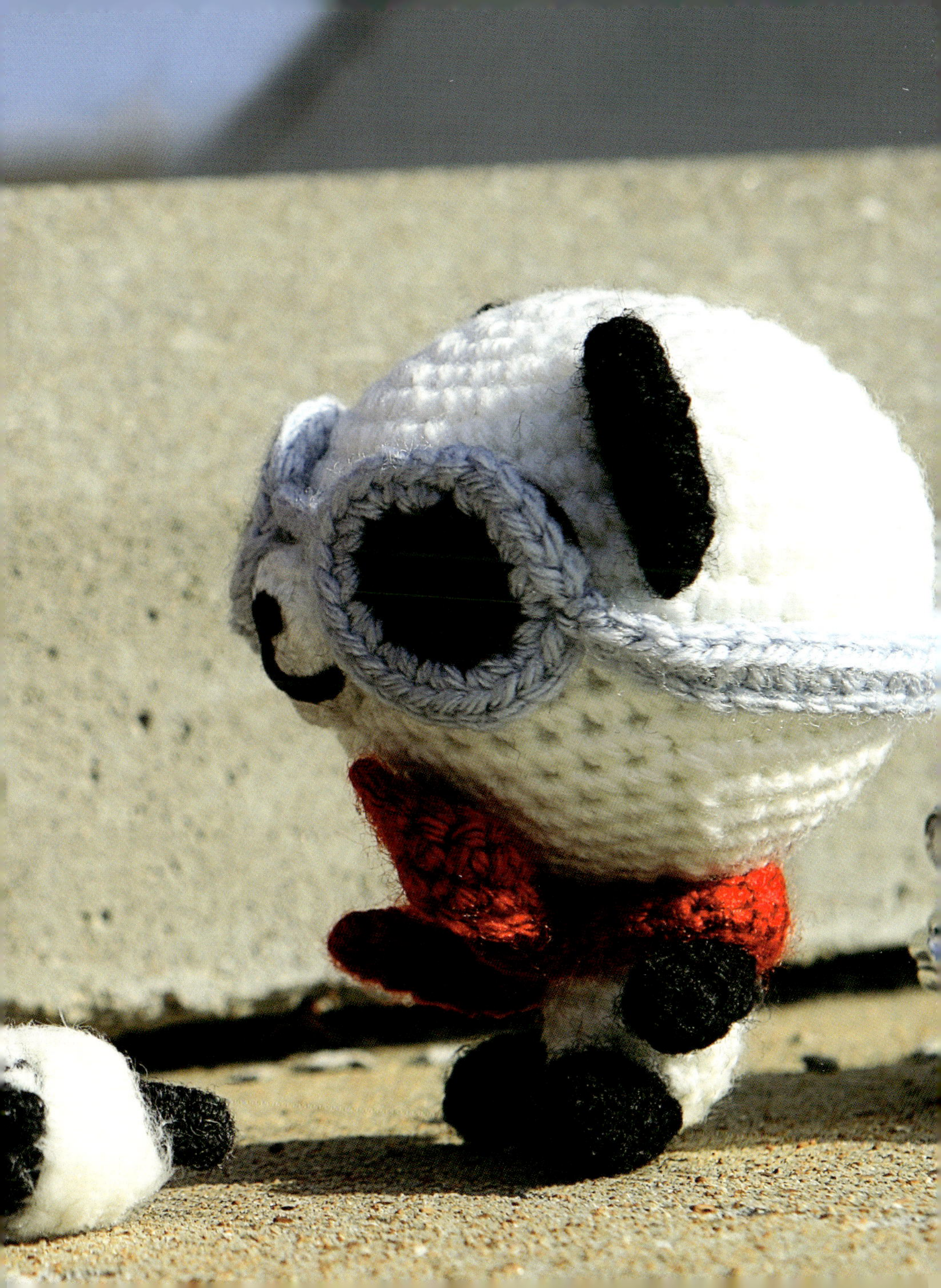

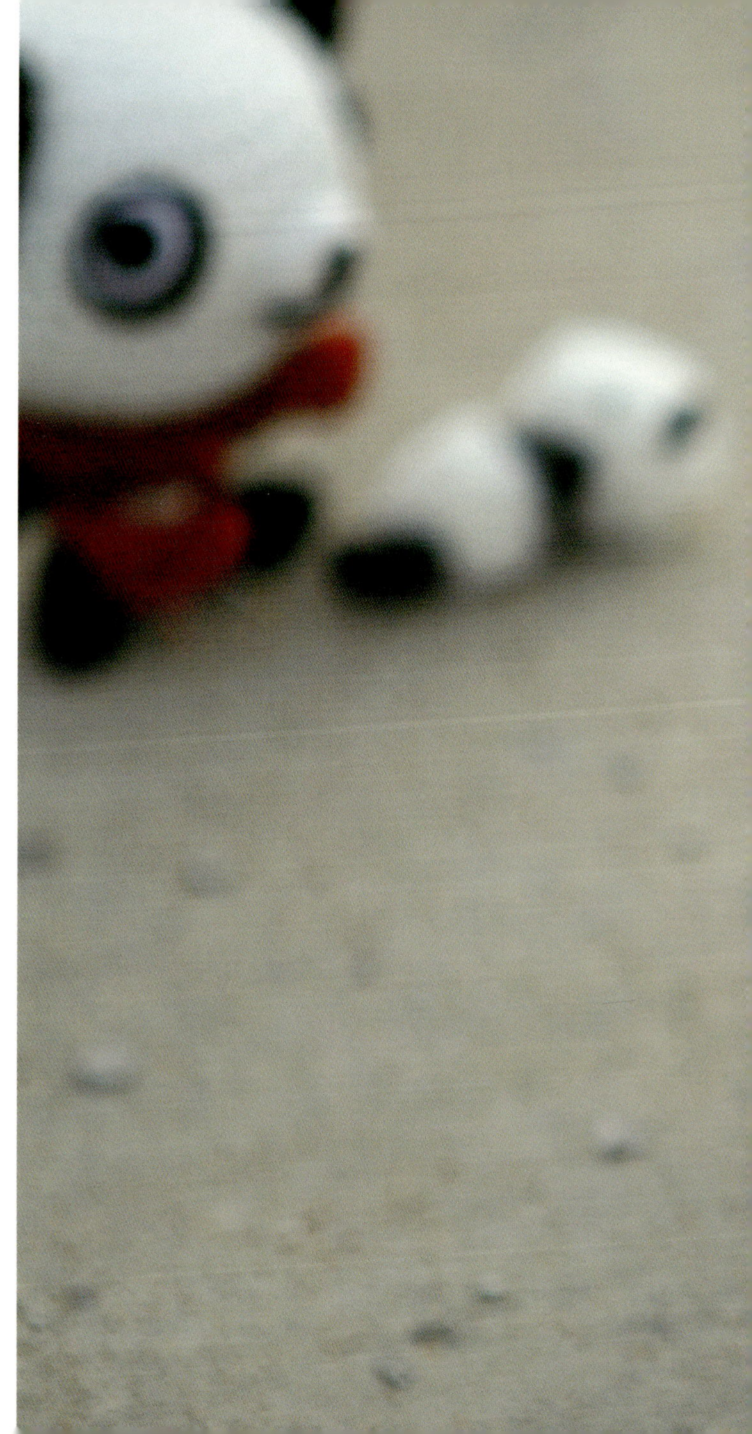

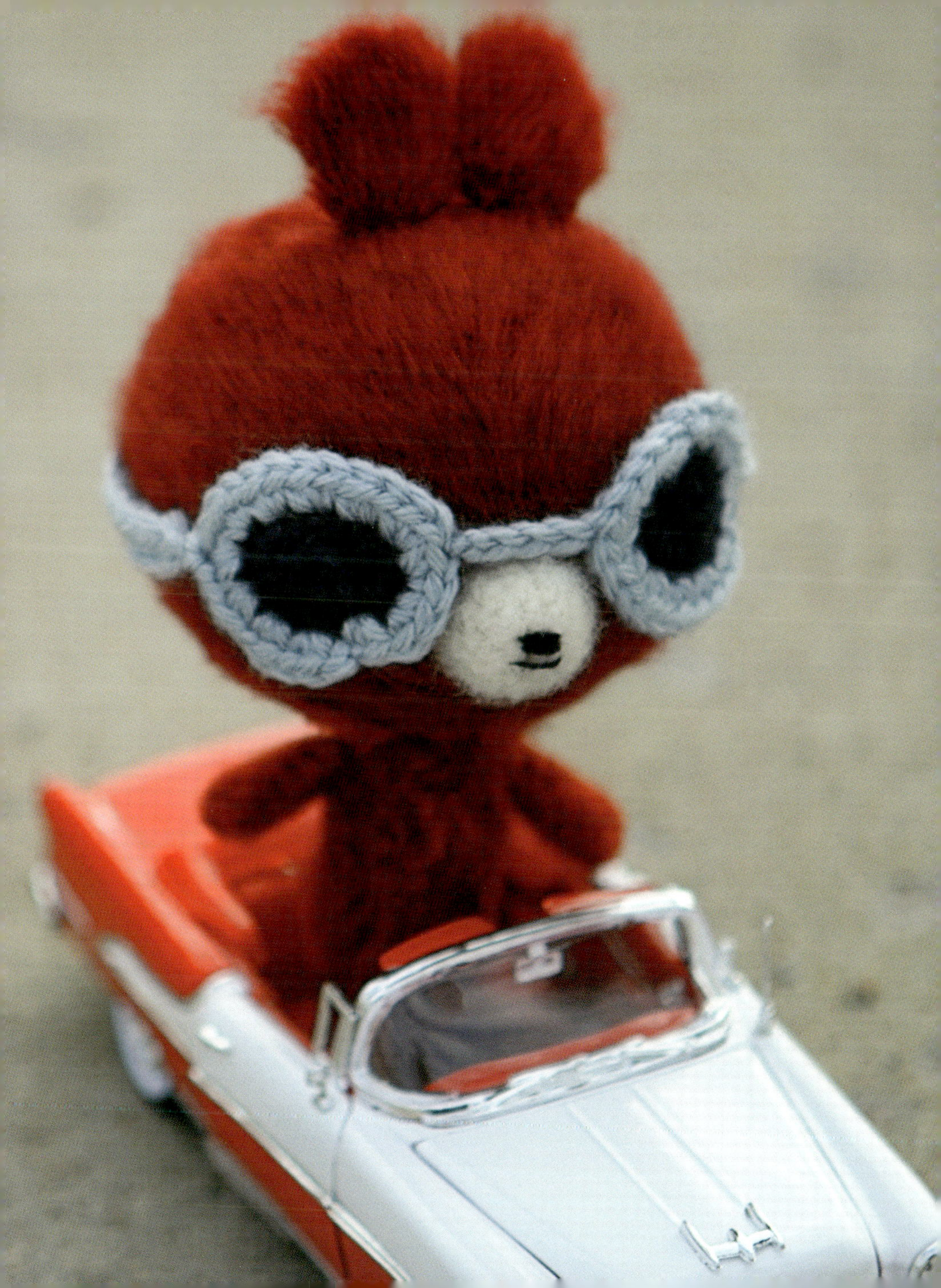

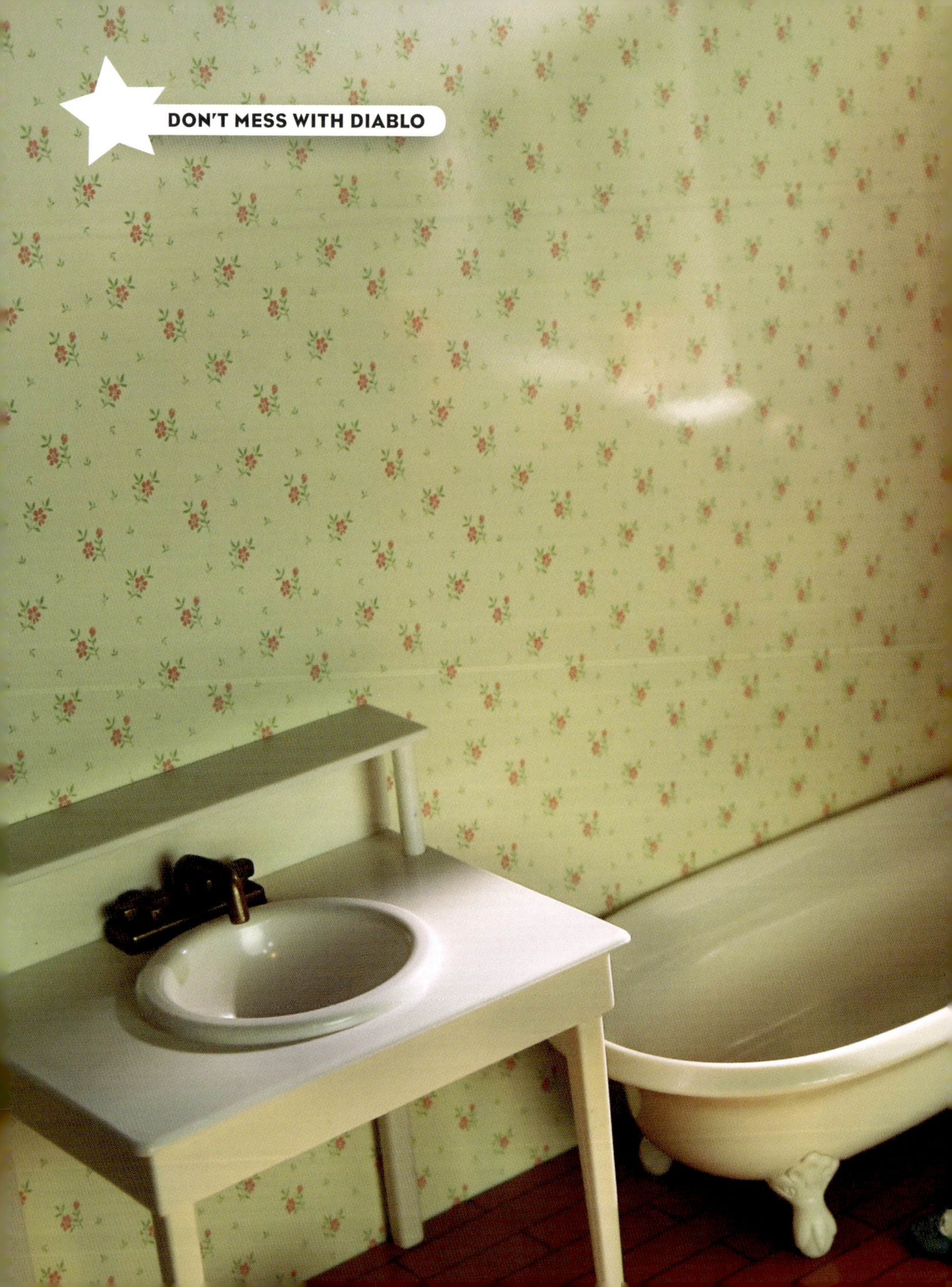
DON'T MESS WITH DIABLO

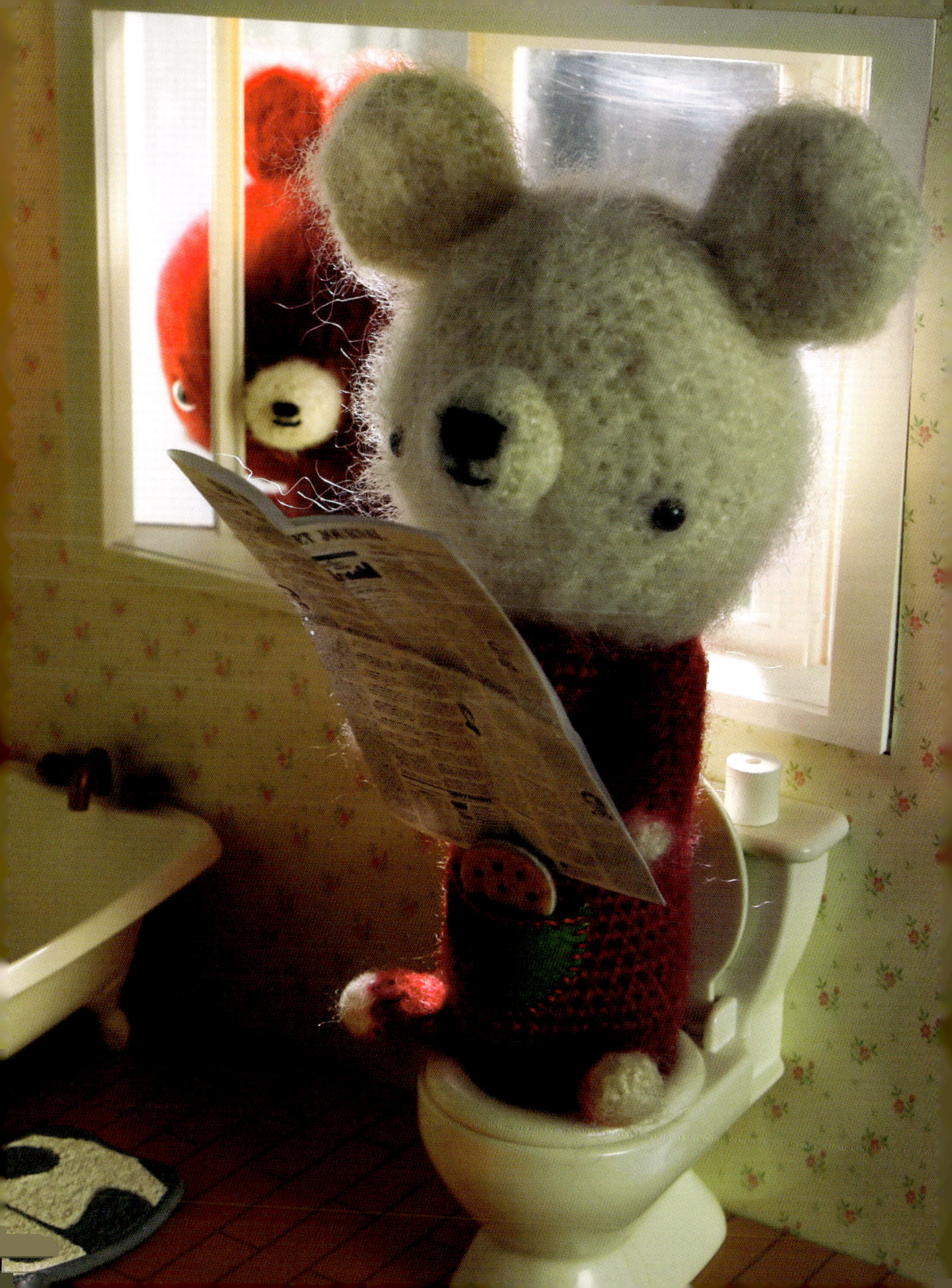

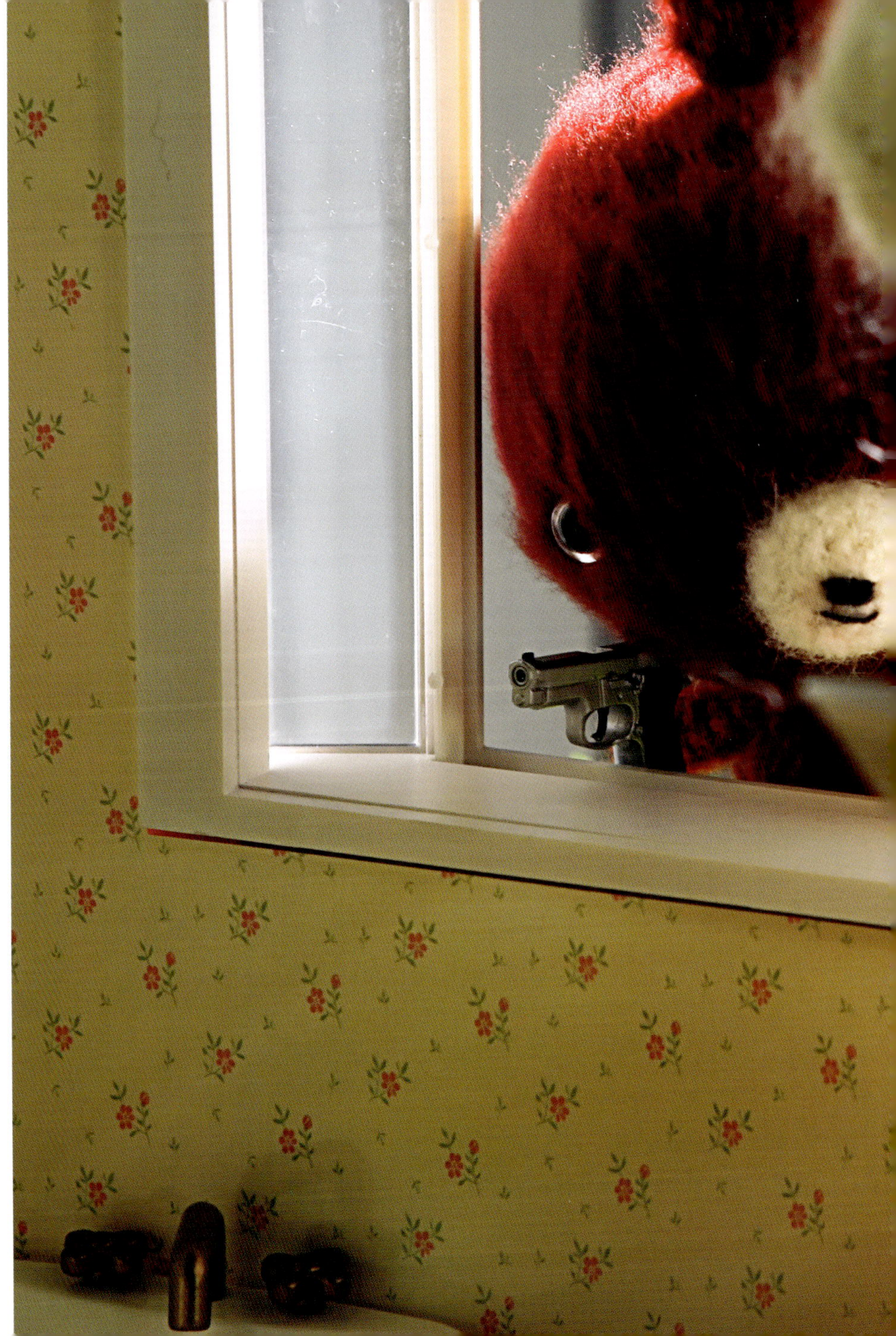

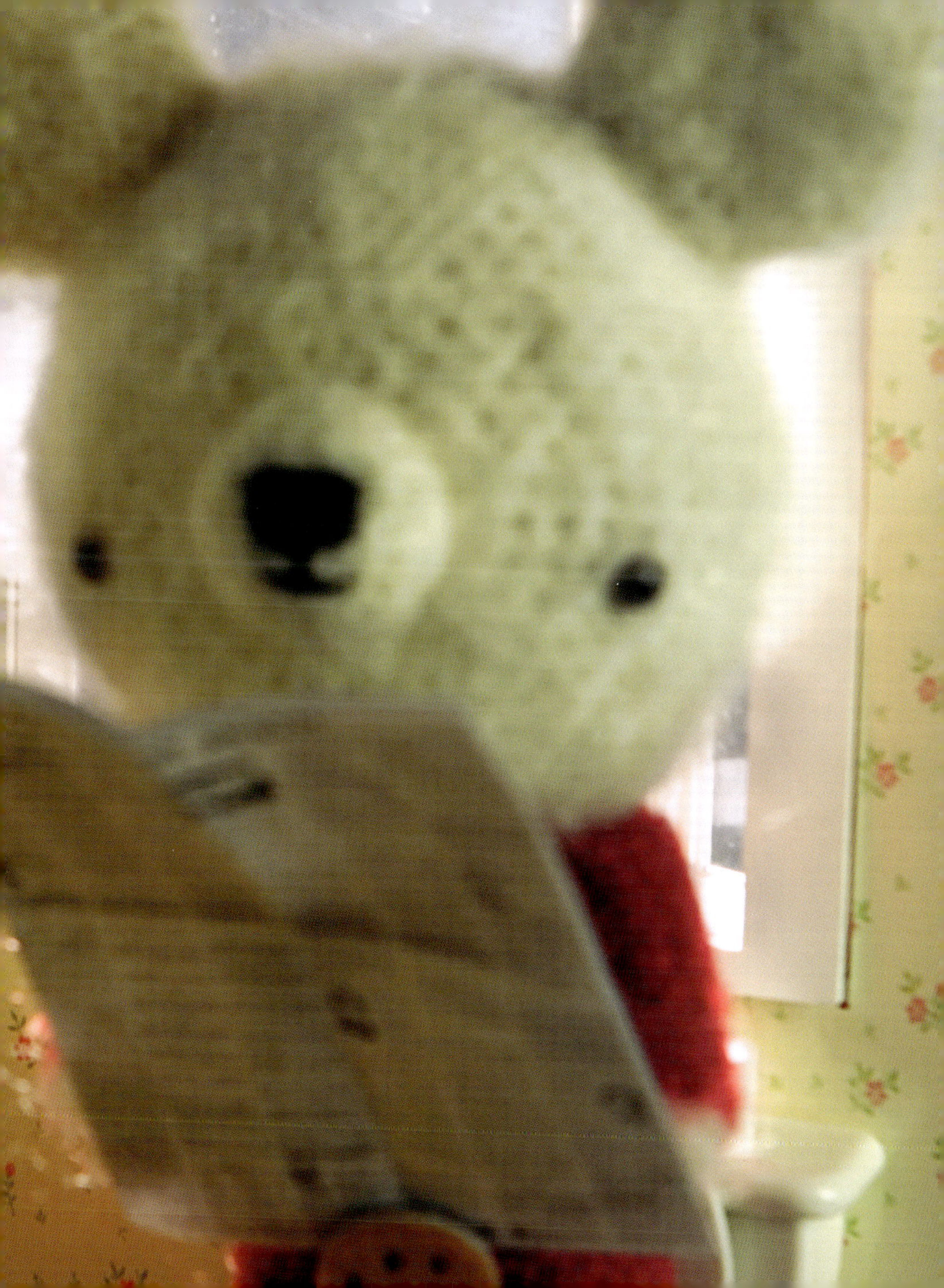

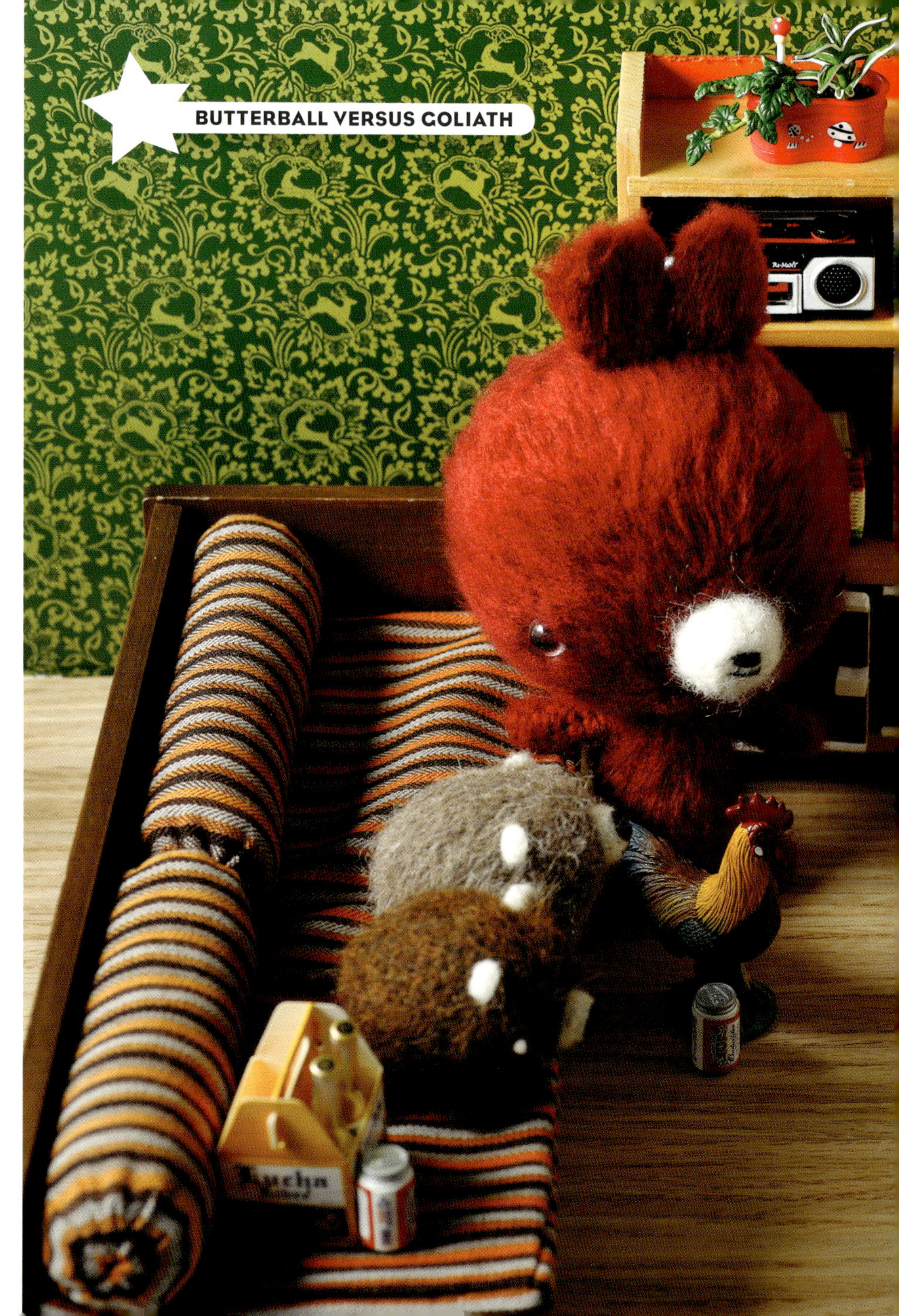

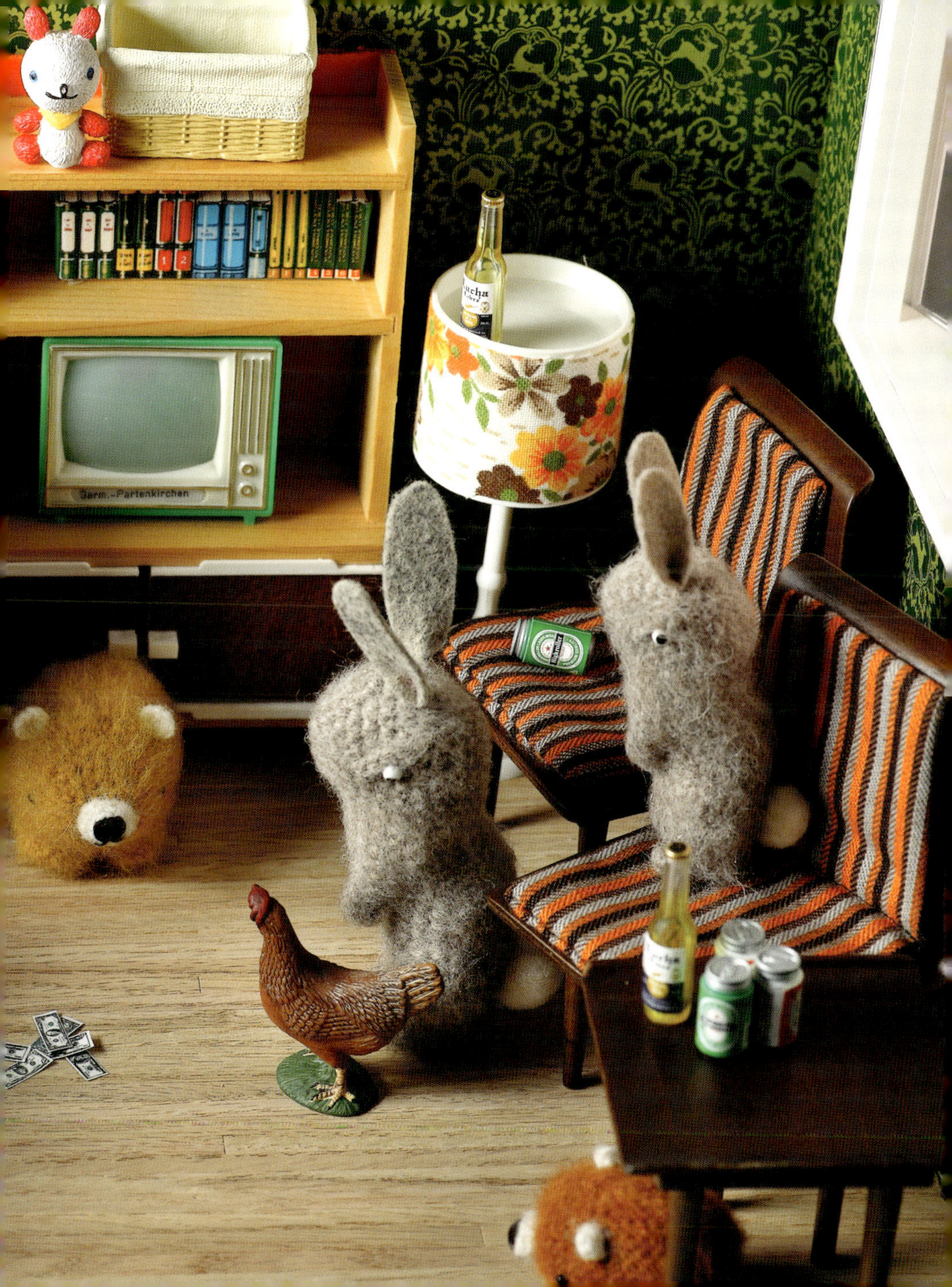

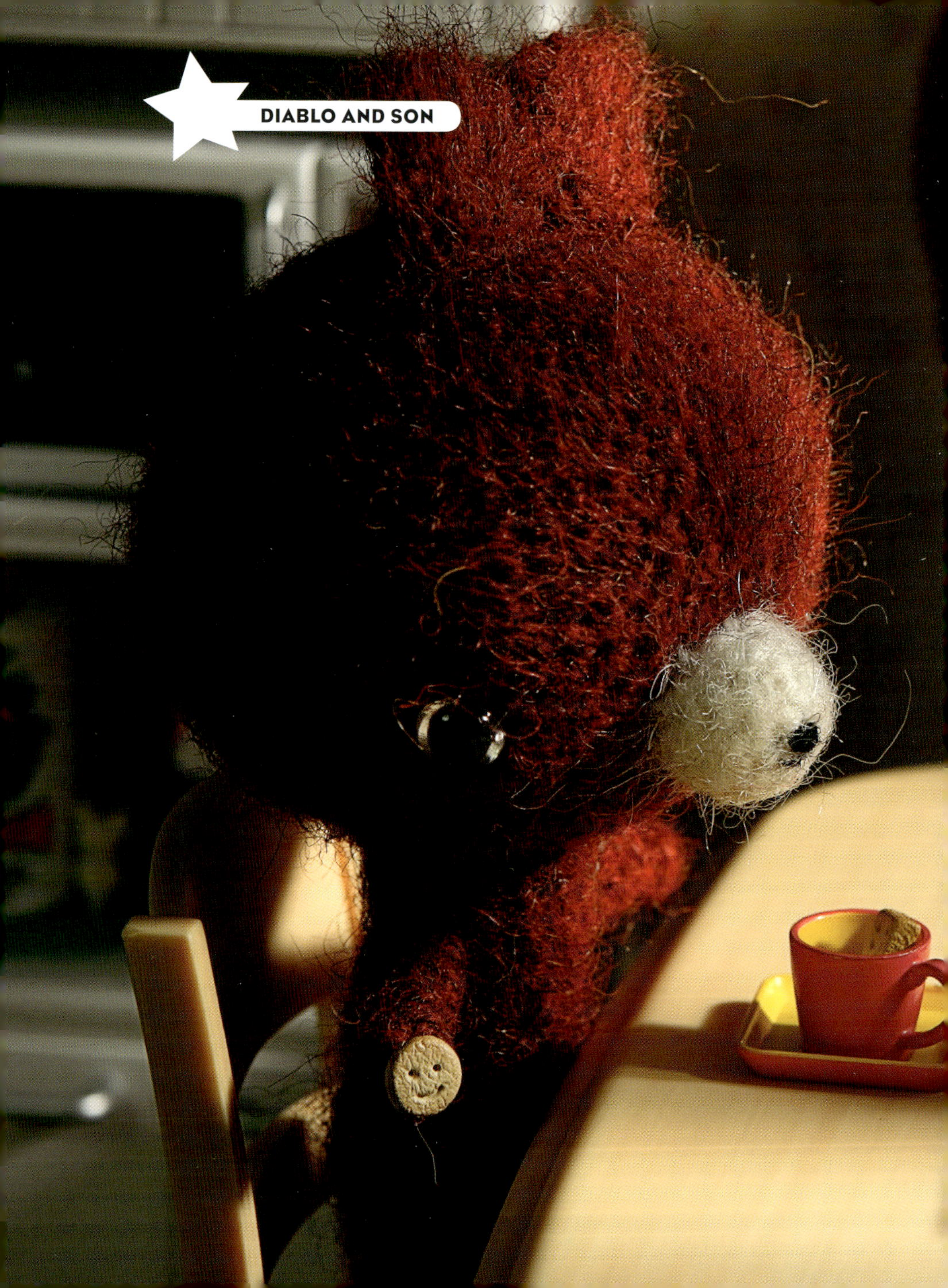
DIABLO AND SON

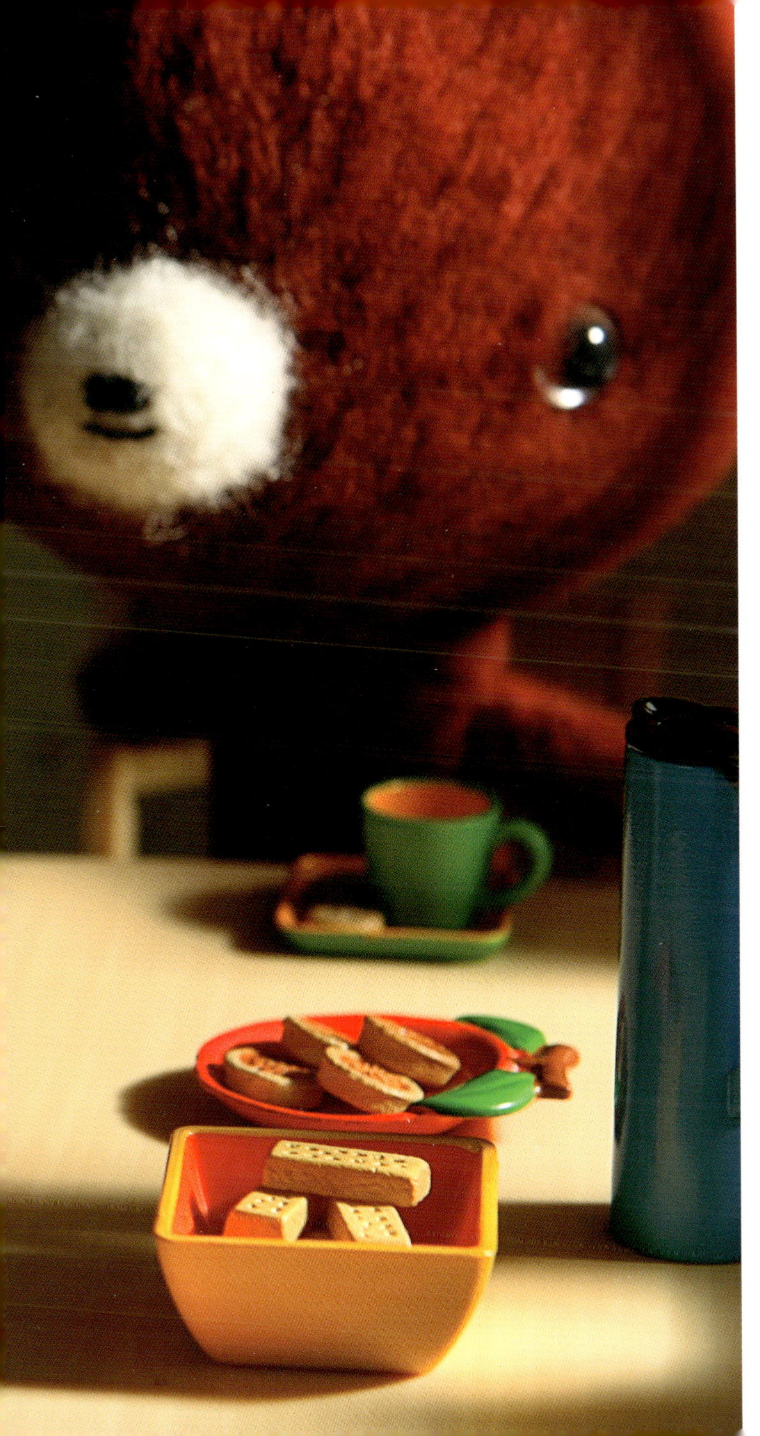

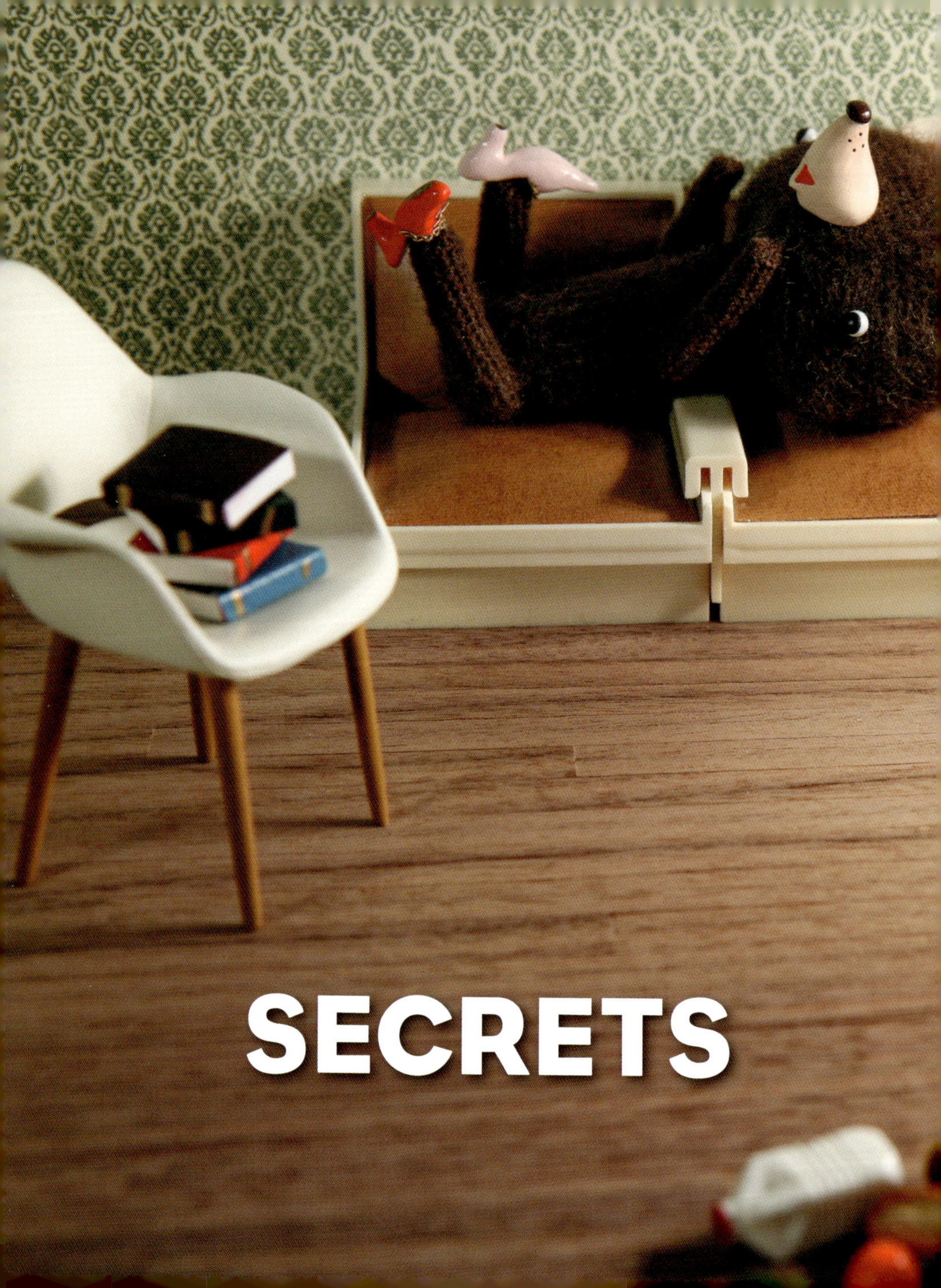

SECRETS

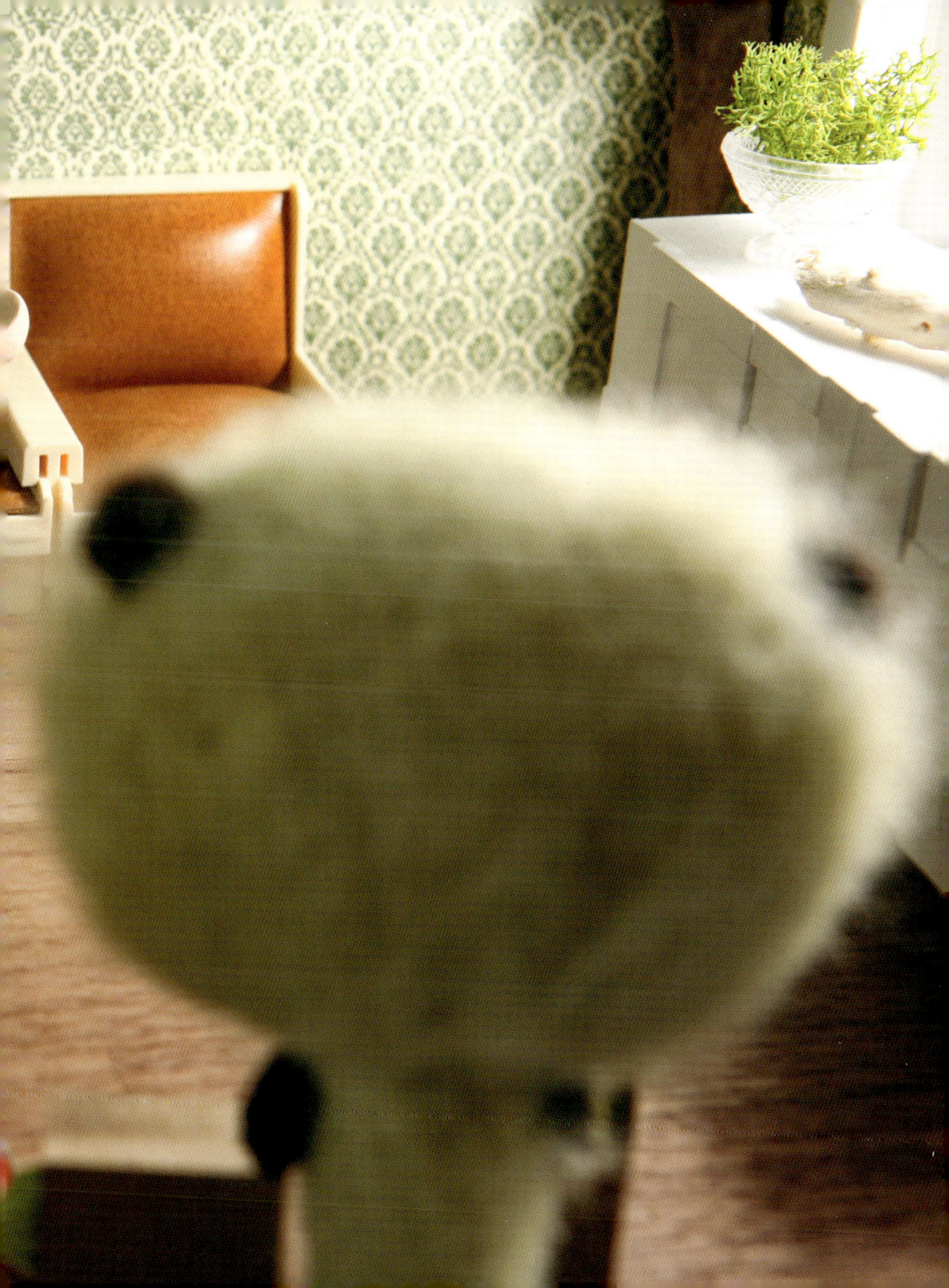

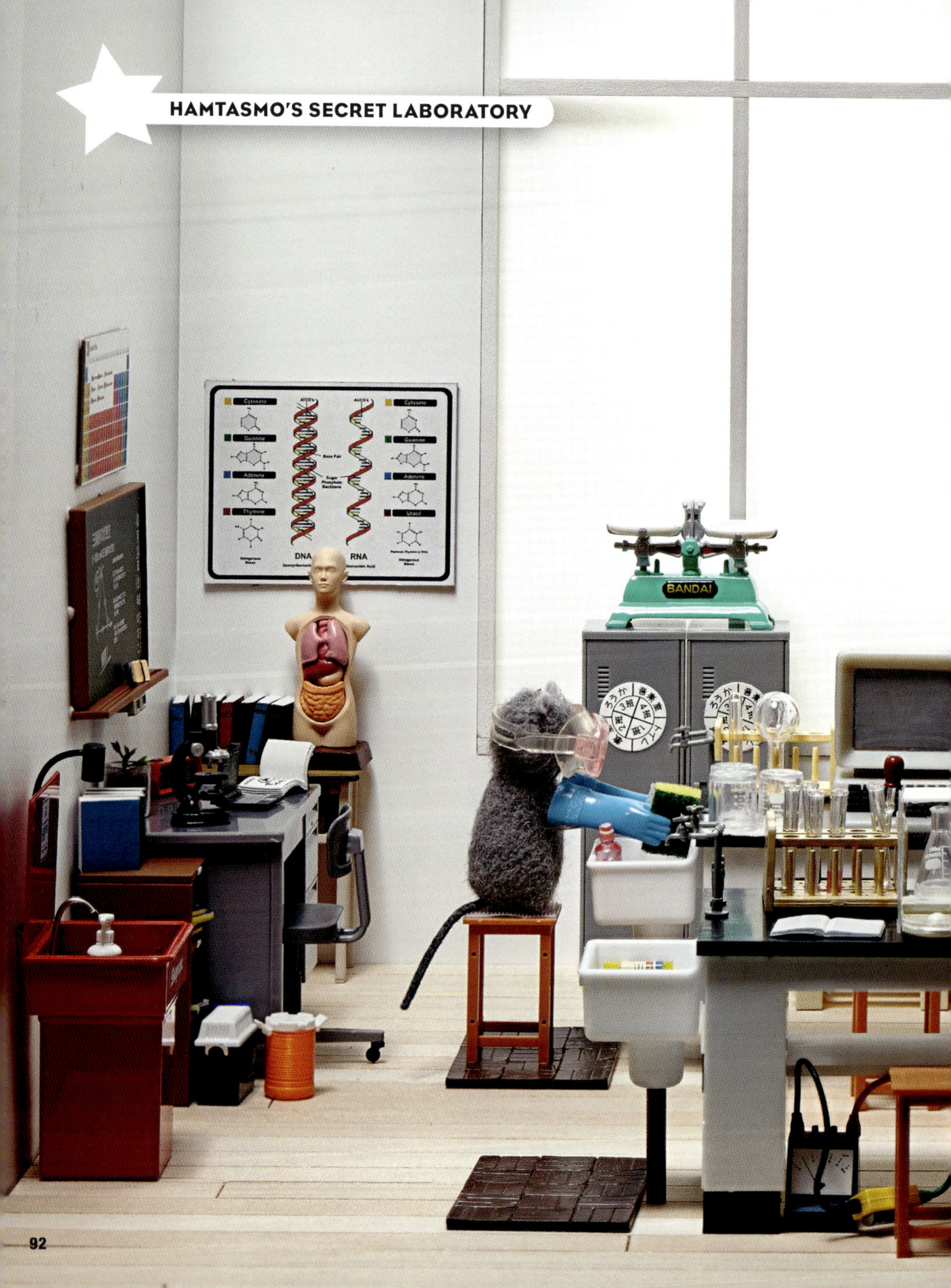

HAMTASMO'S SECRET LABORATORY

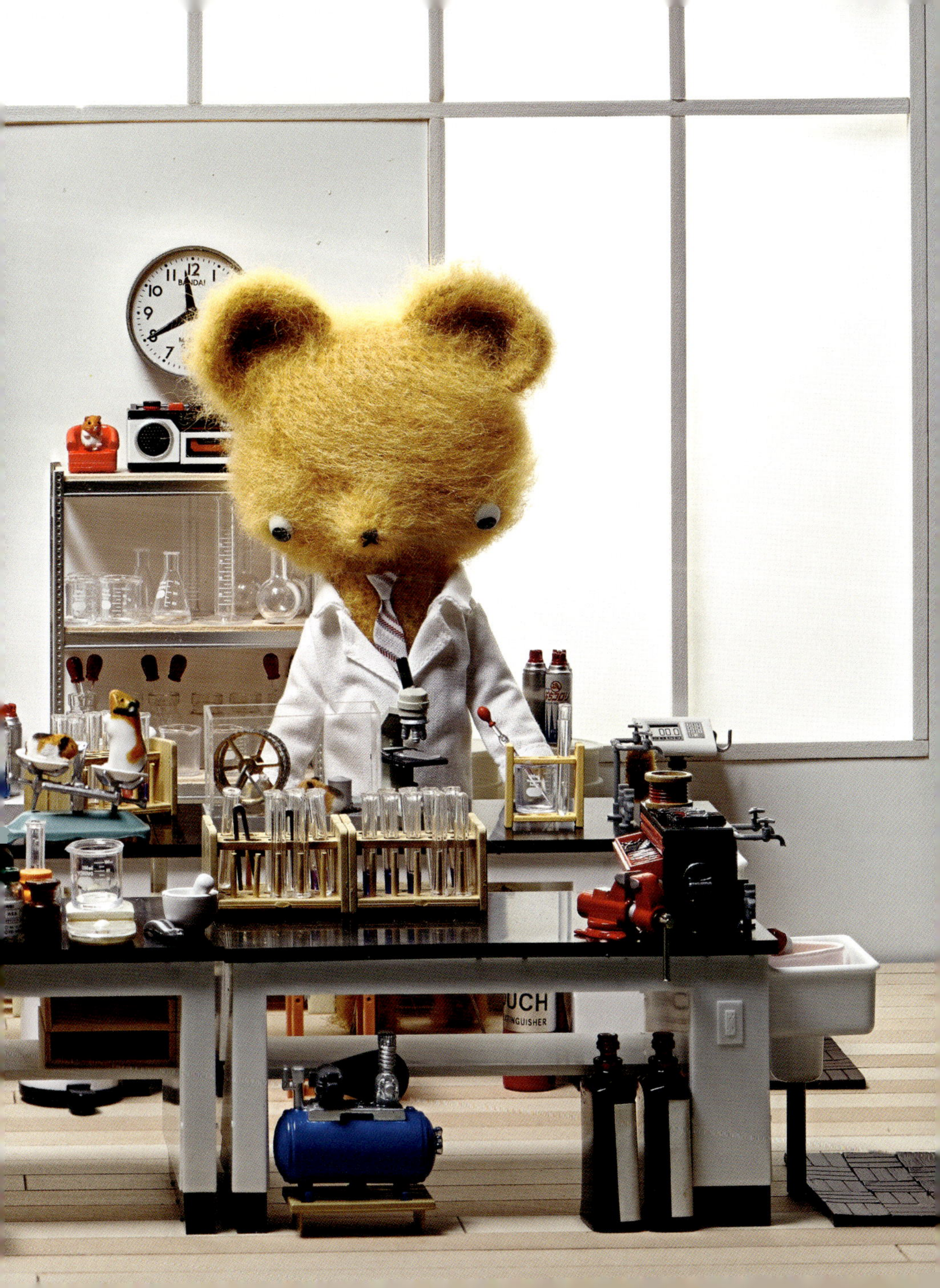

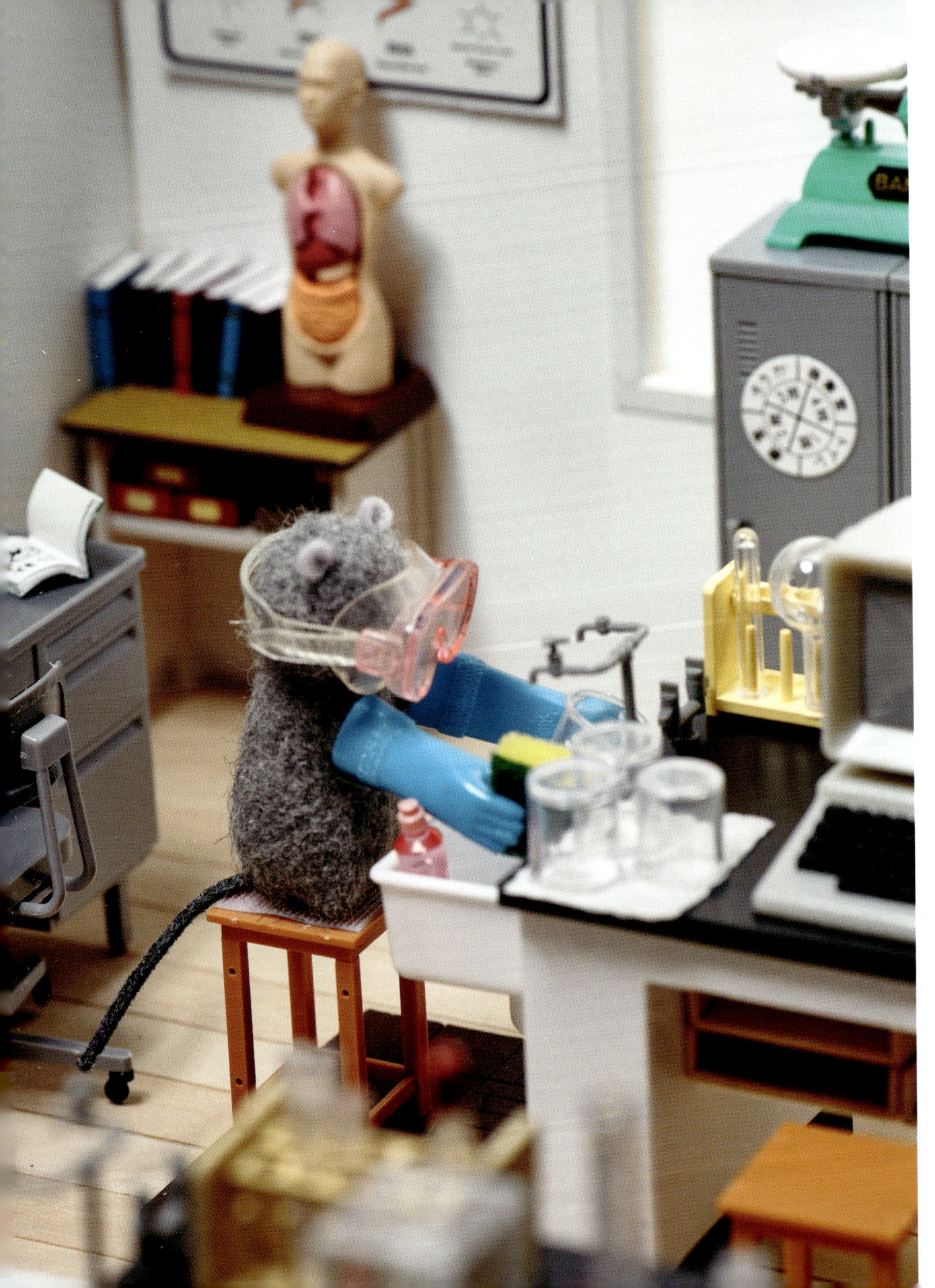

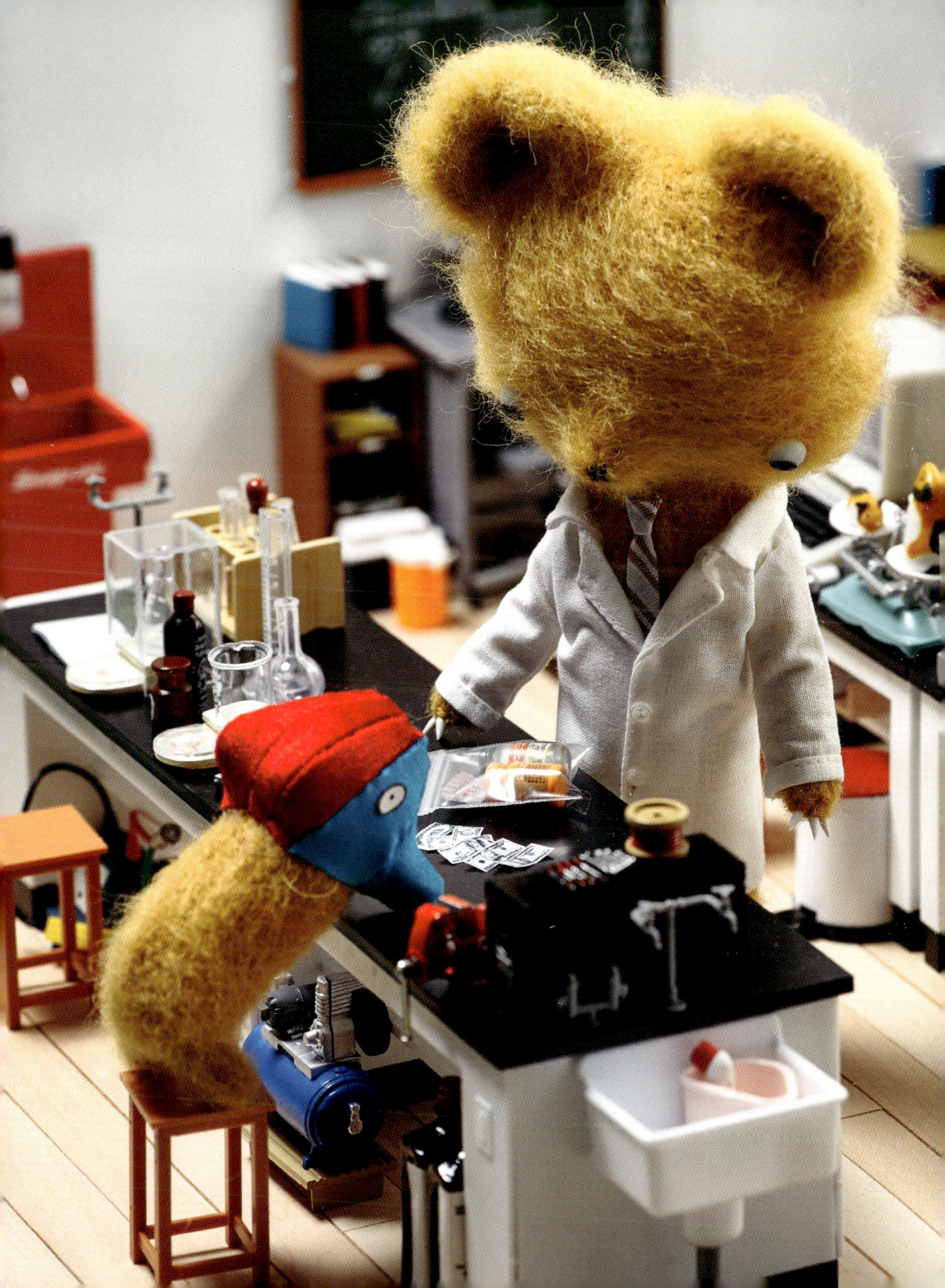

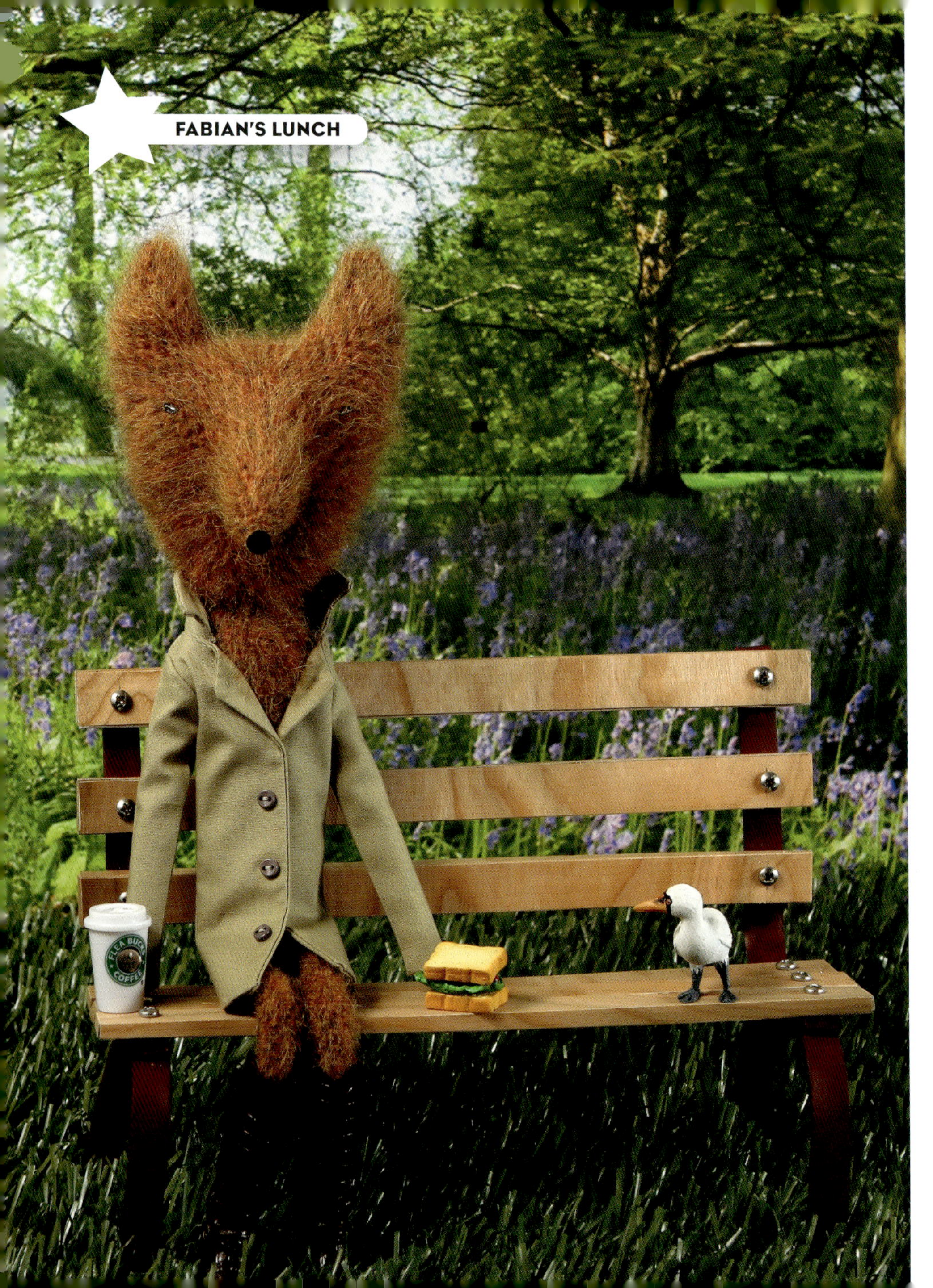
FABIAN'S LUNCH
FLEA BUCKS COFFEE

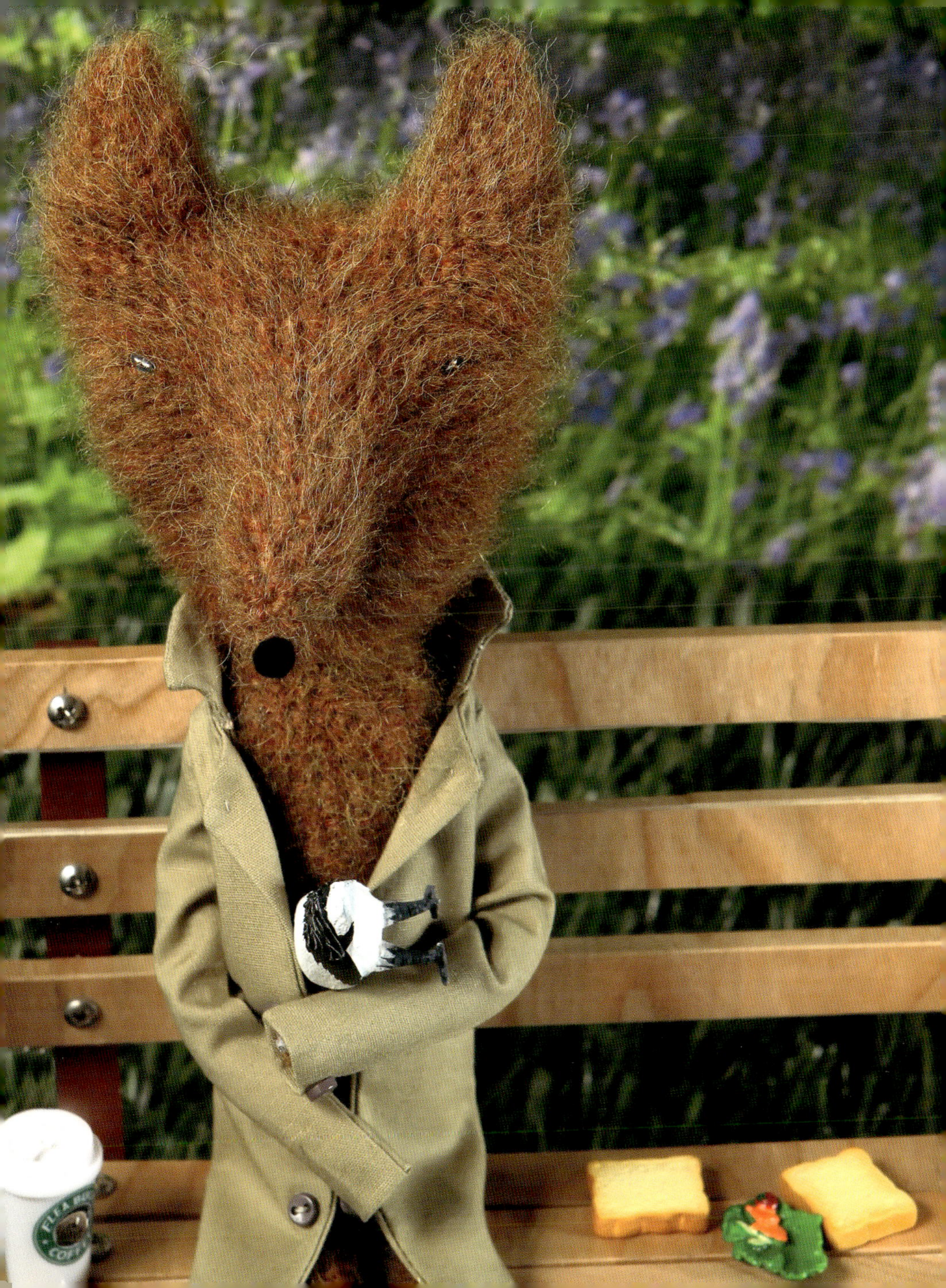

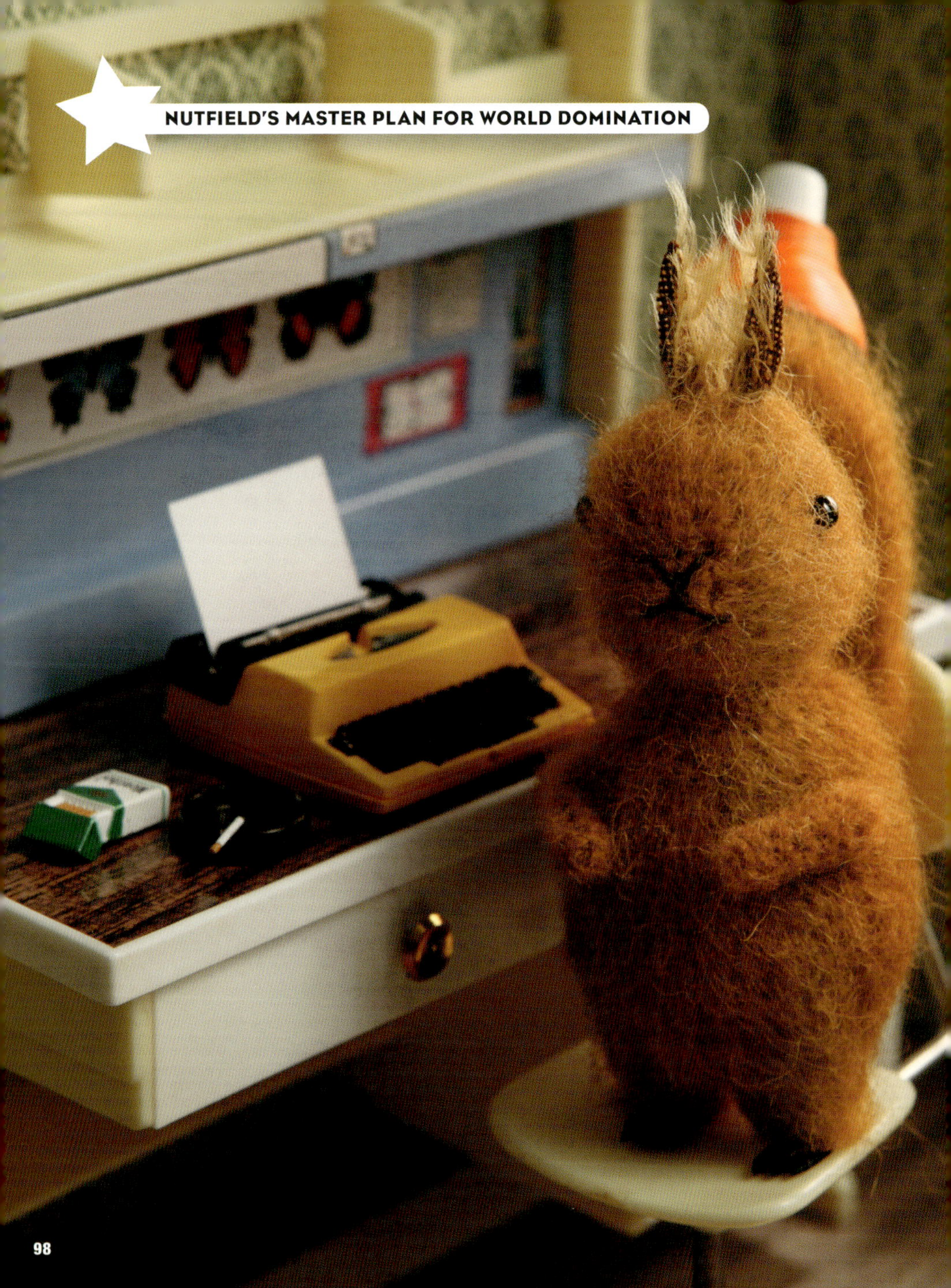
NUTFIELD'S MASTER PLAN FOR WORLD DOMINATION

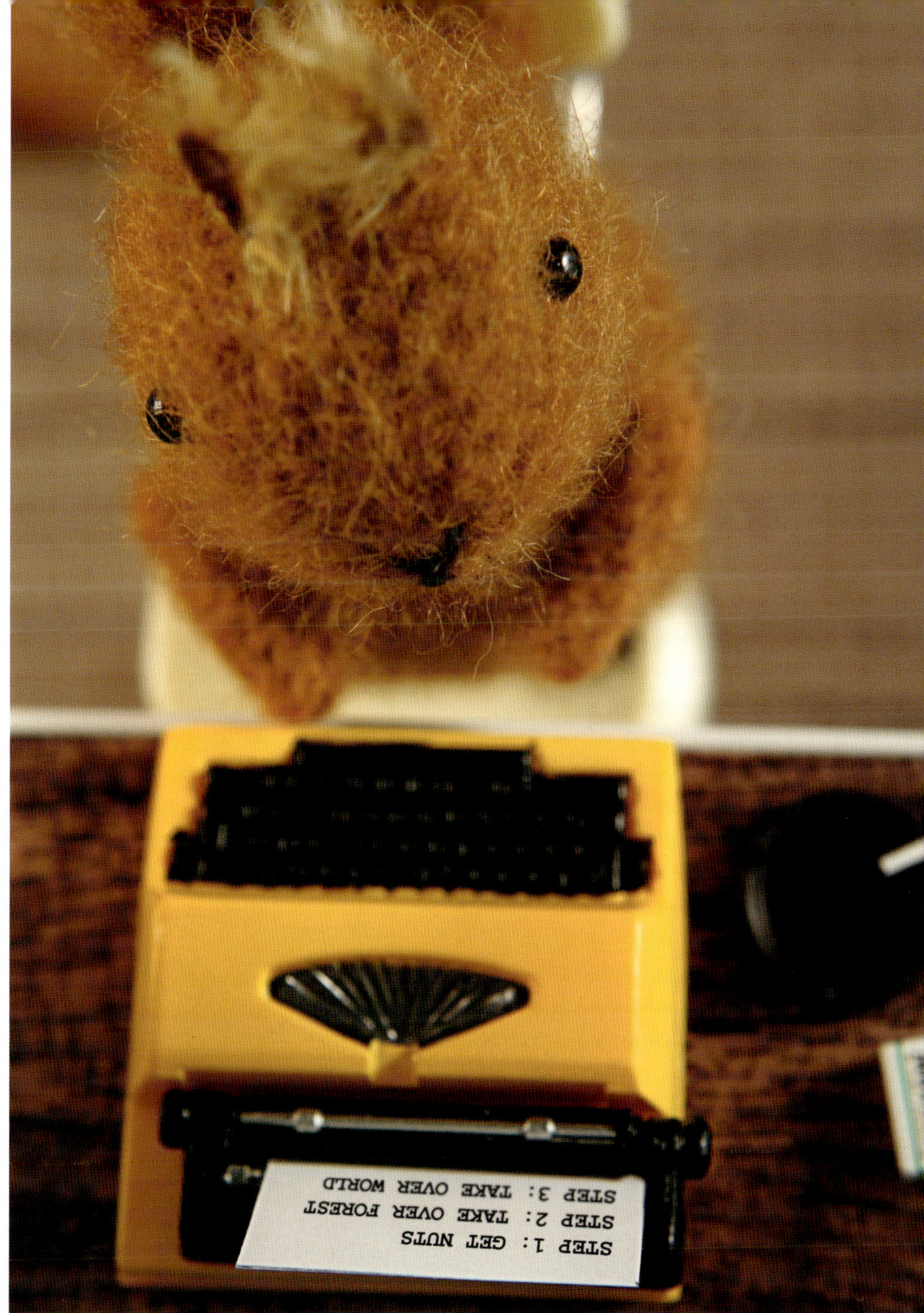

STEP 1: GET NUTS
STEP 2: TAKE OVER FOREST
STEP 3: TAKE OVER WORLD

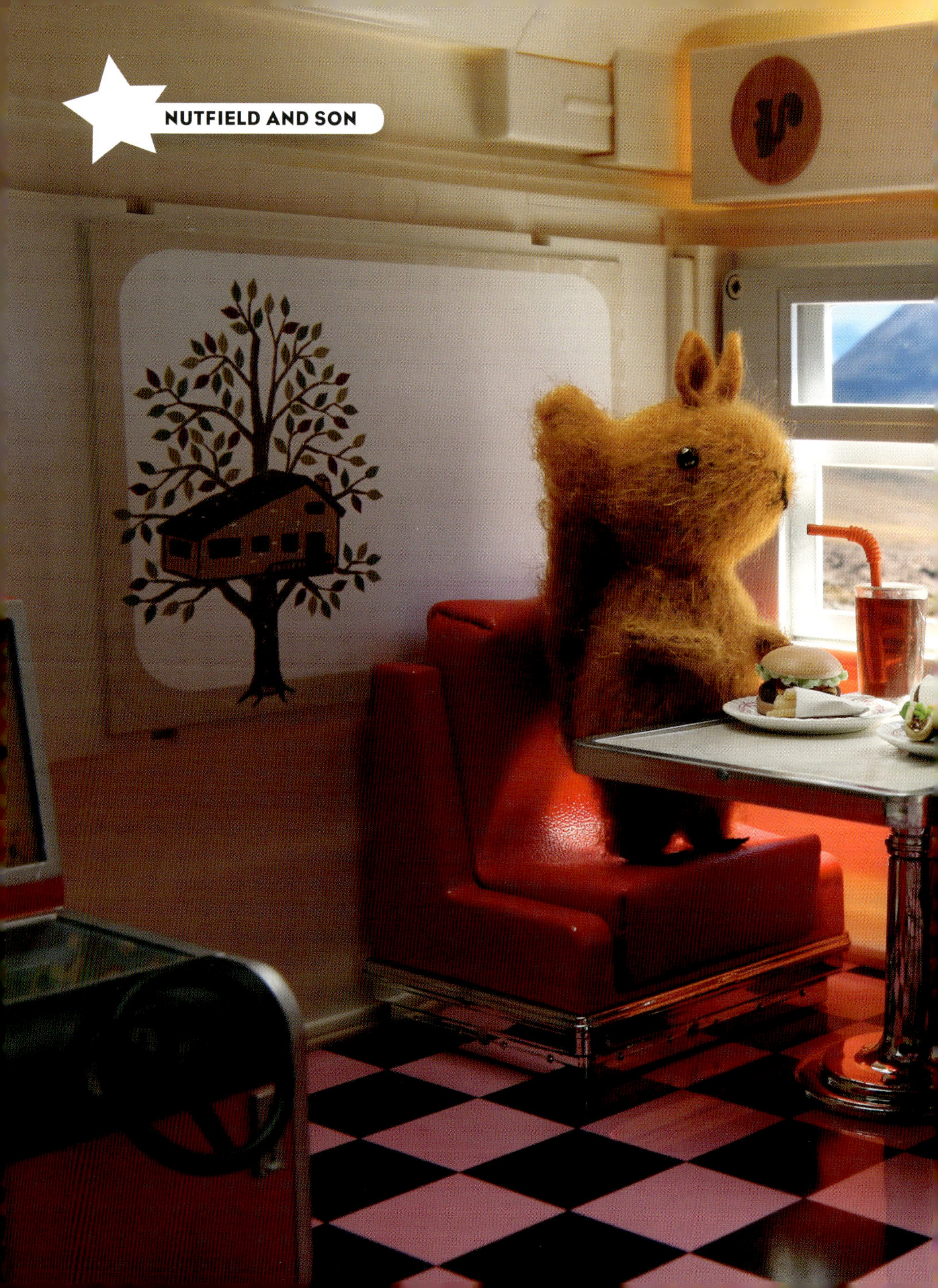
NUTFIELD AND SON

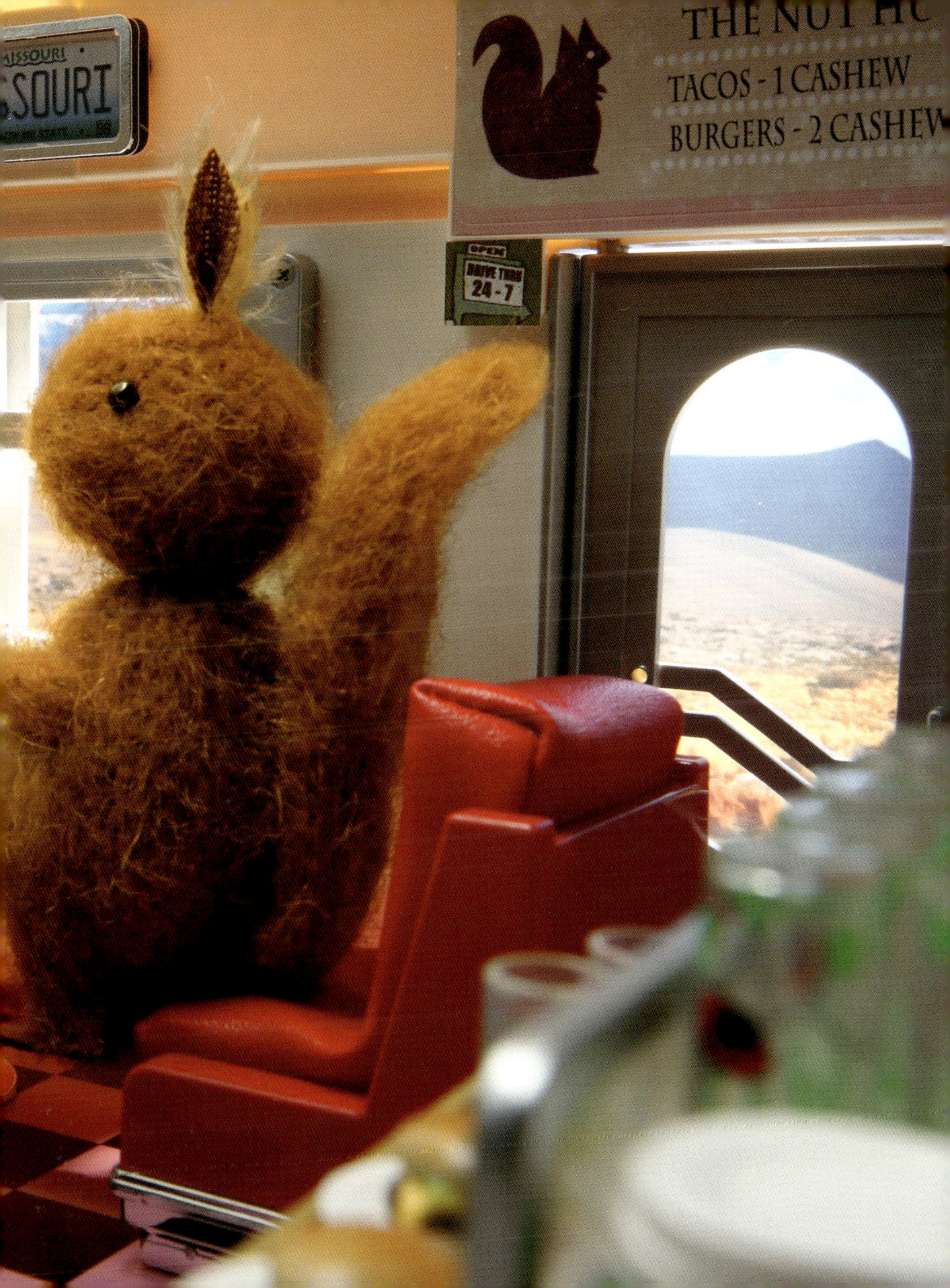
MISSOURI
SOURI
THE NUT HO
TACOS - 1 CASHEW
BURGERS - 2 CASHEW
OPEN
DRIVE THRU
24 - 7

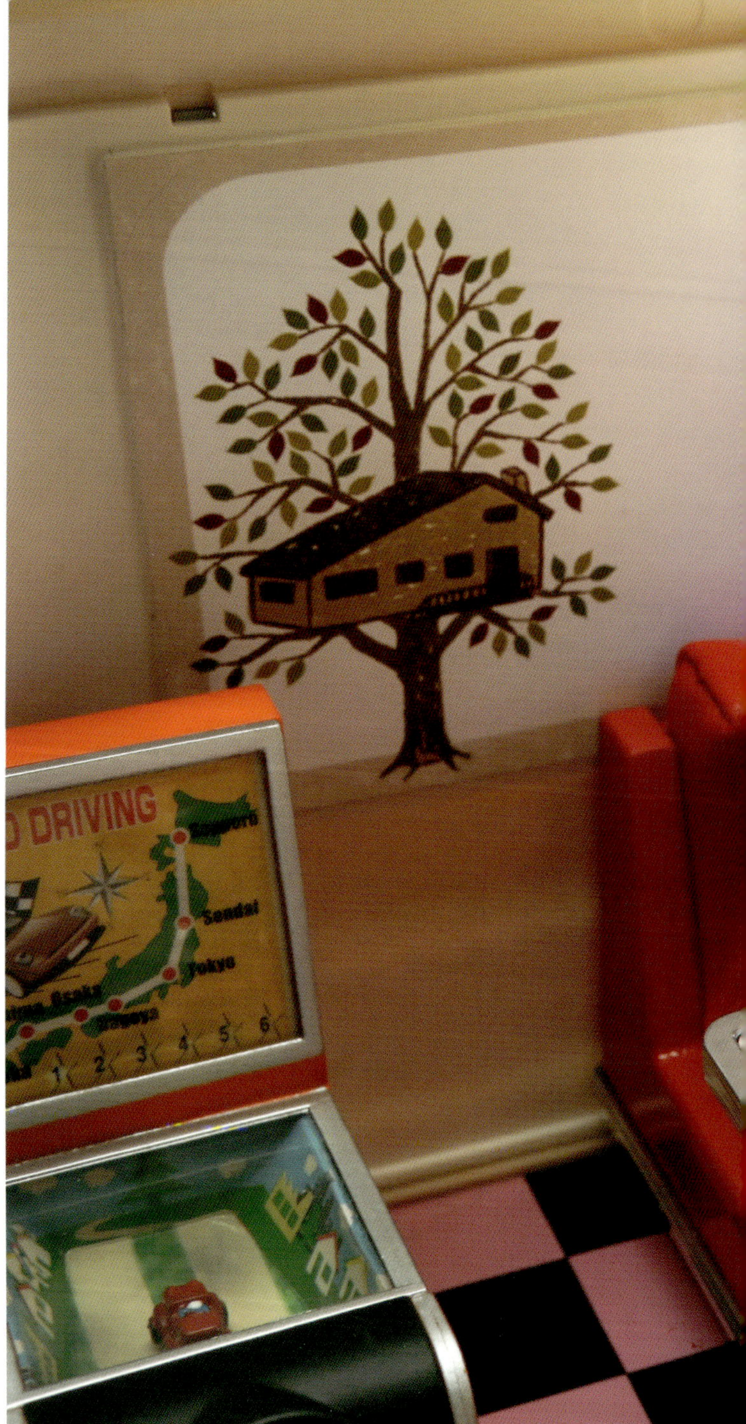
DRIVING
Sapporo
Sendai
Tokyo
Osaka
Nagoya
1 2 3 4 5 6

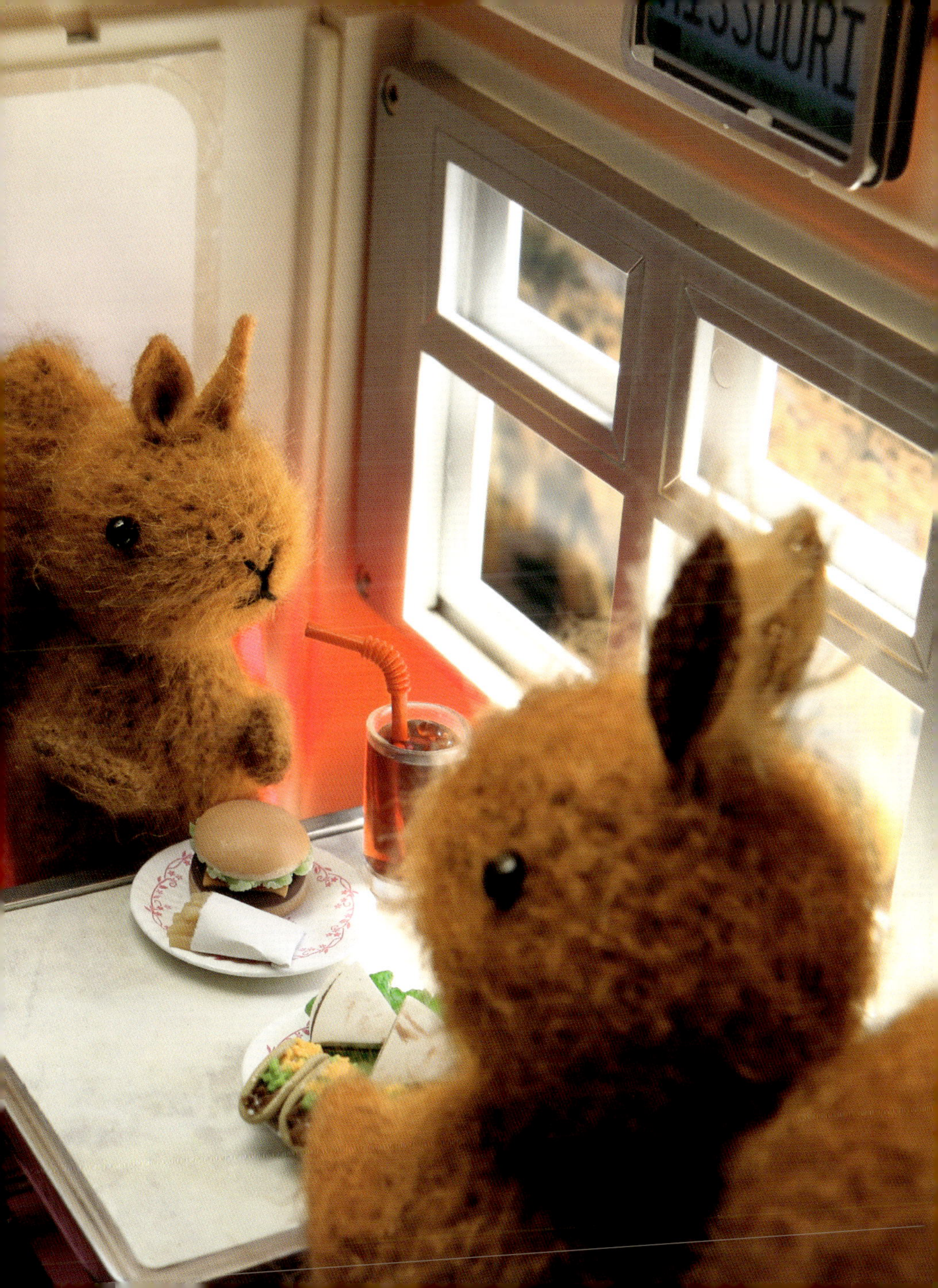
MISSOURI

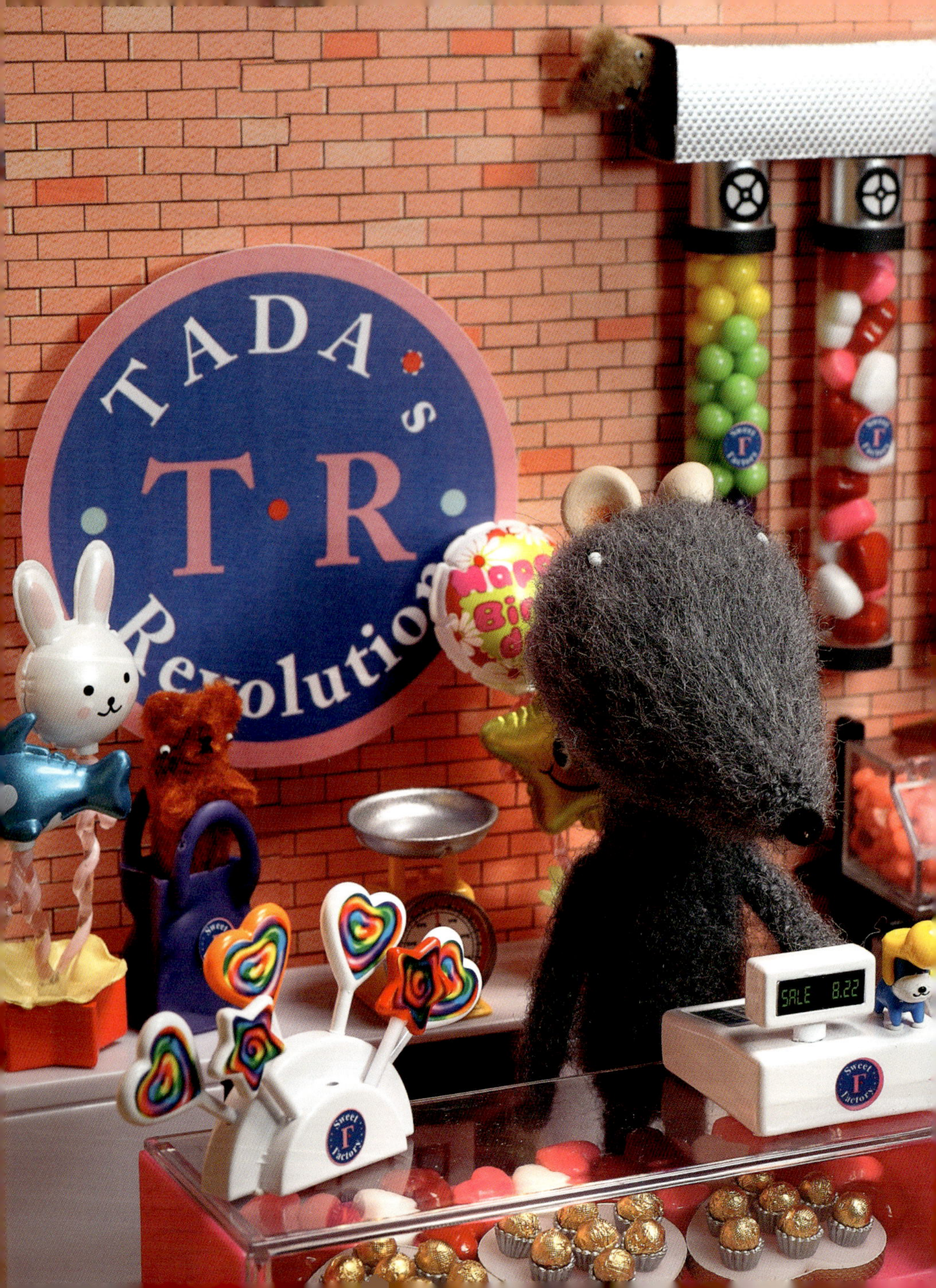

TADA's
T·R
Revolution
Happy Big
SALE   8.22
Sweet
Factory

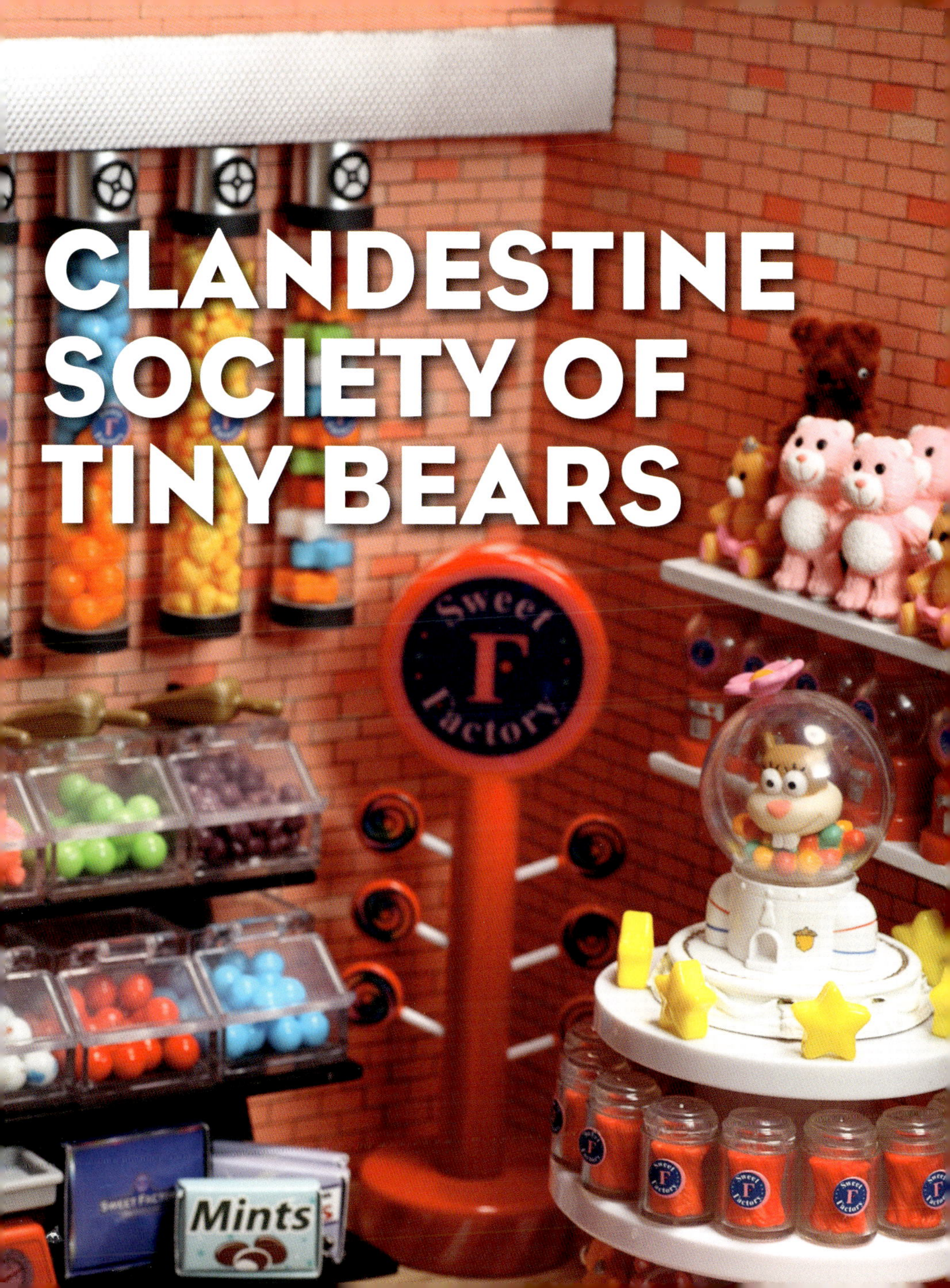

CLANDESTINE SOCIETY OF TINY BEARS
Sweet Factory
Mints

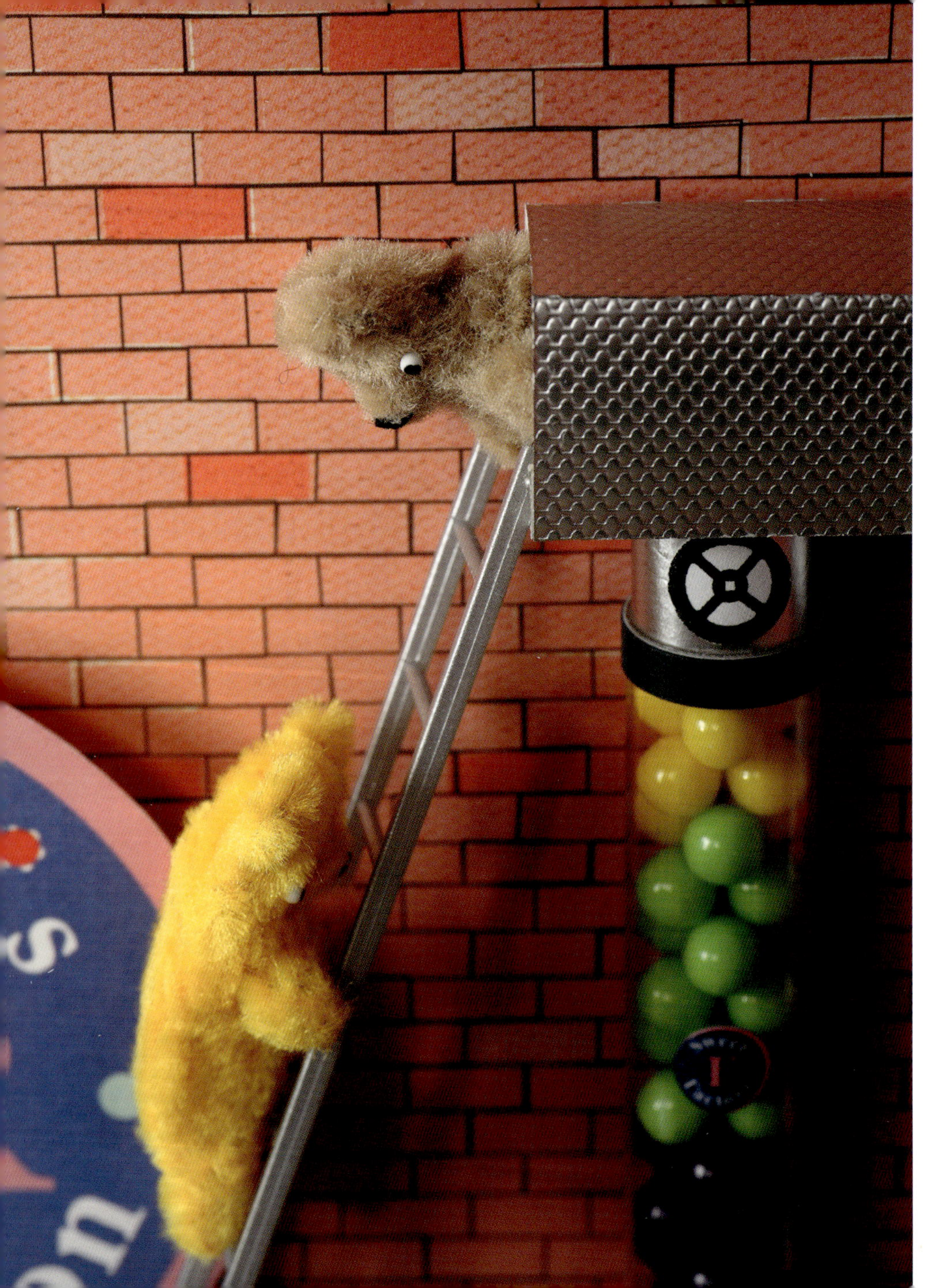

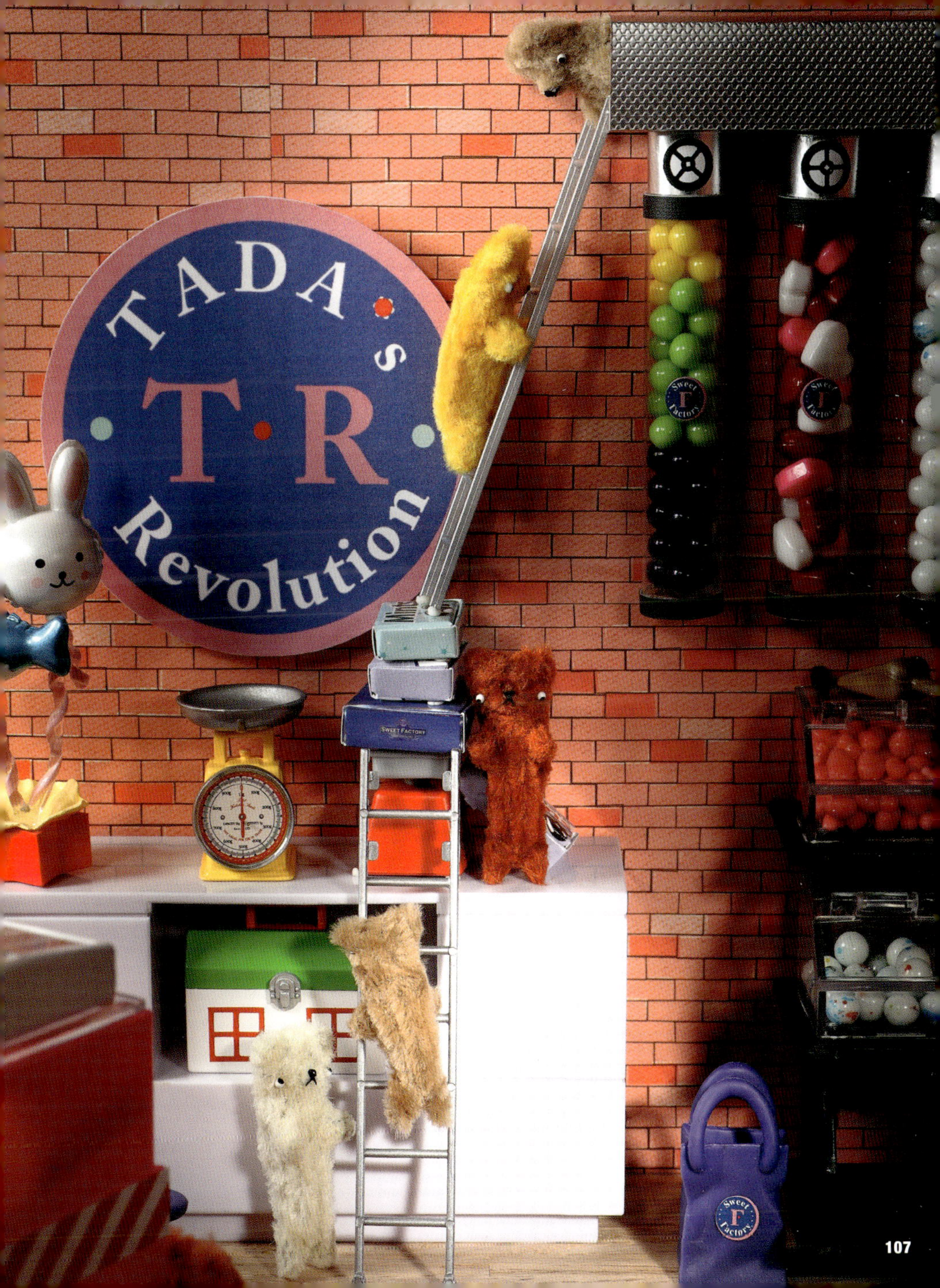

TADA's
T·R
Revolution

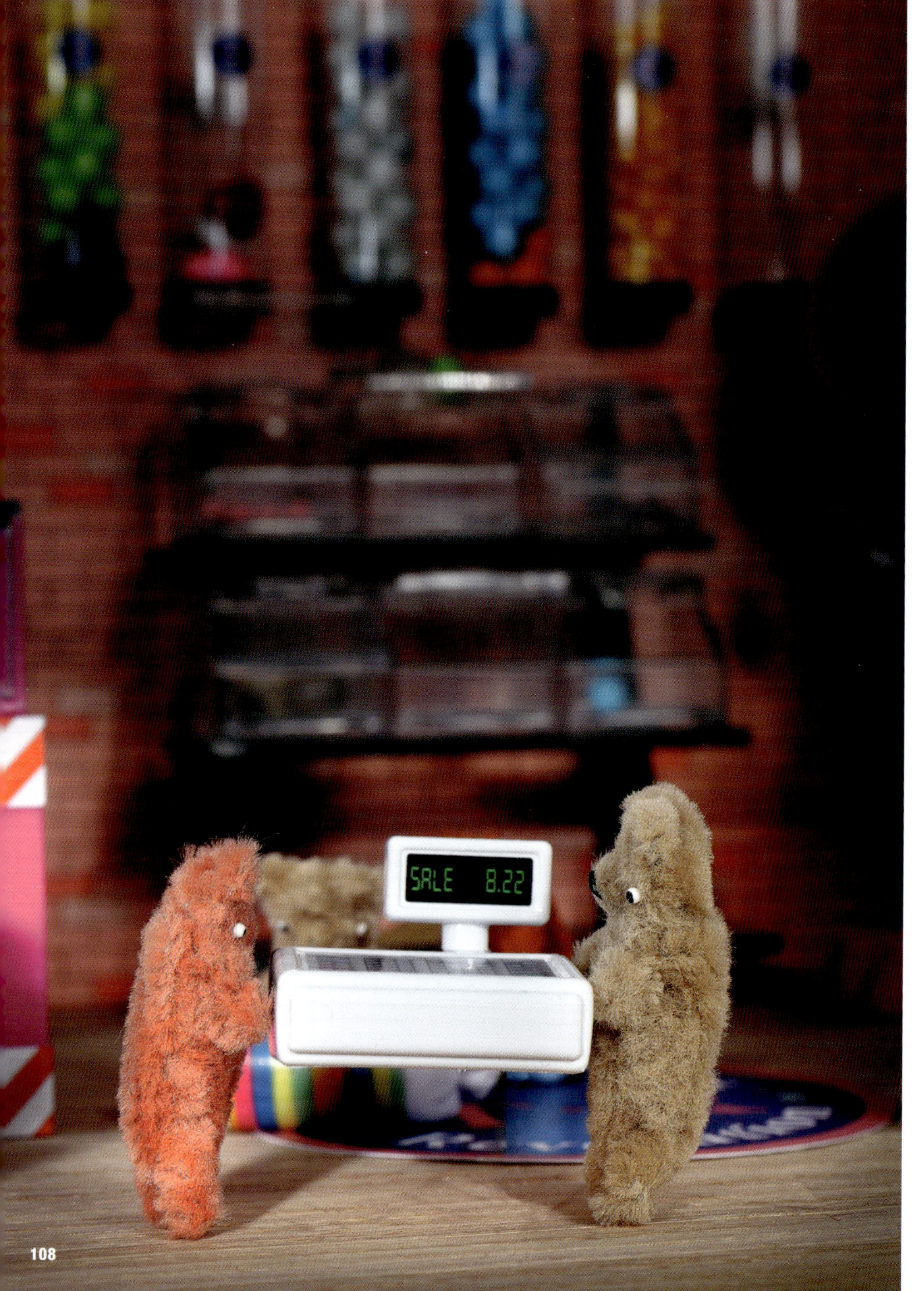
SALE   8.22

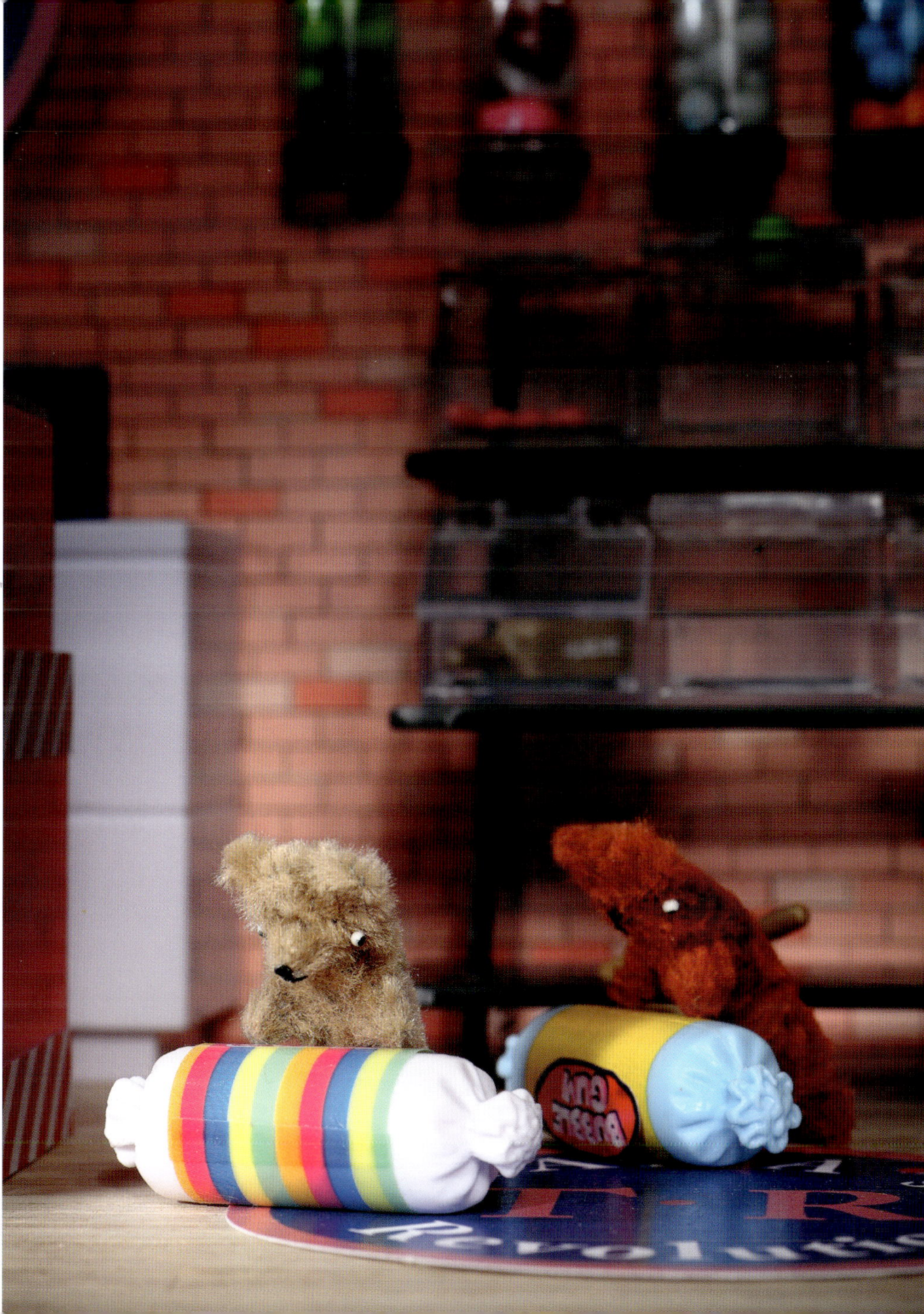

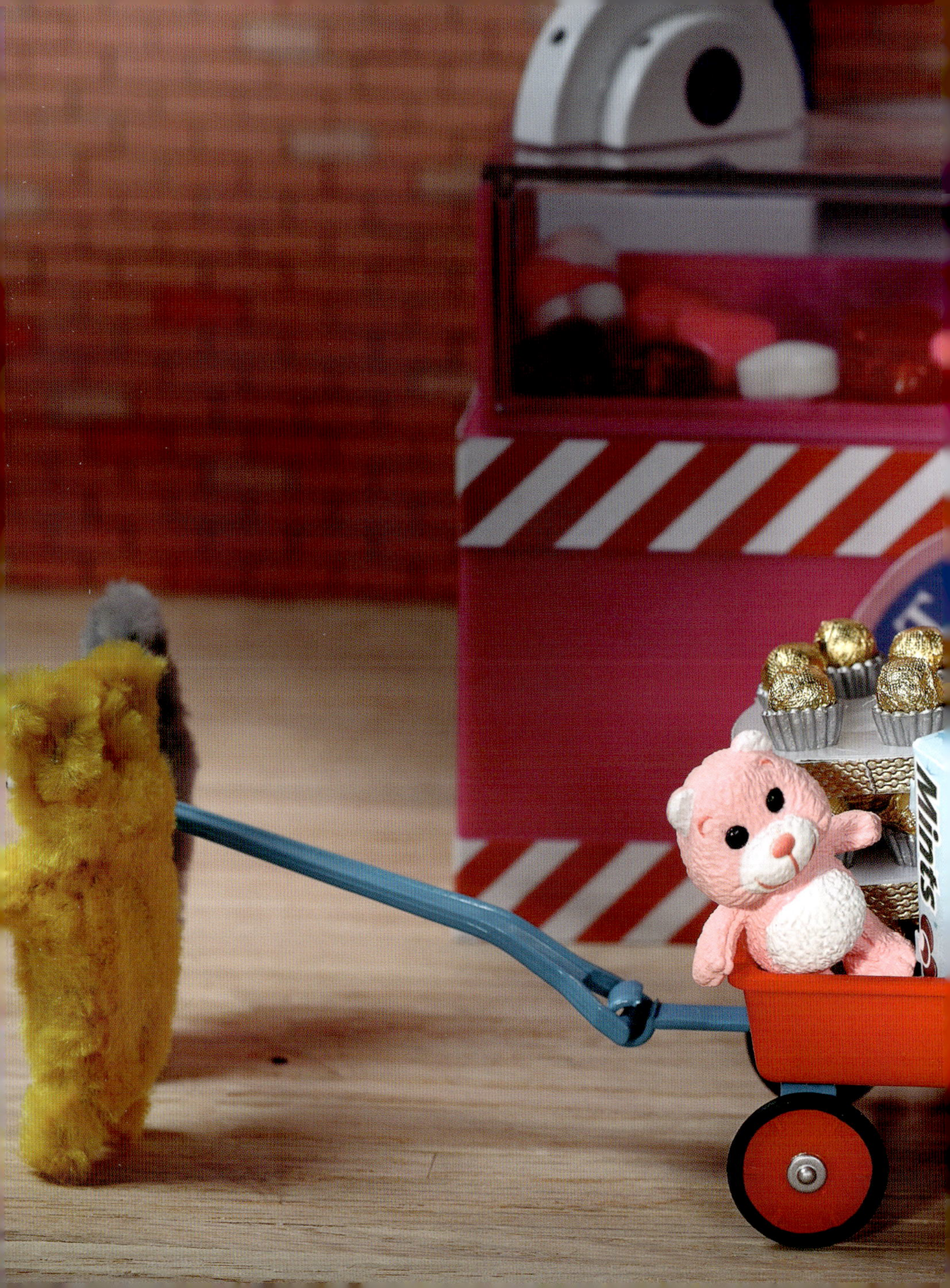

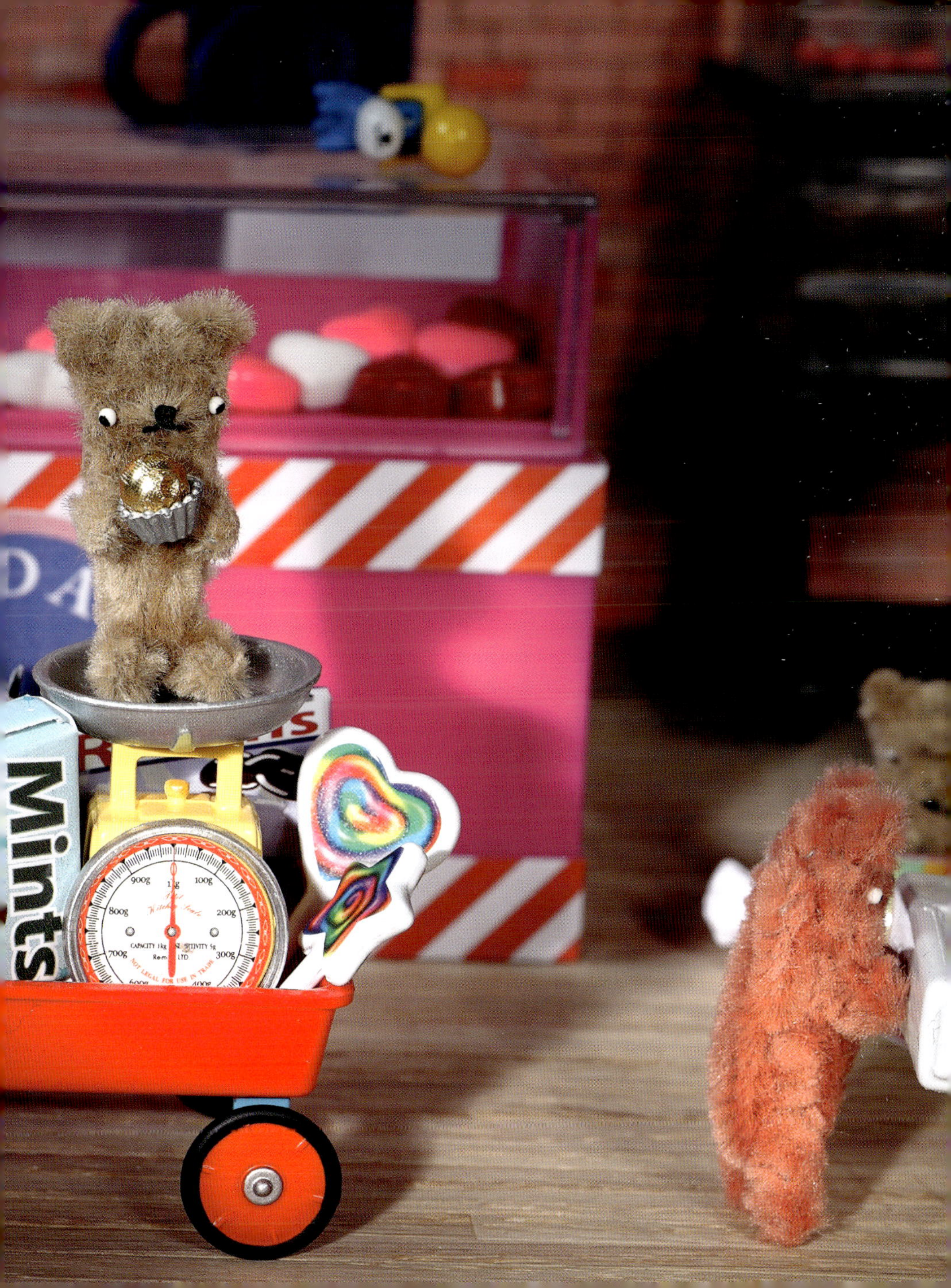

Mints
900g 1 kg 100g
800g   200g
700g   300g
CAPACITY 1kg SENSITIVITY 5g
600g   400g

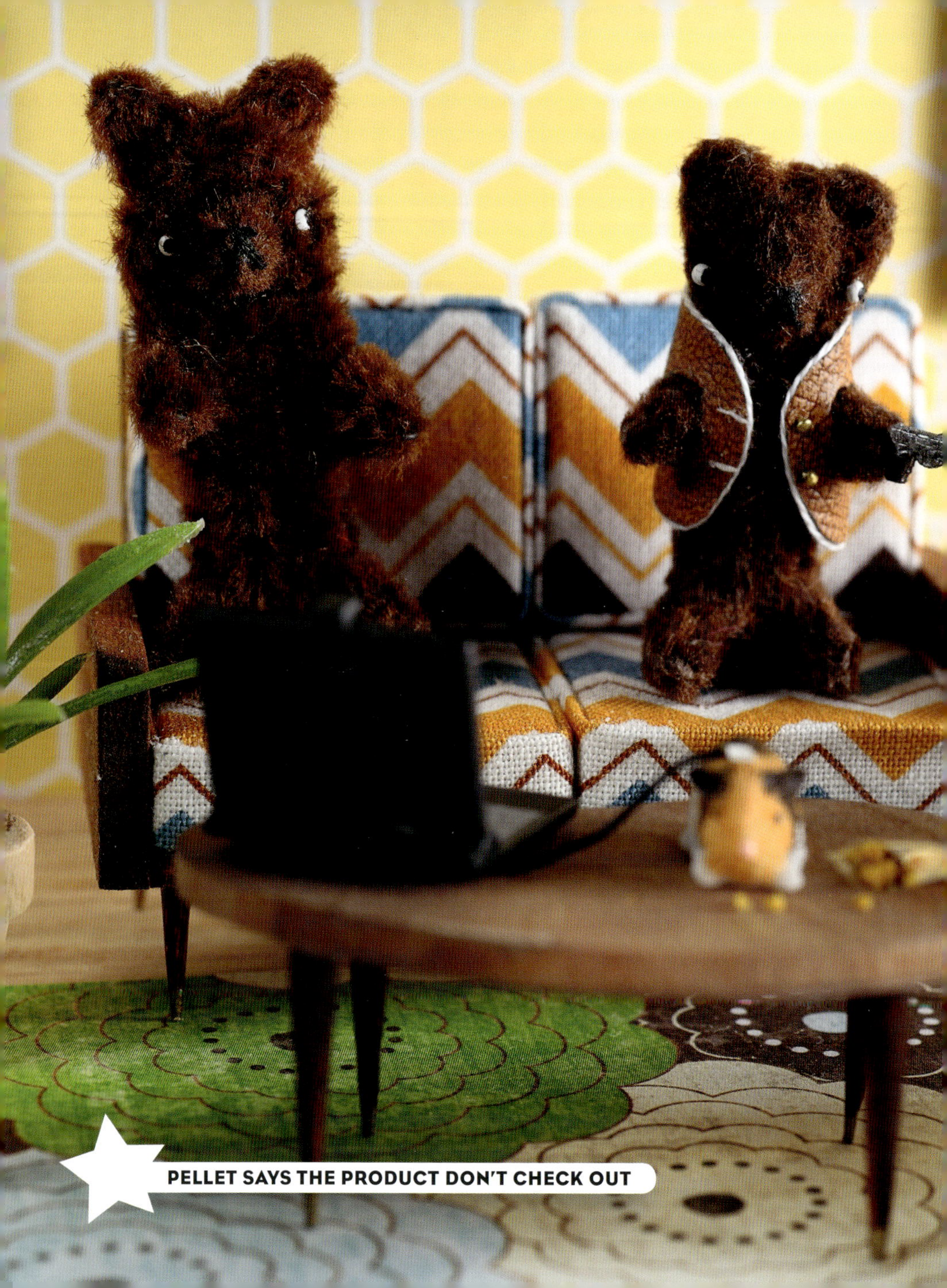
PELLET SAYS THE PRODUCT DON'T CHECK OUT

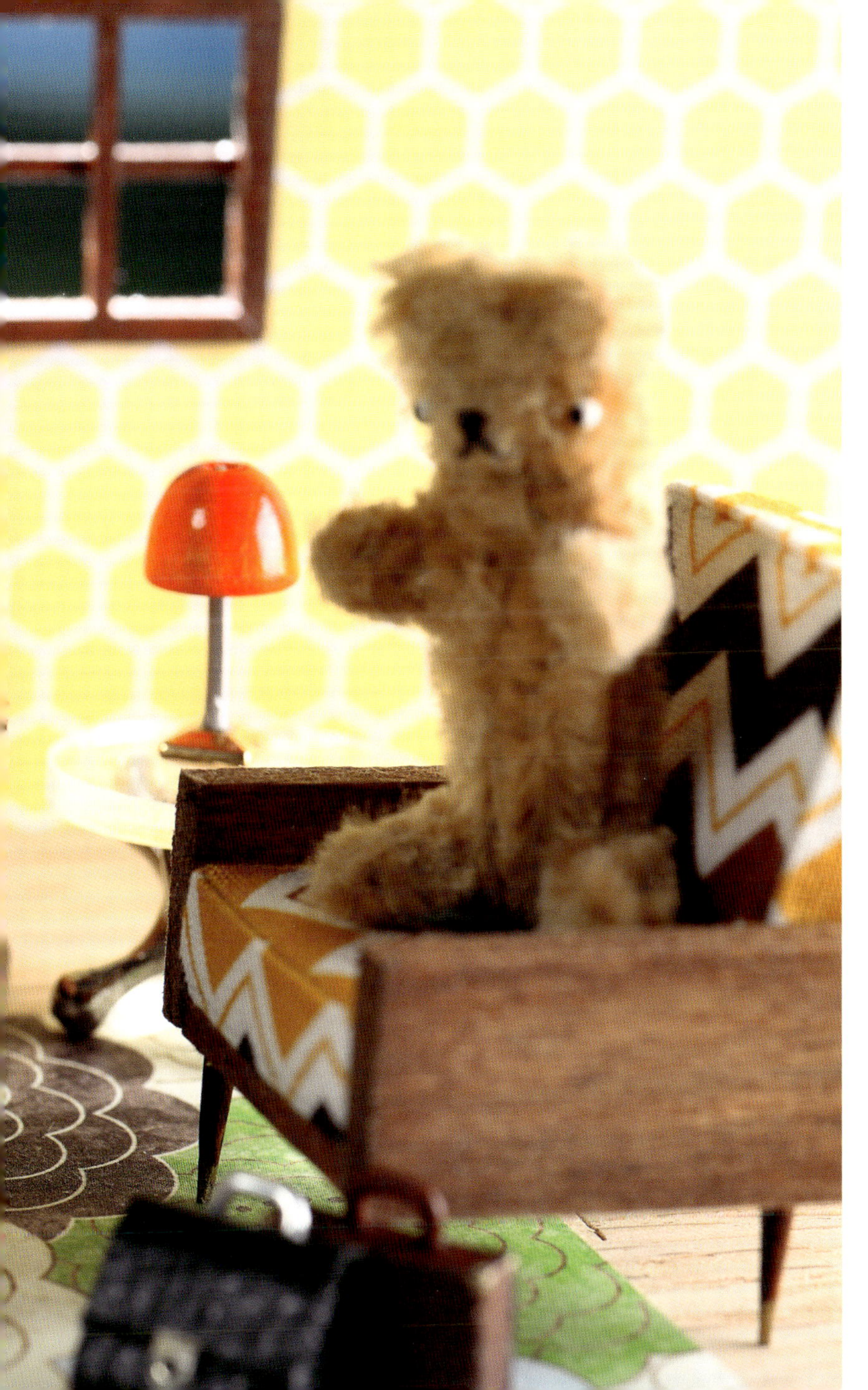

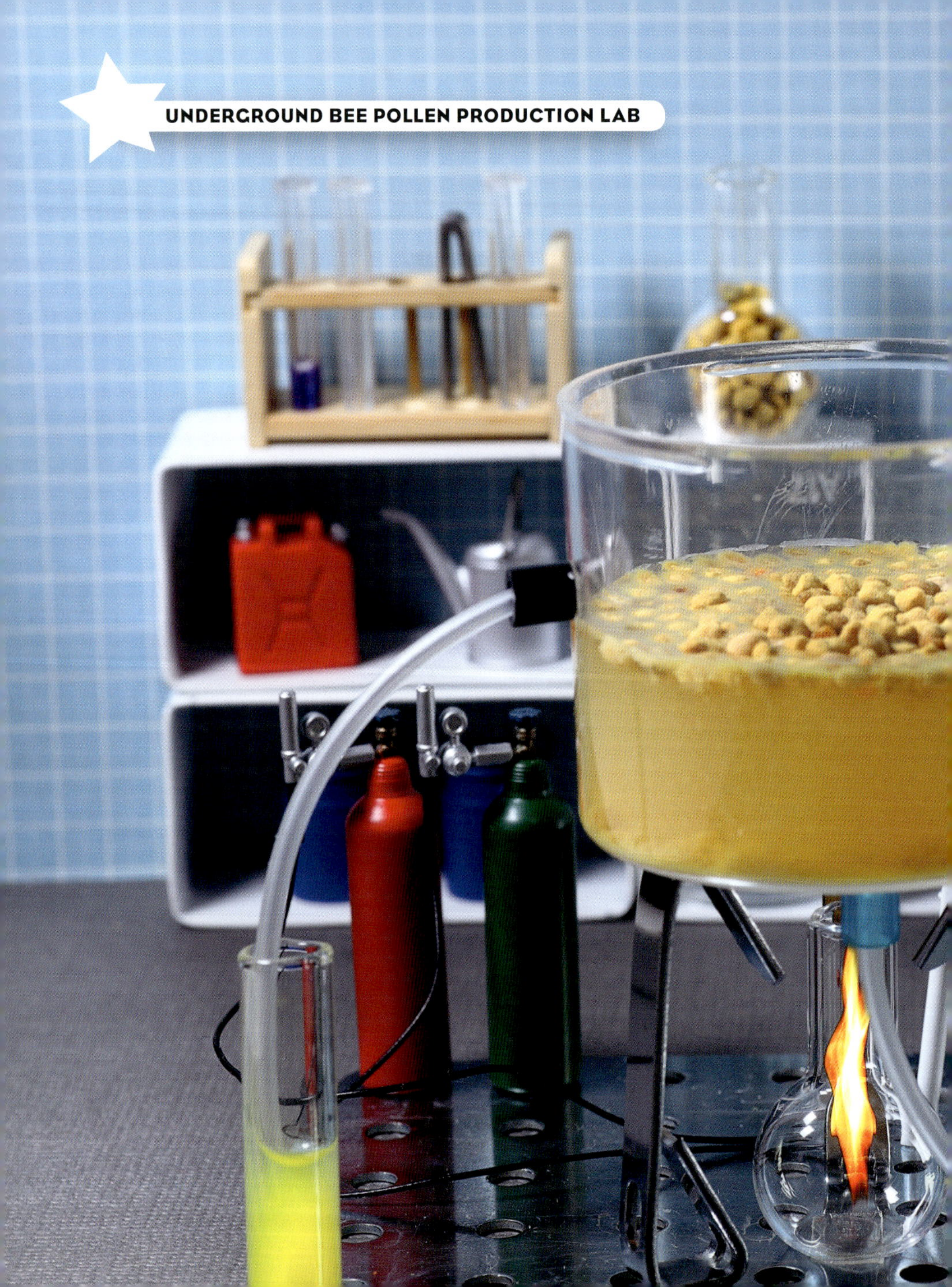
UNDERGROUND BEE POLLEN PRODUCTION LAB

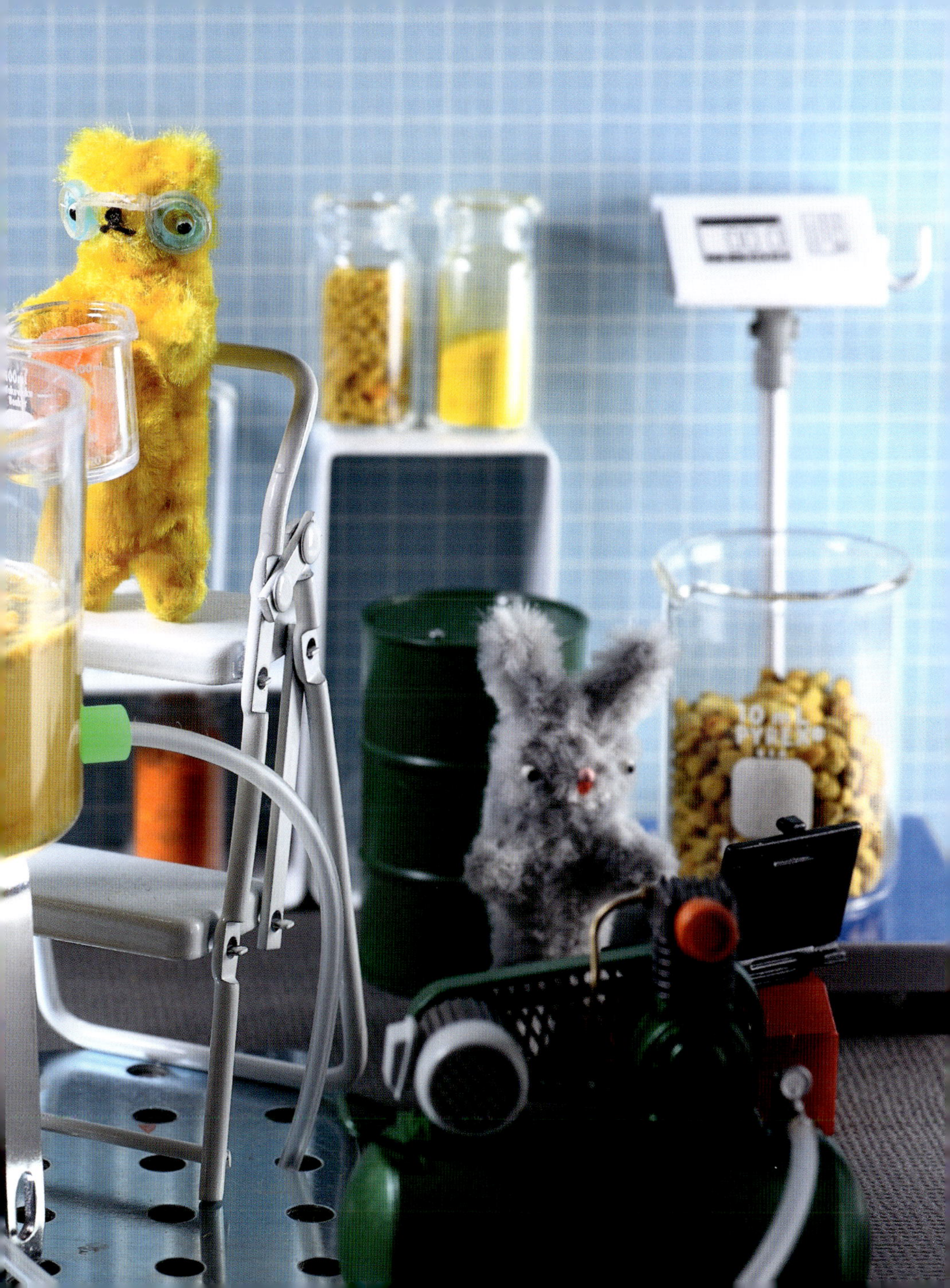

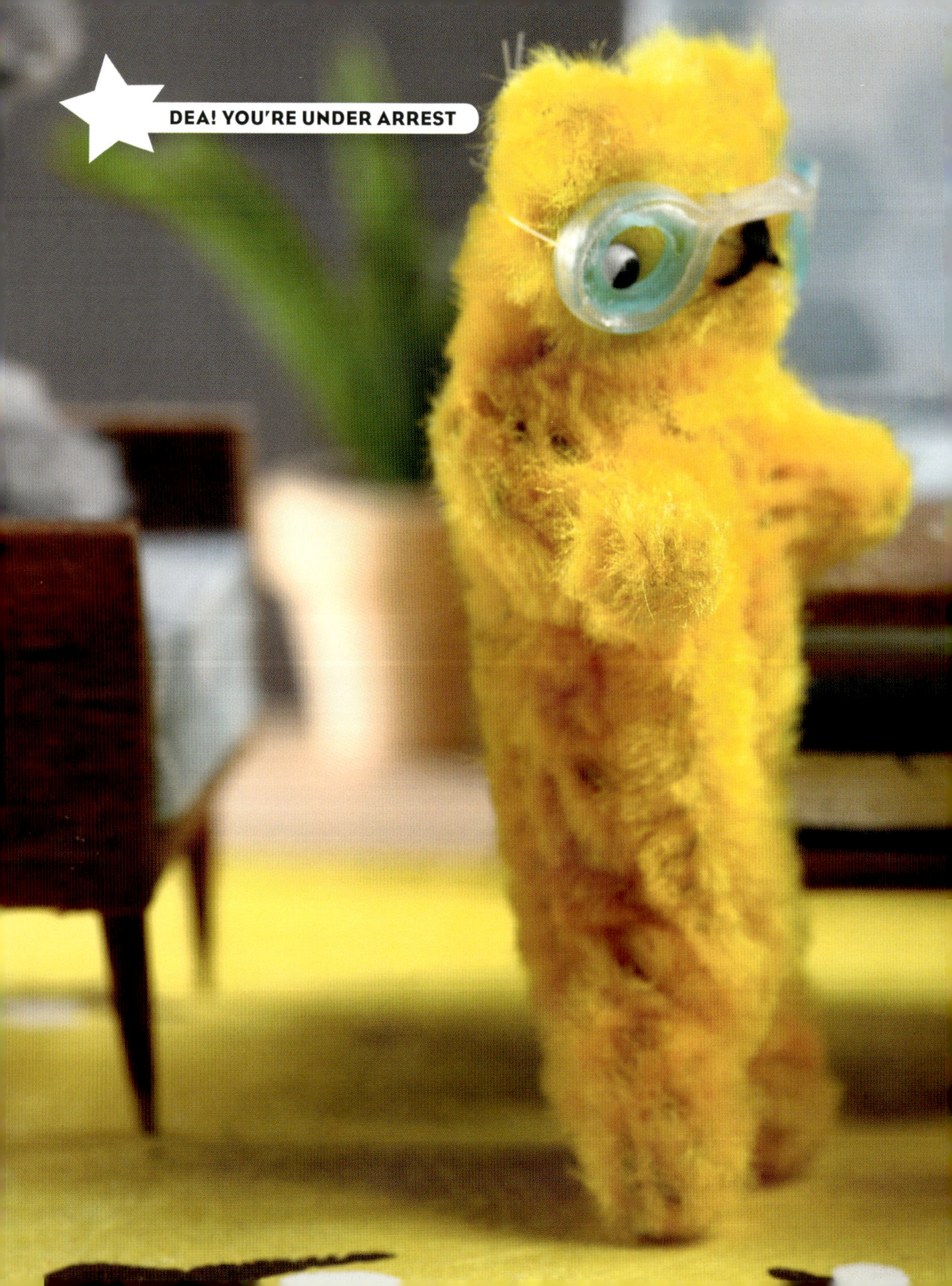
DEA! YOU'RE UNDER ARREST

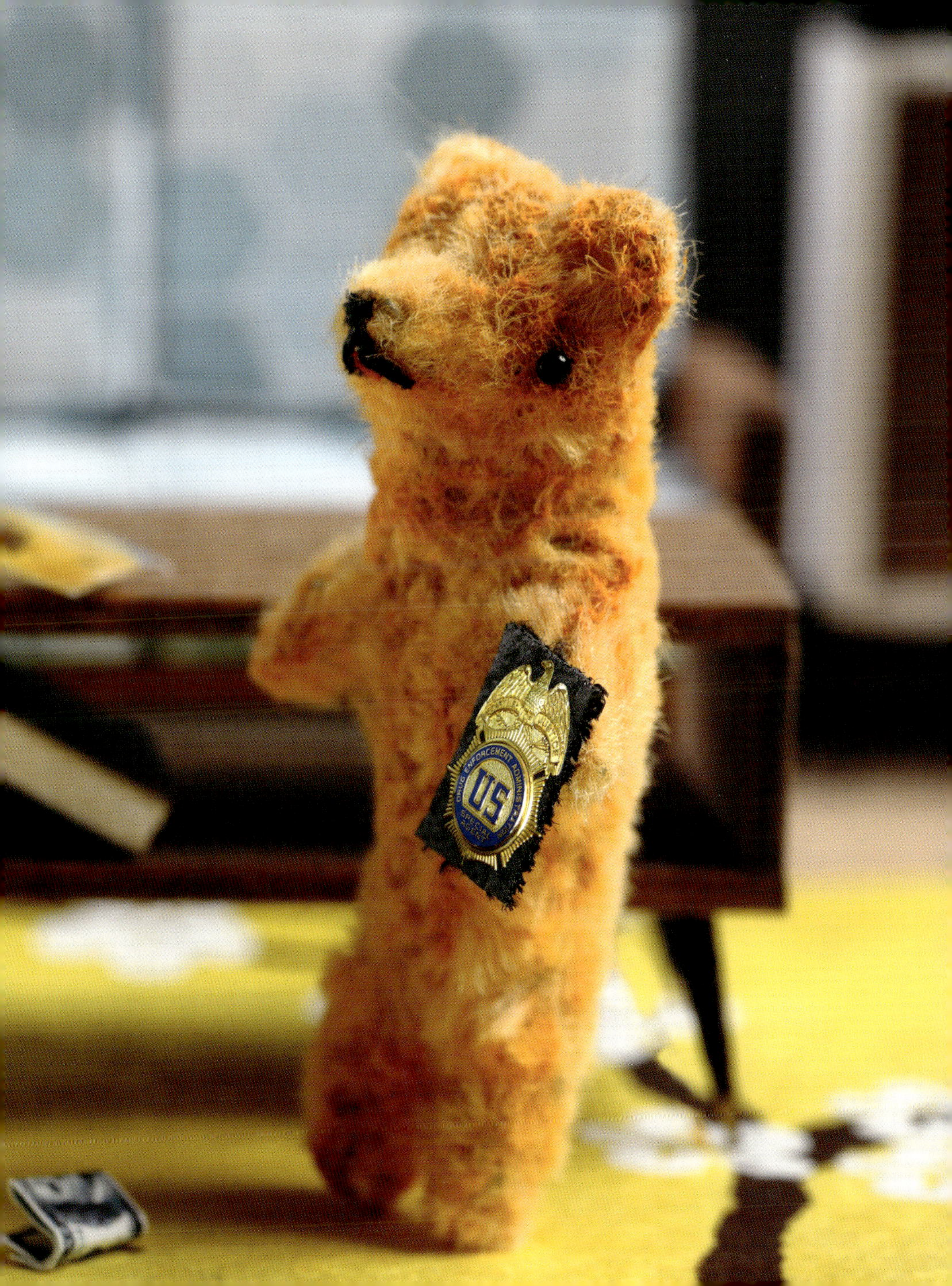

DRUG ENFORCEMENT ADMINISTRATION
US
SPECIAL AGENT

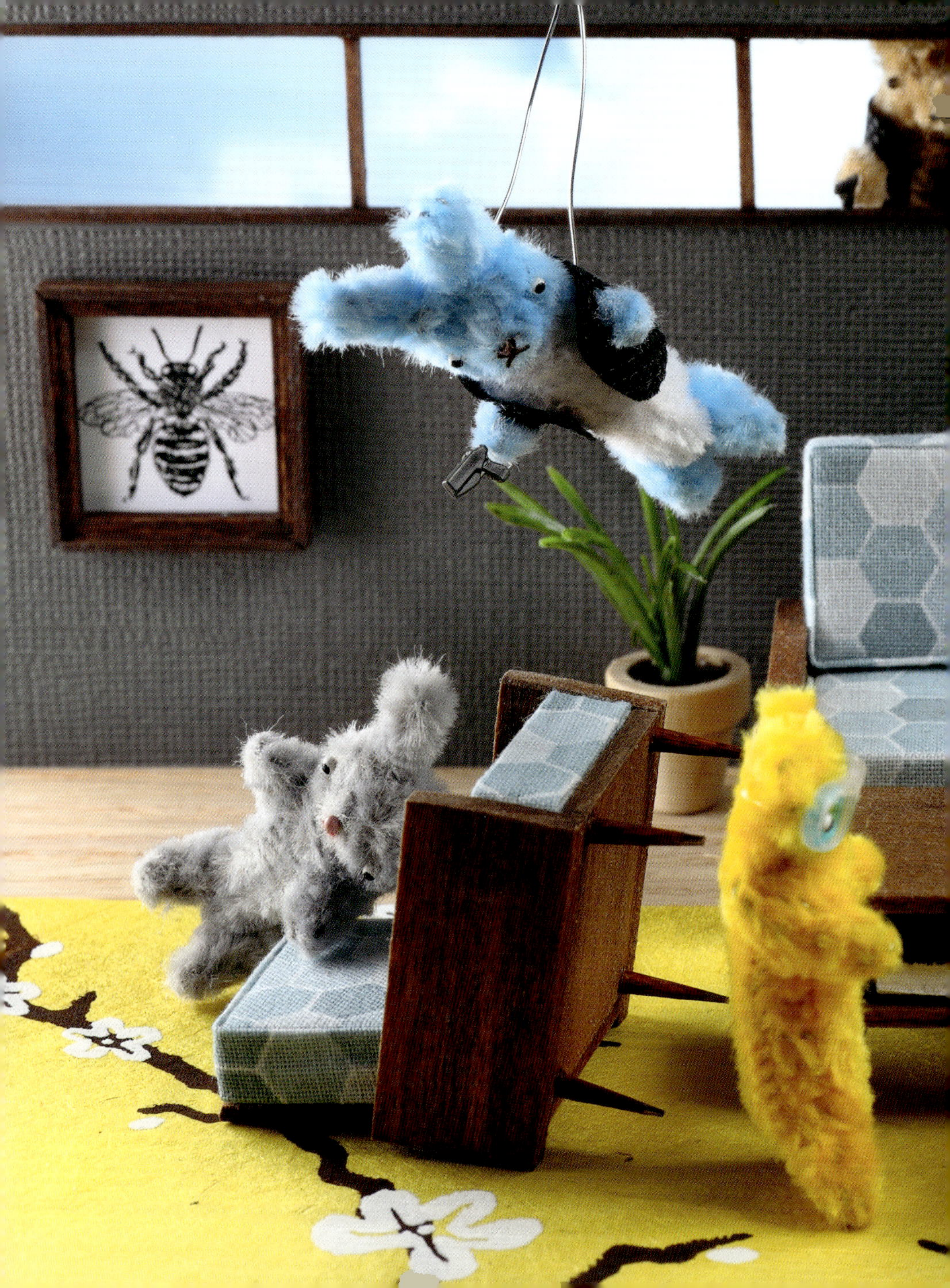

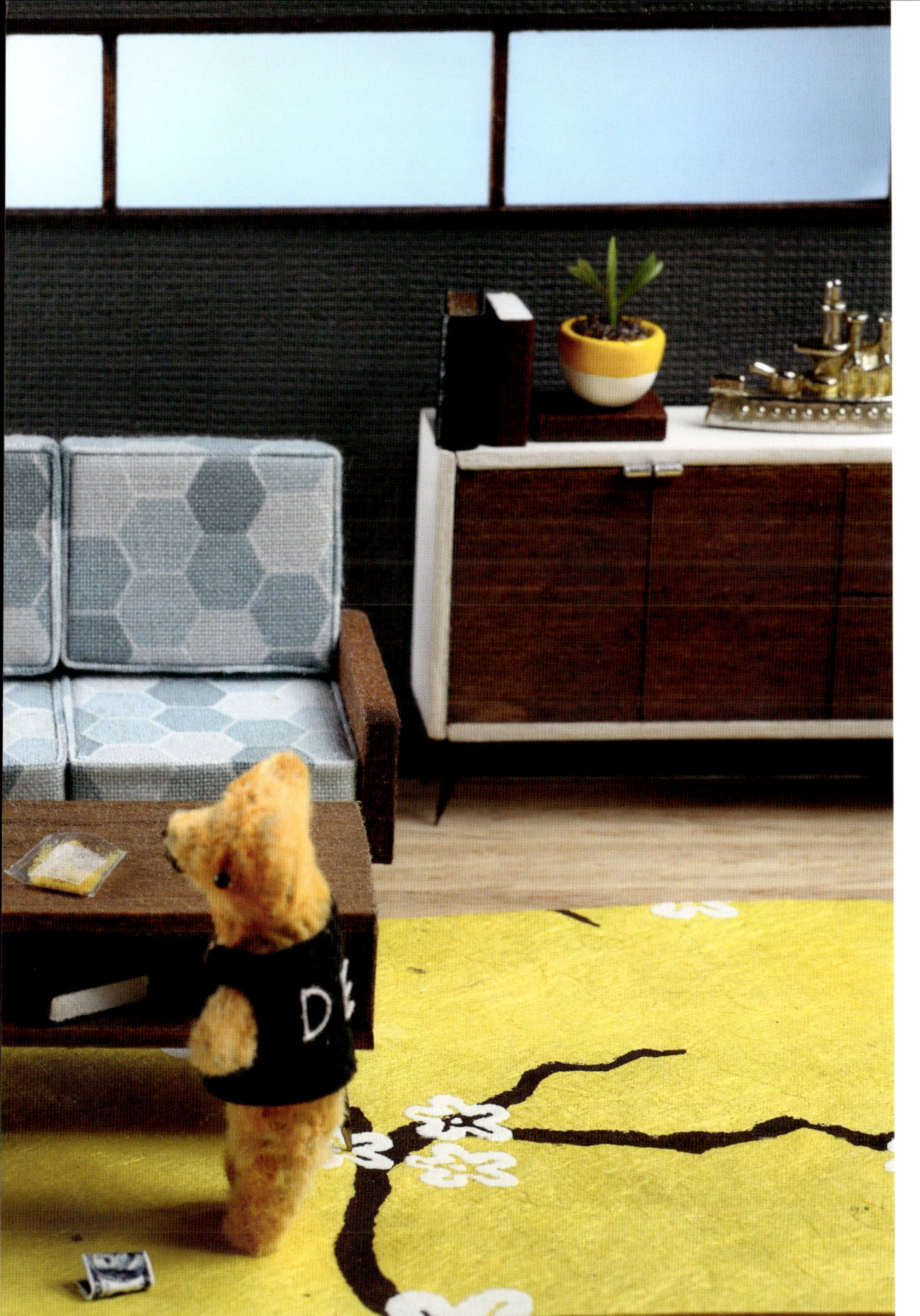

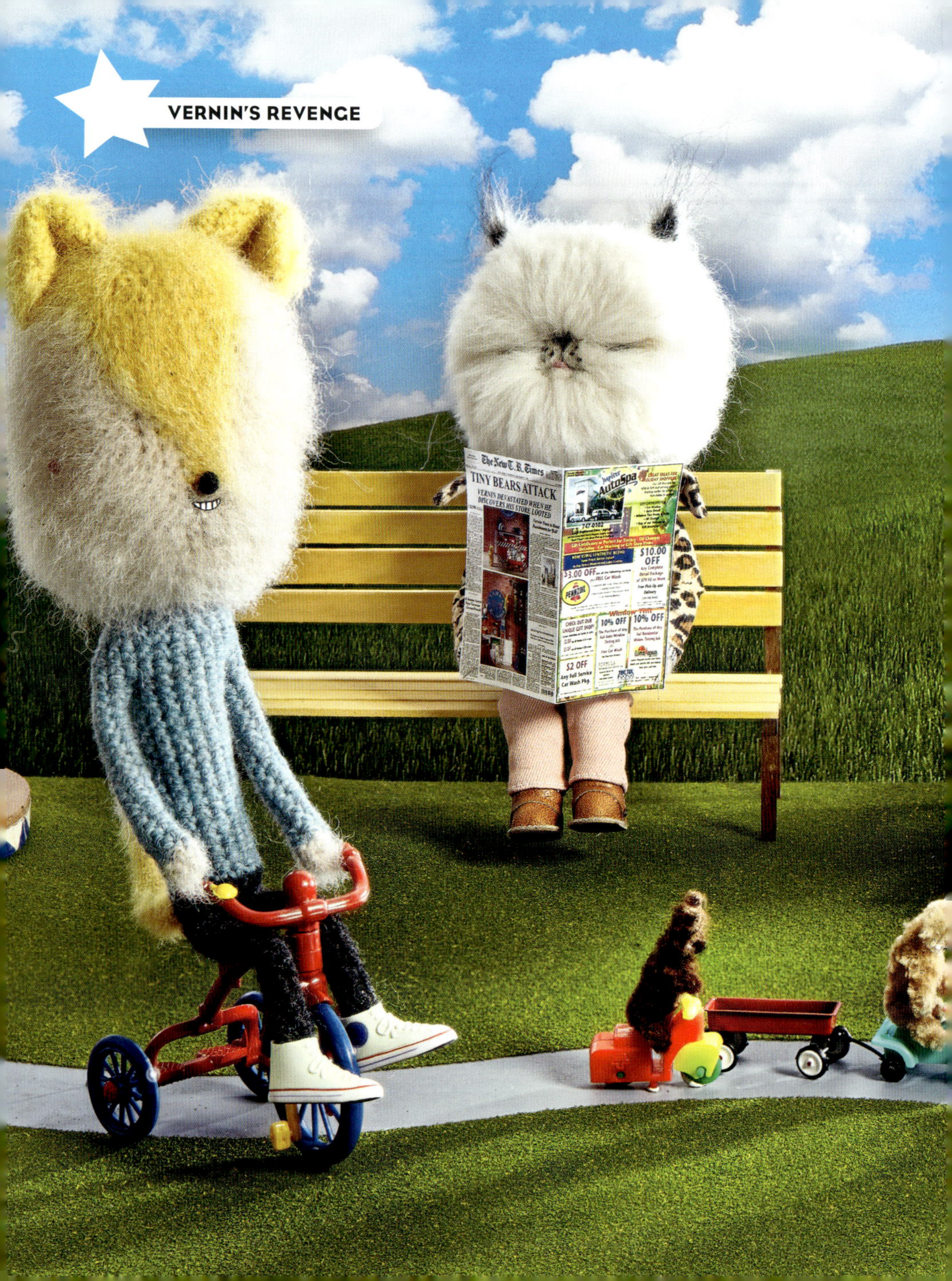
The New T. K. Times
TINY BEARS ATTACK
VERNIN DEVASTATED WHEN HE DISCOVERS HIS STORE LOOTED

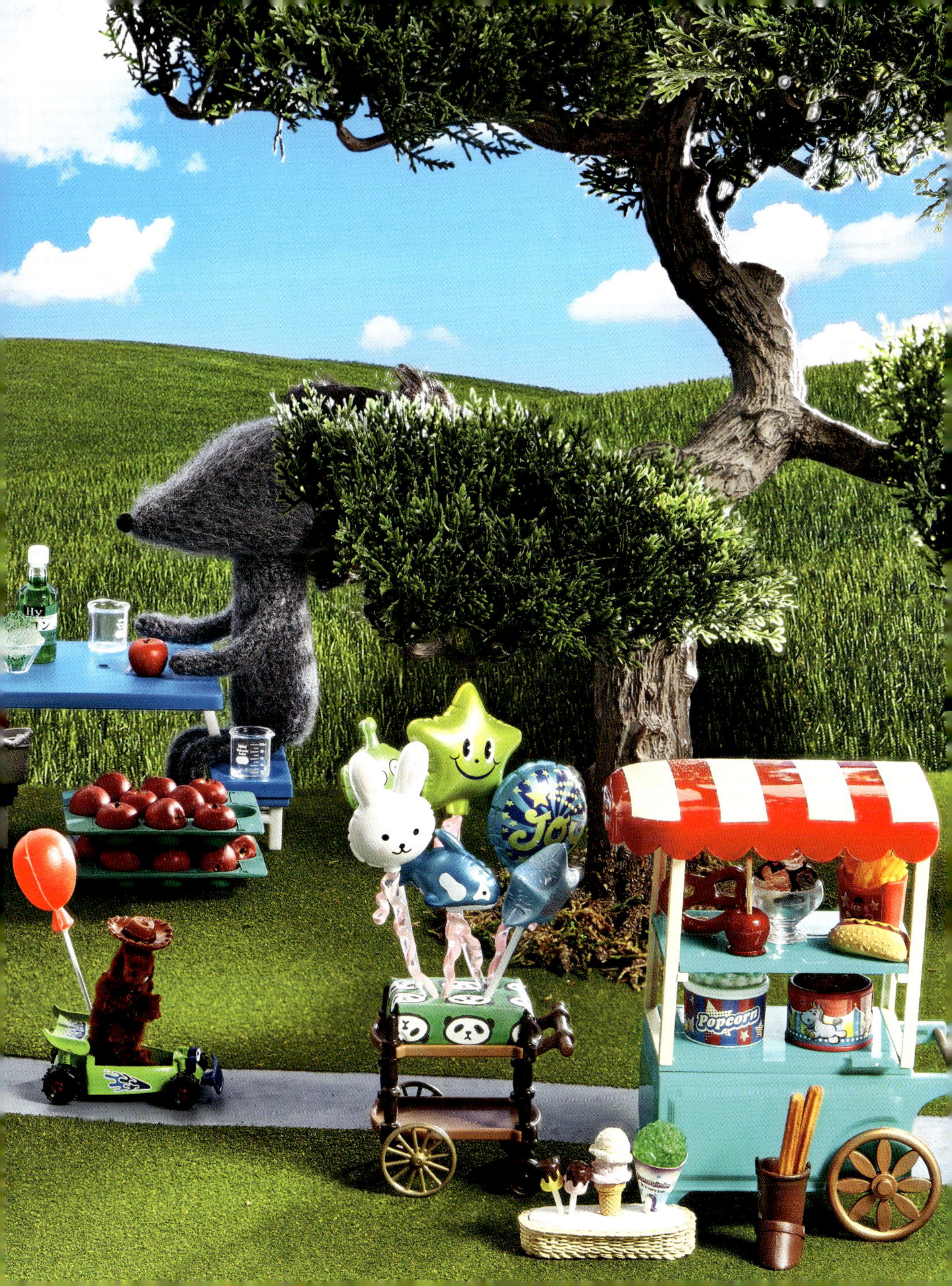

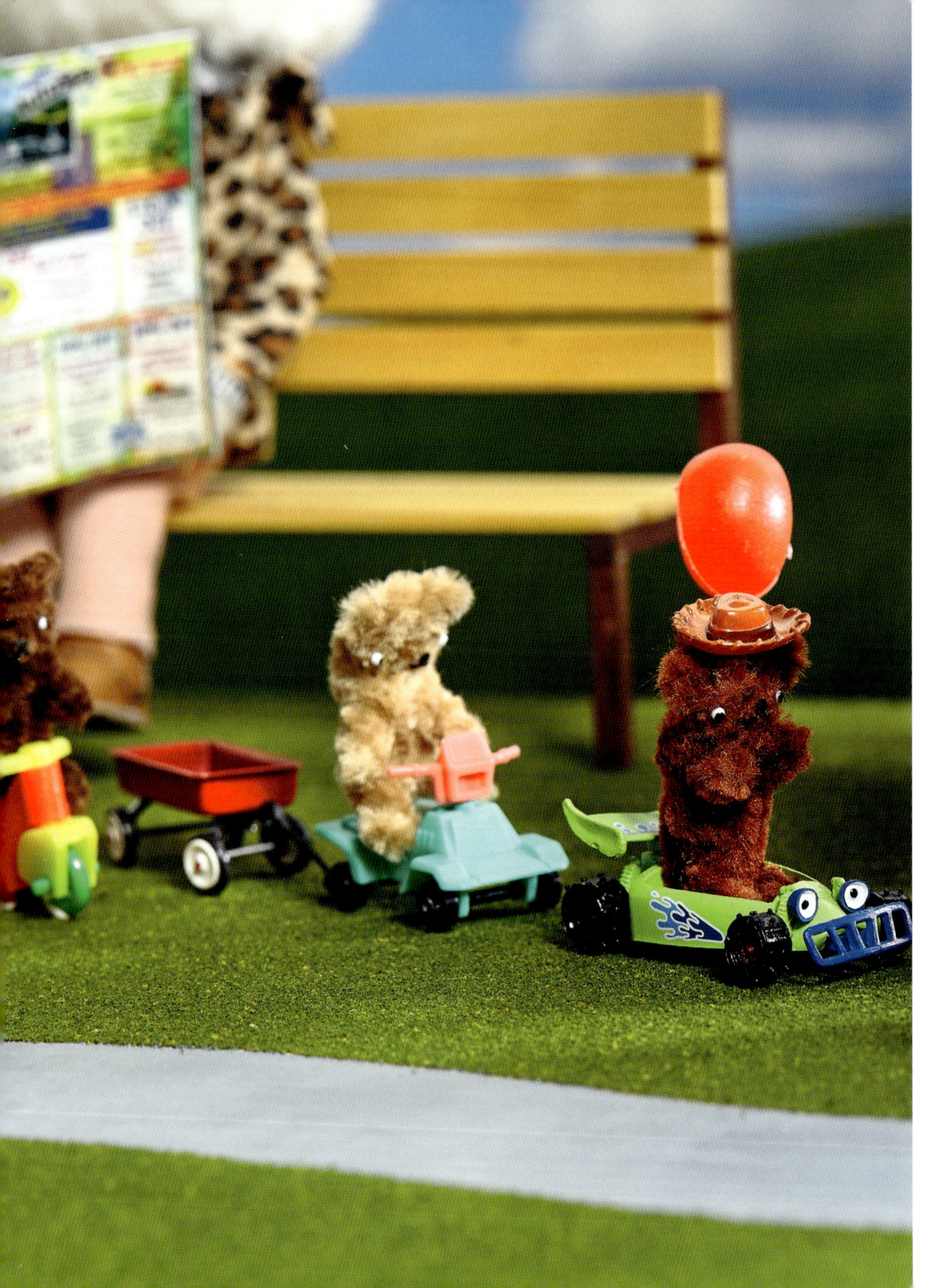

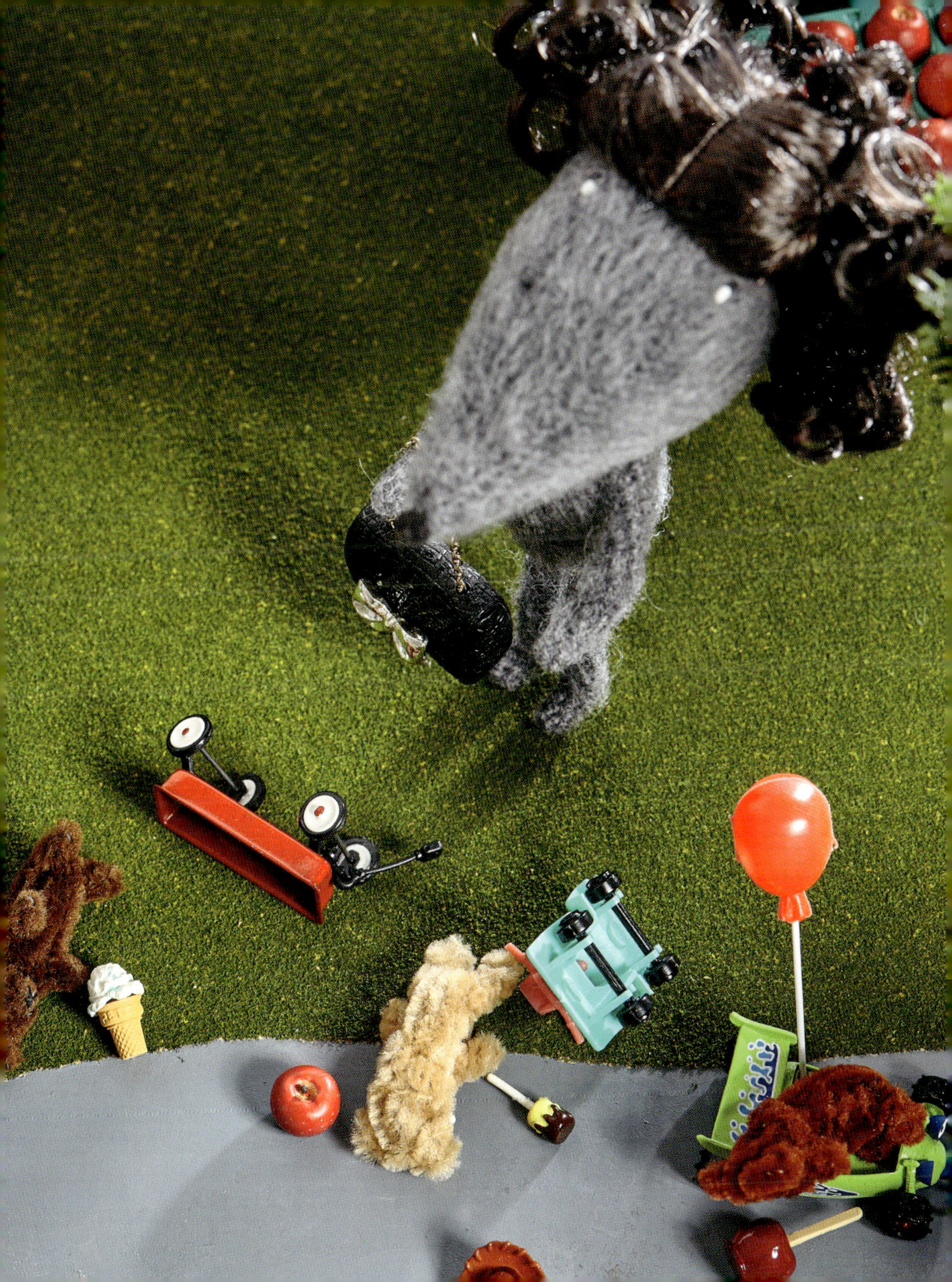

CAST OF CHARACTERS

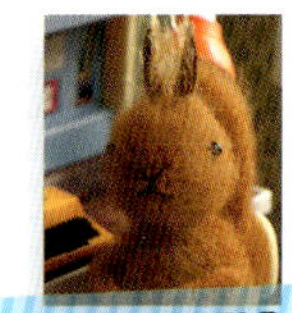

A wealthy tree house mogul, Nutfield has recently focused the majority of his attention on teaching his son Nutzilla the skills to maintain the family business.

NUTFIELD

Son of Nutfield and an aspiring businessman, Nutzilla tries hard to fill his father's shoes in running the family tree house business.

NUTZILLA

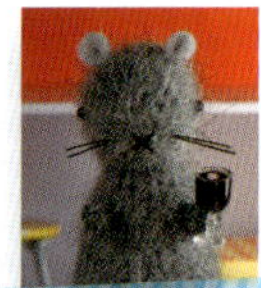

Naïve and oblivious, Prescott is easily swindled and has been the target of many of Haupfear and Bosworth's schemes.

PRESCOTT

Mischievous and irresponsible, Bosworth spends most of his time working on get-rich-quick schemes with his best friend, Haupfear.

BOSWORTH

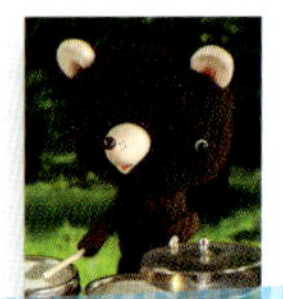

As the top stylist of TADA's City, PB's latest project has been his new fashion line for dogs.

PB

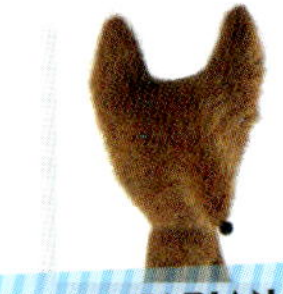

As Captain of TRPD's Street Crime unit, Fabian feels the pressure as TADA's City crime rate skyrockets.

FABIAN

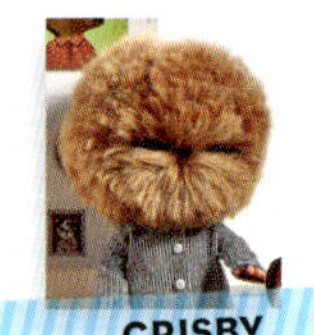

Deputy and Fabian's partner, Gimp Dog, spends his free time hanging out with his roommate and best friend, Green Dog.

GIMP DOG

Immigrants from Bunnimlandia, Haupfear and Mongstad came to TADA's City in search of opportunity, but have been distracted by the many vices of the Big City.

HAUPFEAR & MONGSTAD

TADA's Revolution's former Chief Financial Officer, Grisby, was recently demoted following concerns about his productivity at work. Grisby is now a Personnel Specialist and enjoys playing baseball with his son.

GRISBY

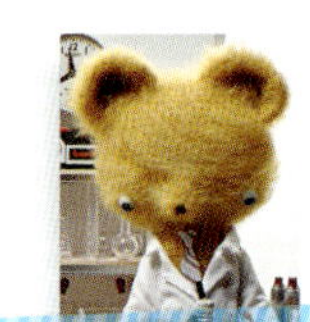

A renowned molecular biologist, Berenson is the Chief Scientific Officer of Hamtasmo Labs and is currently developing a new line of performance-enhancing supplements.

BERENSON

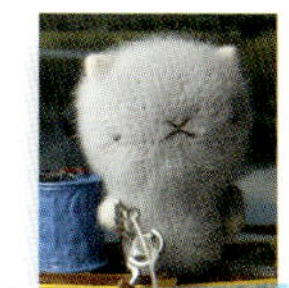

An avid survivalist, Helix has traveled to the world's most extreme locations, but has gotten several injuries along the way.

HELIX

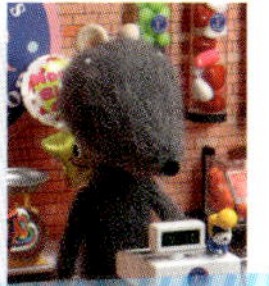

After his candy store was raided by the Tiny Bears, Vernin founded the "Men Against Tiny Bears" and has resolved to put an end to the Tiny Bear menace.

VERNIN

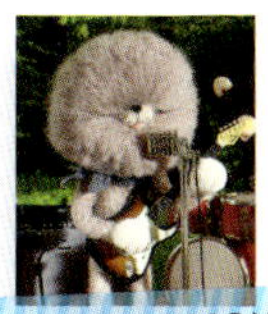

TADA's City's top rock band, Dandelion and the Revolution, are currently touring their new album: *Puffs*

DANDELION

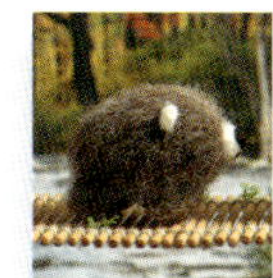

A self-proclaimed "entrepreneur," Cromwell has become notorious in TADA's City for his dishonest and exploitative business practices.

CROMWELL AKA FLEA

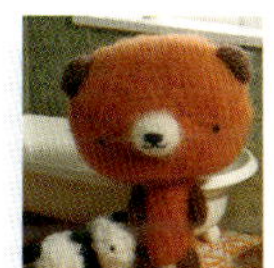

Having been relocated to El Paso under the Witness Protection Program, Slim and Tobby have assumed the identities of Travis and Randy, and work at a taco supply warehouse.

SLIM & TOBINSKI

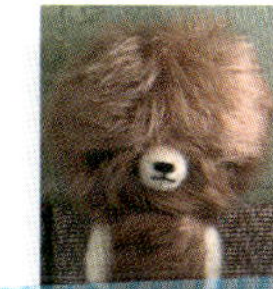

Once a close friend of Slim and Tobby, Leopold severed ties with Tobby after the two had a dispute over the ownership of a cream puff. Lately, Leopold has focused his attention on training his dog, Bradford.

LEOPOLD

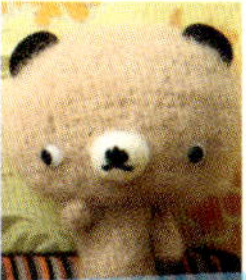

Plagued by bad luck, Guy flunked out of TR Community College and narrowly escaped death at Gimp Dog's Bed and Breakfast. Most recently, his dog, Friendlington, has gone missing.

GUY

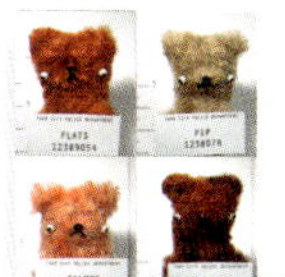

As a career criminal, Diablo has been pursued by Fabian and Gimp Dog for many years, but he remains at large.

DIABLO

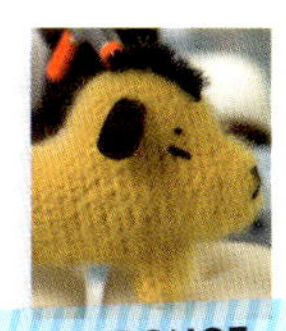

A collection of ne'er-do-wells who have been exiled from their native country of Pipeland, these parasitic nomads have settled in TADA's City and have begun targeting the town's residents.

TINY BEARS

A trendsetter and fashion blogger, Ponce frequents PB's salon and is always experimenting with the latest hairstyles.

PONCE

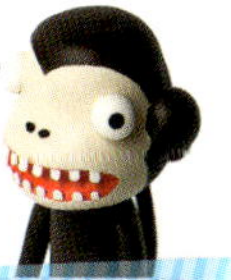

One of the top chefs of TADA's City, Monkey has a discerning palette and will settle for nothing less than the finest ingredients.

MONKEY

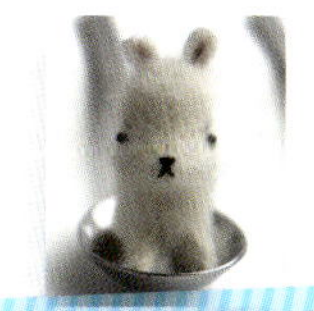

Formerly Guy's dog, Friendlington went missing and has mysteriously resurfaced alongside Vernin.

FRIENDLINGTON

SUSAN CHI

Susan Chi is a self-taught multimedia artist based out of Los Angeles, California. She specializes in fiber and textile arts, miniatures and set building, photography and stop-motion animation. *www.tadasrevolution.com*

ACKNOWLEDGEMENTS

I would like to thank my husband and best friend, Nicholas Nguyen, for his unconditional support and love through the years. His talent and skills in photography, lighting, and image processing have made TADA's Revolution and this book possible.

A furry thank you to our mischievous Pomeranian, Bear Bear, for inspiring me with new ideas for the adventures. A huge thank you to the teNeues team, Carla Sakamoto and Allison Stern, for their hard work and dedication, and for providing us with wonderful ideas and feedback!

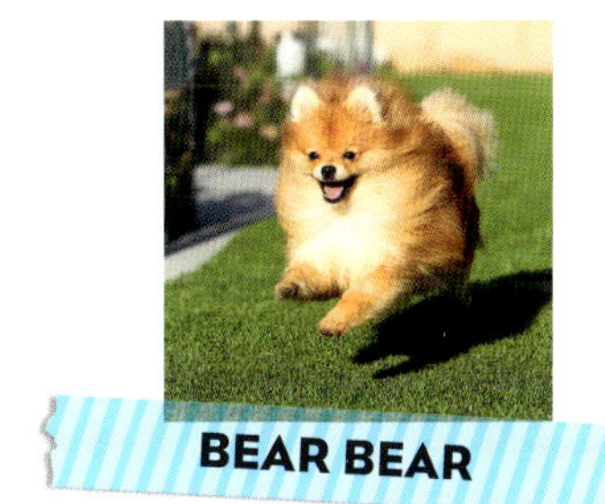

Editor: Carla Sakamoto
Designer: Allison Stern
Production by Dieter Haberzettl
Color separations by MT-Vreden

Published by teNeues Publishing Group

teNeues Media GmbH + Co. KG
Am Selder 37, 47906 Kempen, Germany
Phone: +49-(0)2152-916-0
Fax: +49-(0)2152-916-111
e-mail: books@teneues.com

Press department: Andrea Rehn
Phone: +49-(0)2152-916-202
e-mail: arehn@teneues.com

teNeues Publishing Company
7 West 18th Street, New York, NY 10011, USA
Phone: +1-212-627-9090
Fax: +1-212-627-9511

teNeues Publishing UK Ltd.
12 Ferndene Road, London SE24 0AQ, UK
Phone: +44-(0)20-3542-8997

teNeues France S.A.R.L.
39, rue des Billets, 18250 Henrichemont, France
Phone: +33-(0)2-4826-9348
Fax: +33-(0)1-7072-3482

www.teneues.com

ISBN 978-3-8327-3366-7
Library of Congress Number: 2015953769

Printed in the Czech Republic

Bibliographic information published by the Deutsche Nationalbibliothek.
The Deutsche Nationalbibliothek lists this publication in the Deutsche
Nationalbibliografie; detailed bibliographic data are available in the Internet
at http://dnb.d-nb.de.

teNeues Publishing Group
Kempen
Berlin
London
Munich
New York
Paris

teNeues